Y0-BUN-651

H
ML661 / B7

MUSIC

for the Millions

The Kimball

Piano and Organ

Story

1857-1957

William Wallace Kimball, founder of the W. W. Kimball Company, as he appeared in the piano's golden age. Photograph was taken by W. J. Root "before 1898."

MUSIC

for the Millions

The Kimball
Piano and Organ
Story

VAN ALLEN BRADLEY

ML
661
.B7
West

HENRY REGNERY COMPANY · 1957 · CHICAGO

Copyright © 1957 by Henry Regnery Company, Chicago, Illinois
Manufactured in the United States of America
Library of Congress Catalog Card Number 57-9231

AN INSTITUTE OF BUSINESS HISTORY PUBLICATION

For PATRICIA

Acknowledgments

I must first express my thanks to W. W. Kimball, who joined enthusiastically with me in the firm purpose behind this book: That besides telling the story of one hundred years of company history, it should of itself become a valid contribution to the Americana shelf and the literature of the American music industry. To him and to his associates I am grateful for the complete freedom allowed me to explore the W. W. Kimball Company's offices, factories, and files.

Particular thanks are due to the following Kimball personnel: Vice President W. W. Kimball Jr., for guidance at the factories; Curtis P. Kimball, assistant secretary and sales manager, and Theodore H. Krumwiede, for an understanding of piano sales and advertising; Roy Johnson, for a salesman's view of the factories; Rolla Burke, for background information on piano selling; John Harbison and Charles Fiek, old timers, for their memories of the past; and Julia Boutet, for all but forgotten incidents out of the past.

Among former Kimballites, George L. Hadley of Boston, Carle C. Conway of New York City, John H. Whitney of Elyria, Ohio; Mr. and Mrs. Frank P. Whitmore of Orlando, Florida; George B. Demes of Chicago, and Ben F. Duvall of Glencoe, Illinois, provided invaluable information and help. I am especially grateful to Messrs. Hadley, Conway, and Whitmore for documentary material, drawings, and photographs which supplemented the materials in the Kimball archives.

Especial thanks are due to another Kimballite, James V. Sill, retired vice president and general manager, who read the manuscript.

I must also record my thanks to Paul M. Angle, director of the Chicago Historical Society, and to the society's able Margaret Scriven for setting me straight on much early Chicago history; the Newberry Library and the Chicago Public Library; Thomas L. Sayers, librarian of the Chicago *Daily News,* for locating obscure material, including photographs; Lloyd Wendt and Herman Kogan, Chicago historians who are former newspaper associates of mine, for special assistance; John Drury, author of "Old Chicago Houses," for hitherto unpublished information; Charles Washburn, author of "Come Into My Parlor," for documentary materials; Peter Pollack of the Art Institute of Chicago, for details on the Kimball art collection; and Herma Clark of the Chicago *Tribune,* for early Chicago materials.

John B. Carlson, editor of the *Piano Trade Magazine,* turned his extensive files over to me and allowed me complete freedom in research at his establishment, for which I am deeply grateful.

To Louis Cheskin of the Color Research Institute of America I owe special thanks for encouragement and professional assistance. I know I shall never adequately repay the kindness of Frances Daly Ricketts, who typed most of the manuscript.

Charles Lee, editor, and Eugenia Fawcett, production manager, of the Henry Regnery Company have generously and patiently given me the benefits of their skill and experience.

Finally, I must humbly thank my wife, Patricia, who still puts up with me despite the fact that for many long months our new family room was a cluttered annex of the Kimball company's archives, and my children, Van Allen III, Pamela Star, and Susan, for their forbearance. Especially Susan, who can now turn up the television.

VAN ALLEN BRADLEY

February 4, 1957.

Contents

Contents

Contents

Illustrations

Illustrations

MUSIC

for the Millions

The Kimball

Piano and Organ

Story

1857-1957

1

"Seemed at times he could tear the veil off the future."

IT WAS in the panic year of 1857 that William Wallace Kimball shook the rural dust of northeastern Iowa off his heels and struck out for the roaring young city of Chicago and a new start. On the record it appears that it was pure intuition that impelled him—the same remarkable intuition that in later years would lead his friend William Bates Price, a fellow piano manufacturer, to marvel, "Seemed at times he could tear the veil off the future."

When Kimball made his decision in the summer of 1857 to close out his insurance and real estate operations in Decorah, Winneshiek County, there were in that small but thriving commercial center as yet no visible signs of the economic disaster soon to sweep the country. Nor could Kimball have dreamed that within a few months he would—by merest chance—be launched into the beginnings of a piano and organ business that would burgeon into a considerable industrial empire and make of him the first great pioneer in the bringing of musical culture to the Westward-moving frontier.

1

In time, the company that William Wallace Kimball was to found in Chicago would become the world's largest manufacturer of pianos, and the envy of longer-established rivals in the East. With Singer of sewing machine fame, he would revolutionize the American householder's buying habits by pioneering installment selling. In its first century the house of Kimball would become one of American industry's truly impressive examples of the ability of free enterprise, bulwarked by ideas, imagination, and capital, to contribute to the strength and welfare of society. It would enrich the lives of millions, add a host of brilliant achievements to the commercial development of the piano and organ in America, create new capital, provide jobs for tens of thousands.

A century later, in 1957, as the company prepared for even greater achievements in a splendid new plant—the world's most modern piano factory—it would remain a strikingly successful manufacturing enterprise, still in the hands of the Kimball family.

If there was no portent of the oncoming depression in William Wallace Kimball's decision to quit Decorah in the prosperous midsummer of 1857, there was still an intuitive recognition that this frontier village was too small a sphere to contain his expanding ambition.

The rugged, distinguished-looking, young adventurer from Maine had done well in the four years since he had come to town in 1853. That was the year the town was laid out, a handful of families comprising its citizenry. By 1854 it had grown from this small beginning to an enterprising settlement of more than 100 people and some 15 or 20 buildings—counting stores, stables, hotels, and shops. By 1857 it was the center of commerce for the whole region round about, drawing its trade from as far as 100 miles away, especially north and west.

Now, at 29, young Kimball could look back upon fruitful years of activity in which he had made important contributions to that growth. As the community had thrived, so had the Maine adventurer, who, as his brother-in-law Albert G. Cone would later record, "began business 'on his own hook' as an insurance and real estate agent—a calling which, especially in a new community, rich in its promise of future development, has often proved one of the surest stepping stones to success."

There was a continuous excitement in the air in the middle 50s as prosperity rode into Decorah with the tide of immigrant wagons from the East. In those days as many as 250 to 300 of these prairie schooners were passing daily over the stage road from Dubuque to St. Paul and the great Northwest. To many of these visitors Decorah and the regions round about seemed a likely place to put down roots. It was a pleasant spot, nestled in the lush valley of the Upper Iowa River and surrounded by woodlands and gently rolling countryside.

More than once the beauty of the Iowa hills and valleys reminded young Kimball of the New England of his boyhood. For this reason, he knew that to the New Englanders among the immigrant visitors it would have a special appeal. So it was that many a fugitive from a rocky, rundown farm in the East got his fresh start out West through a land acquisition engineered by the hustling young man from Maine.

Iowa's rich and arable farm lands were everywhere in demand. In 1855, the year the land office of the Turkey River Land District was established in Decorah, "the town was crowded with adventurers from all parts of the country, with a rage for land almost barbarous," according to W. A. Alexander's "History of Winneshiek and Allamakee Counties, Iowa." It was "a wild and curious time. . . . The amount of gold, or its equivalent, then in town was almost incredible—some say not less than a half a million." There were nine banks doing business in Decorah by the spring of 1856.

It was thus a time for making money in land, among other things. Prairie land, river bottom, town lot—any land in the rich Decorah region was valuable in the flush 50s. A speculator could, and often did, make a great deal of money. Even a cautious trader, such as Kimball, could scarcely fail to prosper. The land he bought at moderate prices tended to rise rapidly and to find a ready market as the region grew.

As Albert Cone recorded it, "Mr. Kimball builded wisely but . . . not more wisely than he knew. He foresaw the end from the beginning, and owed nothing to blind chance. A tall, robust youth, straight as the monarch of the forest in his native state, ruddy of complexion, blessed with good health, energy and animal spirits, and calculated by his free and open manner to win friends wherever he went, and in whatever he did, he was not long in gaining a sure foothold, and in acquiring the name and position of one of the most popular businessmen in the village and the vicinity . . . he bought and sold land, and 'swapped' one thing for another, as only a genuine Yankee knows how, and, by dint of his remarkable energy and untiring 'push,' supplemented by a judgment of localities and values which stood him in good stead, and which was wellnigh unerring, he accumulated quite a comfortable sum of money, and might be said to have fairly embarked on the road to prosperity."

We can thus imagine the shock to his Decorah friends and associates when in the midsummer of 1857 the successful young real estate operator began pulling in his chips and preparing to depart. To most Decorah residents, the future looked bright.

But, as seems probable now, the cautious young man from Down East had read his history well. He was aware that "wildcat" banking and over-speculation in real estate—much of which he had observed with his own eyes in the land-hungry atmosphere in which he lived—were endangering the nation's economy. Railroads were over-building; industry and agriculture were over-expanding; the currency was inflated. The basic cause of the impending panic lay in Europe, where stock market abuses and adjustments following the Crimean War led to withdrawal of investments in America. Young Kimball could scarcely know this, of course; but he sensed it was time for a change.

4

Thus it was that he decided to liquidate the major share of his Iowa investments. He had husbanded his capital. Now he would test his business skill in broader fields. Perhaps he would get out of real estate and try something new—if the right opportunity came along.

Chicago seemed a likely place for a new venture. In his early twenties, as a commercial traveler through the South and the Middle West, he had visited the bustling city at the foot of Lake Michigan, had tasted its heady excitement, sensed the vitality that surged through its muddy streets. Here, he felt, lay the great challenge of the future.

Kimball was in Dubuque, 100 miles to the southeast on the banks of the Mississippi, settling some of his accounts, when the panic struck in the Eastern cities in August, 1857. The effect was not immediately felt in the Mississippi Valley towns, although a number of Western banks and insurance companies collapsed under the strain, and the panic slowly spread. After a dozen years of prosperity, due largely to the overland quest for California gold, the United States began to be gripped by its twelfth depression since 1790. Building and manufacture were the first to feel the creeping paralysis. Agriculture, particularly in the North, was hit hard.

By the end of September the paralysis had crept to the Iowa frontier. It was felt first in Dubuque, where the money market tightened and the grim-faced bankers began to loan sparingly at 2 per cent a month; a little later upriver at McGregor's Landing and at Prairie du Chien; then westward in Decorah and in the tens of thousands of big and little towns the length and breadth of the land.

The uncanny Kimball "sixth sense" had paid off. The young man from Maine with the twinkling, steel-blue eyes had put his affairs in good order and was ready to wait out the storm. This knack for making the right decisions was an attribute that was to serve the vast Kimball enterprise well in later years, enabling it to

weather many a national crisis while less fortunate competitors
went to the wall.

Before setting out for Chicago, Wallace Kimball, as he was called
at the time, decided to ride over into Mitchell County, two counties to the westward, and on to the hamlet of McIntire to tell his
younger brother David of his decision.

It was a bright October day, with the rolling world of the prairie
lying blue and bronze and green and gold under a blazing sun.
Here, amidst fertile acres watered by the beautiful Wapsipinicon
River, David and a friend, G. W. Barker, had settled the year before on adjoining tracts obtained through the government land
office at Dubuque. Their little board shanty, the first frame building in Wayne Township, was situated on the line between their
farms, and thereby held their homesteading claims.

The lowly cabin glimmered in the heat of noon as Wallace rode
up, hitched his horse to a sycamore, and dismounted.

2

"He seemed too full of business to make a long stop here."

DAVID WILLIAMS KIMBALL, mending a snow fence at the rear of the house, was surprised to see his handsome, brown-haired brother. He warmly welcomed Wallace's infrequent visits and wished they could last longer.

"Wallace was here last week," he had written on September 3, 1856, in a typical letter to his sweetheart Sarah Moore, back in Worcester, Massachusetts, "but he seemed too full of business to make a long stop here. I could not see that he had anything to do more than to ride through the country, which looks a great deal better to him after visiting those rough and rocky hills East."

On David's lonely farmstead there was little opportunity for him to talk with anyone from the outside world. When Wallace dropped by, he could enjoy a brotherly chat and also catch up on the news. There had been little or no news since early in March, when James Buchanan was sworn in as President and, two days later, the Dred Scott decision had rocked the country. Lately, there had been talk among the neighboring farmers of a panic, and

David wondered if things were really as bad as they said, and what it would mean to him here on the farm.

Now Wallace was here and telling him, with a broad sweep of his hand toward the prairie land around him, "I've seen everything there is to see out here, David. I'm going to Chicago."

As usual, Wallace was eager to be on his way—especially now that his decision was made and his business operations closed. But he knew that this time the separation from David, with whom he had always been close, was going to be a longer one than usual. Noting the anxious look that crept into David's eyes as he told him of his plans, Wallace cocked his head to one side, rubbed his beard, and grinned.

"Have you got a bed for the night?" he asked, as he slapped his brother reassuringly on the back. David scuffed the toe of his work boot in the dust and broke into loud laughter.

The Kimball brothers, alike in habits of thought and speech as they were in bearing and facial expression, and in gaunt stature, talked long into the October night. They were avid to get the last shred of enjoyment out of this final time together before Wallace set off on the morrow for Chicago and the future that awaited him.

Eagerly David told of the improvements he was making on the farm, of the night raids of the Indians, who stole harness and tools from the barn and, only the night before, had taken a cow. He was full of plans for the future: Next spring, panic or no panic, Indians or no Indians, he was going to build himself a real house, 16 by 20 feet, of wood frame construction. The lumber was already cut and laid aside.

Then he would go back to Worcester, which had been his home from 1843, when he had gone there at the age of 13, until the winter of 1855, when he had come West with Barker. At 27, David was in love with the beautiful Sarah, 23, daughter of Nathaniel Curtis Moore of Worcester. He would marry Sarah and bring her back to the new home he had planned. From under the Bible he pulled out a set of neatly drawn plans and showed them to his brother.

To all this Wallace listened with quiet pleasure. It was good to know that Sarah had accepted. A man isolated, as David was, needed the companionship of a woman. In turn, Wallace told his brother of his own dreams of the future. Vague they were, it was true; but neither of the Kimball boys doubted for a moment that whatever Wallace chose to do he would make his mark.

The talk turned to boyhood pleasures, as it always does when brothers long apart are brought together. It seemed a long way from this rude prairie shack to the old Kimball homestead near Rumford, in Oxford County, Maine. Memories came flooding back to them—fishing for flashing trout along the lovely Androscoggin River, which flows through the heart of Rumford, its cascading waters dropping 180 feet in a mile; the smell of roasting ears for which the Oxford County farms were famed; the luscious apples; the beautiful lake country and the mountain resorts along the western border of the county, which touches the foothills of the White Mountains; the long days of work on the farm, beginning at 4 A.M. and ending at dark; the frolicsome black bears they ran into one day while hunting for raccoon in the forest of white pine, fir, spruce, and hemlock back of the old homestead; the grandeur of the scenery at this time of year, with beech and birch and rock maple and elm ablaze in all their autumnal glories of red and brown and gold.

Yes, it was a long way from Maine to Iowa. Wallace had made it first. Born on March 22, 1828, at Rumford, he was one of eleven children of David and Lucy Williams Wheeler Kimball, both descendants of long established New England families. His brother David Williams was born two years later, on February 14, 1830.

The first of the Kimball clan to live at Rumford was Wallace's grandfather Moses, a soldier of the Revolution who served in Col. Gilman's regiment. A son of John Kimball, a carpenter, of Exeter, New Hampshire, Moses settled on the farm at Rumford in 1785 with his wife, the former Phebe (Cole) Smart, who bore him ten children, including David, the father of Wallace and David Williams.

Most of the Kimballs in America are descended, the genealogists tell us, from one Richard Kimball, a Puritan wheelwright of Rattlesden, England, who came over with his family on the ship *Elizabeth* in 1634 and settled at Ipswich, Massachusetts. He was a member of the "Kemball" family (originally "Kymbolde"), which has been established in Suffolk County, England, for the last 450 years. He changed the spelling of the name to Kimball after emigrating to America. From John Kimball, the father of Grandfather Moses, the line goes back through Caleb, a mason, of Wenham, Massachusetts, to Richard of Wenham, a wheelwright and son of the original Richard, who came to America with his father on the *Elizabeth*.

The life of a farm boy has never been beer and skittles, and this was particularly true of the life that Wallace and David lived on their father's farm at Rumford in the middle years of the last century. Father David was a man of limited means, and he had a large family to provide for.

This meant that everybody pitched in. It was the kind of experience to develop a spirit of struggling self-sacrifice and self-dependence in all the children, and neither Wallace nor David ever forgot it. In later years it was a characteristic of the wealthy Wallace in particular to see that the members of his family were well provided for. Even as a boy, as Albert G. Cone later set it down, he was "a loving and dutiful son" who "devoted a generous portion of his earnings . . . to the care and comfort of 'the old folks at home.' "

Both boys received their early education at the country school, and Wallace, at 18, became a teacher himself at Rumford for two winter sessions. Next he clerked for a year at a village store. He was paid a salary of $8.33 a month, with sick days and holidays deducted at the time of settlement. It was a small wage but a good one for a young man in those days.

"The country store," as Cone wrote, "gave him his first start. From running errands, he became a clerk, trusted by his employer—a favorite with everybody. . . . The little village store with its curious but orthodox assortment of drygoods, groceries, hardware and what not—its calico, its flour and sugar, its ten-penny nails, and its old-fashioned plows, its knickknacks and its gewgaws—claimed his time and abilities until the age of 21, when he removed to Boston, where a clerkship of a more responsible kind awaited him in one of the large establishments. . . ."

One of the stories that David Kimball used to tell was of the time when Wallace packed his bag to go away to Boston, where he had located a job through the "Help Wanted" columns of the Boston *Globe*. Father and mother and all the children decided to bid him goodbye at home and have the hired man drive him to town to take the train. After many a tearful farewell, the young man left, but only a short distance down the road Wallace discovered that he had left behind a book that he had wanted to take along. So the hired man turned the old gray mare around, and back they went to the farm. The entire family rushed out into the farmyard to learn what had happened.

As his mother threw her arms about her six-foot, two-inch son, she exclaimed, "Why, Wallace, are you back already?"

His reply was quick as his eyes danced:

"Yes, damn it. Why didn't you write?"

It was typical of the kind of humor Wallace Kimball most enjoyed, even in his earlier days.

The years have obscured the life and times of Wallace Kimball in his Boston period as a clerk, as well as his subsequent activities as a commercial traveler before he showed up in Iowa in 1853.

For all his charm and geniality of later years, Kimball was difficult to know. His really intimate friends were few, although thousands thought they knew him well. Apparently he preferred to let many of the details of his life remain a mystery. He was often aloof and enigmatic in his statements and in his replies to questions. There are notable gaps and conflicting testimony in the various published accounts of his career, and often the historian must make what seems to be the most reasonable choice. The discrepancies Kimball never bothered to correct. They are of little real significance, we must assume, alongside the record of his achievements.

A typically vague sketch, in the "Century Encyclopedia," reports simply that Kimball, after going to Boston, "secured mercantile employment, and soon became a traveler, doing business first in New England and afterward in the Middle, Southern and Western states." It adds: "As a result of these years of travel, he acquired an intimate and comprehensive knowledge of Western mercantile geography, which proved of inestimable practical advantage to him later on, in supplying those various latitudes and communities with the product of his own manufactory."

After Boston, the next we hear of Wallace at first hand is in a letter from David Williams Kimball to Sarah Moore, written from Dubuque and dated February 1, 1856. More than a dozen years before, in 1843, young David had left the Rumford farm and gone to Worcester to live with an uncle and to apprentice himself to Mason H. Morse, a well-known architect and builder from whom he learned the carpenter's trade. In the winter of 1855, having heard of his brother's success in Iowa and of the fine farming opportunities there, he said goodbye to Sarah and left with his friend Barker for the West. En route they stopped for a few days at Chicago and looked unsuccessfully for work. Then they went on to Dubuque, where they were temporarily employed as machinists.

In his letter of February 1, addressing Sarah as "My dear Friend," he wrote in part:

"After leaving Worcester we soon made the acquaintance of half a dozen live Yankees going West. It made the journey very pleasant, much more so than I expected, though we were delayed at Albany four hours on account of the snow blowing on the track.

"We left Albany at 11 in the evening, arriveing at Buffalo at 11 next morning half an hour behind time to connect with the regular train, had to wate till 12 at night for the next train. After leaving Buffalo we made good time changeing cars at Cleaveland & Toledo reaching Chicago at 11 oclock thursday evening where we stopped four days & made arrangements to stay till spring to work in a car shop but their engine broke down so as to stop business a few weeks.

"then we drove on to this place stoping at the Junction 20 minutes for dinner & crossing the river here at 12 at night, in an open wagon the coldest ride I ever had yet. It has been so cold here that I have not been out much yet, not enough to see how the place looks, it is from 10 to 25 below Zero so that people keep quiet as possible if they can get in a comfortable place.

"I am stoping at a place known as the Bothwell house with 30 or 40 boarders mostly from the Eastern states, Mass'ctts is well represented in number if nothing more.

"My brother has gone to Decorah a place 100 miles north west from here. I was something disappointed in not finding him here & half a mind to be homesick but not quite. . . . I hope to hear from you soon though you may have reason to think I have little claim on you for a communication. Truly yours D. W. KIMBALL."

Another letter to Sarah—"My dear Friend"—dated at Dubuque on March 3, 1856, reports a reunion with Wallace at last:

"Yours of 13th was re'cd 26 inst which was the first communication from Worcester. I began to think it would be a very nice thing to receive even a bit of blank paper from that place. I gladly offer many thanks for your kind letter & for not following my example of delay. When I think of your many friends, pleasant times & 'rounds of disipation' I almost wonder I should be thought of at all. For me I am quite alone most of the time though thy presence round me lingers chasing each wayward thought that tempts to rove and driving away that 'common hue' which is sometimes troublesome. It has been really thawing out here for the last few days: the snow is nearly gone & instead of cold weather we have any quantity of mud.

"Three weeks ago I started for Decorah to see Wallace but stopped 10 miles from here to take Breakfast & met him coming down. I hardly knew him at first he looked so much better than I expected & was so swallowed up in over-coats & shawles. No one thinks of riding all night in a stage without as much clothing on as they can well carry. then if they are not frozen they think they have been very fortunate. He has since gone back to Decorah & I expect to go there soon as next week but do not think to stop there a great while. I am going from there out West to look at some farms that Uncle Sam has in the market perhaps trade with him for one & build a log house on it about 8x10. The country is filling up very fast every one that come out here gets land enough for one farm at least, some of them get all they can wheather they go onto them or not. Mr. Colton need not flatter himself that he is the only one that can leave Worcester to come out here without returning in the course of two or three weeks. Though in many respects he has the advantage of me for being contented away, as he does not leave half behind, I think it is more unpleasant being away from there, than being here. . . .

"You may think by this writing I have got the ague, but that is not so. My candle gives such a flickering light that one eye will rest while the other keeps watch. So you must not be severe with me for not filling the sheet with something of more interest. . . . Truly yours DAVID."

The loneliness of which David wrote to Sarah would grow in intensity until the summer of 1858, when he and Barker would build their separate homes and he would set off to Worcester to bring back a bride.

David and Sarah were married on August 16, 1858, and began the slow and uncomfortable trip back to Iowa, traveling partly by train and partly by stage and horseback across the rough country.

Already, in faraway Chicago, the name of W. W. Kimball, as he now chose to sign himself, was getting to be known.

3

"The panic of 1857 had a musical accompaniment."

A STRANGE, quiet elation possessed the handsome, bearded young man from Decorah as he picked up his key at Chicago's Sherman House the evening of November 16, 1857. Slowly he strolled through the lobby of the famed hostelry at Clark and Randolph streets and headed for his room. In his thoughtful mood he might well have been mistaken, as he often was, for a minister or a professor.

All that Monday afternoon, as W. W. Kimball walked through the busy streets, he had pondered a decision—a simple enough trading transaction, as such things go, but, as time would prove it, the most important decision he would ever make.

It was by chance at breakfast that morning that he had struck up conversation with a Yankee piano salesman, down at heels and homesick for his native New York. Like hundreds of other Easterners who crowded the teeming town, the salesman had come West to seek his fortune. Now, with prices falling and "Panic Sale" signs on store front after store front, he was ready to give up the quest.

Nobody seemed attracted any more, he confided, by the merchandise he offered—four Grovesteen & Truslow square pianos, all that remained of a stock he had brought out from Albany. For weeks now they had sat, gathering dust and imperiled by the dampness, in a squalid warehouse on South Water Street, in the wholesale district on the banks of the foul-smelling Chicago River.

Would Kimball take them off his hands?

Warily at first, then with mounting interest, Kimball sparred with his new acquaintance. What, he laughed, did a real estate salesman know about pianos? Why, he couldn't even play a note. Then, giving rein to his Yankee instinct as a trader, he casually let it be known that he still retained the title to some valuable lots in Decorah. Wonderful country, Iowa. Often reminded him of New England. Just the place for a man wanting to get into something new.

The New Yorker's eyes lit up. Before many minutes had passed he was offering to swap his four pianos for the Decorah property, sight unseen. Because he had no idea what a piano was worth, Kimball cannily suggested that they sleep over the question and meet again at breakfast tomorrow, when he promised a decision.

In the afternoon he had satisfied himself that the pianos were worth at least as much as, perhaps more than, the land parcels he held. Now his mind was made up, and his step quickened as he walked down the Sherman's gas-lit corridor to retire for the night. He would go through with the deal in the morning.

Kimball's two days in Chicago, now boasting a population of 93,000, had convinced him that regardless of panic and depression there would be no holding back this town. Chicago was going ahead, and he intended to go with her.

For months now, since deciding to leave Decorah, he had weighed and analyzed the manifold promises of the expanding frontier. Long ago he had convinced himself that if he could anticipate the needs of the pioneer people he could in all likelihood build himself a solid future. Here, at last, seemed to be the chance of which he had dreamed.

The piano was a scarce commodity in the cities and towns of the West. Kimball remembered the drawing rooms of Cincinnati, where pianos were often found. In Chicago and Detroit they were also becoming fairly common in the wealthier homes. But in the prairie towns and on the farms they were seldom to be seen. In four years at Decorah, he reflected, he had heard only one old wreck of a piano, in the home of a Norwegian settler. It was probably the only piano in all of Winneshiek County.

Why shouldn't there be a thriving market for pianos all through the country, particularly among the music-loving newcomers from Europe? Especially if a moderately-priced instrument of quality could be found. In the cities, too, there were heavy concentrations of foreign born moving in—Germans, Swedes, Norwegians, Italians, Poles. The piano had long been a familiar musical instrument in Europe. These newcomers could be the backbone of a real business if he could cater to their love of music.

So it was on the next day—November 17, 1857, a brisk, gray Tuesday with the wind blowing cold off the lake and along Lake Street, the great "Street of Merchants"—that W. W. Kimball traded his Decorah lots for four square pianos and launched his business career in the face of a national depression. In that very fall 117 Chicago business houses would go out of business.

Nearly 80 years later, in 1933, as another great depression gripped the land, the noted editor Merle Thorpe, writing in the magazine *Nation's Business,* would cite Kimball's decision to defy the 1857 panic as an example for all business men to ponder:

"What is darkness to one man is to another an inviting chance to strike a light. . . . The panic of 1857 had a musical accompaniment because a man named Kimball decided it was a good time to make and sell pianos. . . . Rewards will likewise come to those who today have the simplicity to wonder, the ability to question, the power to generalize, and the capacity to apply."

With the land-piano swap completed, Kimball bundled himself to the ears in greatcoat and shawl, bent his gray beaver hat to the icy wind, and set out for the retail district of Lake Street, hunting up and down among the three, four, and five-story buildings for a likely place to store his merchandise. He must get them out of the riverfront warehouse before the dampness did its dirty work.

This was the year in which George M. Pullman, another Yankee, a cabinetmaker who was already working on his Pullman car invention, raised an entire block of Lake Street buildings four feet out of the mud with 6,000 jackscrews turned by 600 men. In later years he would be a close friend and neighbor of Kimball.

Striding along the wooden sidewalks of Lake Street, Kimball took note of the feverish activity all around him. At Dearborn Street, he paused to watch the passing vehicles—drays and barouches, Rockaways and slide seats, top and open buggies, Concords and sulkies. Everywhere there were people on the go.

In the retail district an undercurrent of optimism prevailed, in the face of the distress sales signs in the windows. Kimball had observed, too, that the more aggressive business men were holding their own against the panic. The pioneer drygoods merchant Potter Palmer, for example, freshly established in larger quarters at 139 Lake, was setting sales records with low prices that undercut his competitors.

True, Kimball told himself, it was going to test his own skills to the utmost to make his way in this competitive atmosphere. But if a man proceeded with caution there seemed to be every chance of succeeding. After all, his small stock of pianos had been acquired on bargain terms; they were, in effect, distress merchandise. Now he must find a low-rent space in which to store them.

Tomorrow he would move out of the Sherman House, with its elegant furnishings, and conserve his assets by engaging a cheaper room. Until he learned the piano business, there was always his real estate experience to fall back upon.

Among the various—and conflicting—accounts of this notable day and what followed in Chicago piano history, the most reliable appears to have been one that was published in the New York weekly *Music Trade Review* of June 27, 1896, under the title "A

Leaf from the Past." The article presented what purported to be the text of an old manuscript "written more than a decade ago from points furnished by Antonio de Anguera, who held for many years a confidential position with the W. W. Kimball Co."

De Anguera was a Lake Street piano tuner when Kimball came to town in 1857. For many years he tuned instruments for Kimball, and later he became a salesman in the retail division of the company. Drawn from memory, his account is confused on a number of facts, as we shall subsequently note, but it is among the more authentic records left by Kimball's early associates.

It contains enough essential, verifiable information to lay at rest several variant tales of the legendary land-for-pianos deal, reconstructed here in semi-fictional narrative form with the aid of the best available evidence. One of the apocryphal tales puts the scene of the trade at Dubuque; another has Kimball in business selling pianos and sewing machines in Decorah before coming to Chicago.

De Anguera's story is worth quoting, in part, as background for what is to follow:

"Some thirty-three years ago a tall, fine looking young man was hunting up and down Lake Street (which, by the way, was the retail street in Chicago in those days) for a place to put four Grovesteen & Truslow square pianos that he had traded some Iowa land for. He walked up and down the street until he stopped opposite an auction store, where a number of express wagons were unloading a lot of sheet music, musical merchandise and melodeons. The express men were carrying this stock upstairs, over the auction store.

"This was his chance. Up the stairs he went, and upon investigation, found it was the stock of the B. K. Mould Music Co., who had just made an assignment. The assignee had hired this upstairs wareroom to sell the stock off in. The melodeons were the property of the Geo. A. Prince & Co., of Buffalo; and Chas. Prince, the manager of the company in Chicago, had taken a portion of the room to sell his goods in. The young man [Kimball] proposed to the assignee to rent him space to put his four pianos in. The arrangement was made, and so began the career of the young piano dealer. He sold his pianos at a good profit. He liked the business, and saw clearly before him a fortune in it, and the possibilities of building up a big trade. He bought more pianos, and after a few months hired a wareroom for himself across the street. He increased his stock of pianos, added some other makes and hired a piano tuner.

"After a while he got Geo. A. Prince & Co. to consign him a half dozen melodeons, found they would sell, and bought the next lot for cash. He remained in this room a year, devoting his entire energies to the business, and added to his stock some Taylor and Farley melodeons. Then he moved into a down stairs wareroom (on same street) which he shared with a jewelry house that was just starting in Chicago. Here he took the agency of the J. & C. Fischer and other makes of pianos. He stayed in this store several years; prosperity smiled upon him; he hired a polisher and a traveling man; then he began to go East to buy his stock. This young piano man was spreading out. He thought he had kept his own books long enough, so he bought a big safe, a set of books, and hired a bookkeeper. He kept on his firm, straight march to success and fortune.

"His next move was to hire one of the elegant big stores in the New Crosby Opera House, then just built on Washington street, near State street; here his business rapidly increased, and he was fast climbing to the top. He took the agency of the Hallet & Davis piano, and made it his leader—the piano that by his skillful handling has become so famous. He also took the F. C. Lighte & Co. pianos and the Smith American organs, hired more bookkeepers, traveling men and tuners, advertised more liberally, and now he was beginning to be a rich man. He was recognized as a first-class merchant, and was making his power felt in the music world. The different piano and organ manufacturers were all anxious to sell to him; his success was an established fact; his money talked, and his clear, quick intellect took in all that was worth having in his line of business. He bought a big stock of J. P. Hale pianos . . . then began a renting business, such as had never been in Chicago before.

He inaugurated the monthly payment system, and it placed pianos within the reach of the working classes. Now fortune was within his grasp.

"When so near the top came the great fire; destruction stared all in the face. But his face never changed; calm and quiet he stood on the eventful morning after this great calamity, that made the civilized world shudder. He looked at the fallen ruins where his fine store had stood, his big stock all buried in the debris before him, his big safe buried under an immense pile of yet burning brick; he looked at the pale and anxious faces of his men; then he turned and walked out a distance to where the broken telegraph wires had been repaired and connected and sent a message to New York and Boston: *'Send me a stock of pianos and draw on me for what money you want.'* This was the kind of stuff that this piano man, this future king of the piano and organ industry of Chicago, was made of. Cities might burn down, but nothing could *down him!*"

4

"The point to arrive at is a large volume of trade."

Antonio de Anguera's brief and romantic memoir has come to be accepted through the years as one of the starting points for the various accounts of the Kimball beginnings in Chicago.

While basically correct, it contains discrepancies that are not always easy to reconcile with the more prosaic facts disclosed in actual records of the day.

It is, for example, of no real consequence to the Kimball story whether Brook K. Mould's early day music establishment, situated in 1857 at 83 Lake Street, went broke in that year, as the De Anguera manuscript suggests, or later. But the record shows that the Mould firm was still operating in 1858 at 104 Lake, where both Kimball and De Anguera shared its quarters.

Of more concern to one trying to set the record straight is the erroneous impression given by De Anguera that W. W. Kimball plunged immediately into a full-fledged music trade career after renting storage space for his four Grovesteen & Truslow squares on November 17, 1857.

Actually, his progress was much slower. With no knowledge whatsoever of the new instruments he possessed, Kimball realized that he must proceed with caution, learning step by step, if he wished to succeed.

Because he knew real estate best, his first operations as a Chicago business man would be in that field. New construction, particularly on the West Side, was going forward, despite the panic, and his observation of the real estate market had already shown him that prices were holding fairly close to their 1856 peaks. In such a market he could operate successfully.

Accordingly, his first business mention in the Chicago city directory, inserted in the 1858 edition, was as a real estate dealer with an office at 104 Lake. Apparently this was the location referred to in the De Anguera account as "across the street" (from 83 Lake), although it was in the next block to the west, across Dearborn Street.

Curiously, this first listing reverted through a typographical error to an earlier English spelling of the name, appearing as "William W. Kemball."

It was not until a year later, in the 1859 directory, that Kimball began to list himself as a dealer in pianofortes, while retaining a separate directory listing as a real estate agent. It was not until 1860 that he abandoned real estate entirely and turned his full attention to the musical instrument business.

The B. K. Mould storeroom at 83 Lake in which Kimball rented space was on the south side of Lake, between State and Dearborn streets. After engaging a drayman to transfer his musical merchandise from the South Water Street warehouse, he went looking for less expensive living quarters. He found a modest room in a lodging house at 125 Edina Place, off Jackson Street, at the south end of the business district. That evening he relaxed by watching the actress Miss Emma Logan and her co-star H. A. Perry in a performance of "Guy Mannering" at James H. McVicker's brand new theater on Madison Street.

Several of the accounts of these early years say that Kimball first began his business by renting his pianos, and this is confirmed in

A. T. Andreas' generally reliable "History of Chicago," which reports:

"In the fall of 1857, W. W. Kimball came to Chicago, and when he reached this city, trade was in a state of depression. He commenced renting pianos, and, in 1858, was located on Lake Street near Dearborn, with a small stock of music. Notwithstanding the dull times, his business prospered, and, in 1859, he removed to the Larmon Block. He subsequently went to No. 142 Lake Street, where he remained until the opening of the Crosby Opera House, where the fire destroyed his stock."

Albert G. Cone noted that in moving into his first Lake Street quarters Kimball "made one rent and one salesman suffice for both establishments." This arrangement apparently continued through 1858, when the Mould establishment moved to its new quarters at 104 Lake.

By 1859, Kimball had made another move, this time to 51 South Clark Street, where he continued his real estate operations and began to expand his piano business. This location was apparently the one referred to by De Anguera as "a down stairs wareroom (on same street) which he shared with a jewelry house that was just starting in Chicago." It was not on the "same street" (Lake Street), as De Anguera indicated, but in the Clark Street block to the south, between Lake and Randolph streets.

Other writers, including the piano maker William Tonk, in his "Memoirs of a Manufacturer," have referred to a jewelry store in connection with Kimball's early headquarters. One writer, in an article that appeared in the Minneapolis *Times* in 1898, described it as "a little room, 10 x 11, in the rear of a jewelry store." If Kimball indeed did share such quarters, it seems likely that the jeweler was Simon Bruenn, who was at the 51 South Clark address in 1858.

Kimball's own living quarters by then were in the Massasoit House, a popular boarding house on Central Avenue at the corner of South Water Street.

His business operation at 51 South Clark was for a short time only, and his next move was to 95 South Clark, between Randolph and Washington streets and a block farther south, where he opened a wareroom for pianos and melodeons. In 1861 he moved his stock into a music store in the Larmon Block at 99 South Clark operated by Julius Bauer. Bauer later would establish a piano maufacturing business absorbed eventually by the Rudolph Wurlitzer Company.

To be nearer his business, Kimball moved his residence from the Massasoit House to the Stewart House, on the northwest corner of State and Washington streets.

Tonk was a nephew of Bauer and an employe in his uncle's store in this period. In his "Memoirs" he erroneously identifies the place of Kimball's start as a jewelry store on Lake Street "between Clark and La Salle." The Larmon Block, Tonk writes, "was one of the most imposing brick and limestone structures erected up to that time, dealing in musical instruments and sheet music only." He adds that when Kimball moved in and "took part of the rear of Mr. Bauer's store . . . he kept, on a platform, say 25 x 20 feet, as many pianos and organs as the space would accommodate."

That Kimball was already beginning to prosper is indicated by the fact that he moved out of the Stewart House in 1862 and into a more expensive room at the Sherman, where he had stopped for only a few nights when he first came to town in 1857.

"I now had two masters," Tonk's recollections continue, "each of whom paid me one half the wages originally agreed on. The business grew as times got better, and Mr. Kimball moved out, taking quarters on Washington Street, between Clark and Dearborn. At that time Washington Street was in a state of transformation from residential homes to business establishments."

Tonk is in error again in confusing Kimball's next move—from 99 South Clark Street to 142 Lake Street, where he had warerooms in 1862, 1863 and part of 1864—with the move in the latter year to Uranus H. Crosby's splendid new combination opera house, art gallery, and office building at 63 Washington Street, where he occupied a first-floor store at the east end of the building.

In all accounts of these early years, there is an emphasis on the shrewdness and energy with which Kimball set about learning the ins and outs of the music business.

"Mr. Kimball made it a point," wrote Cone, ". . . to fulfill his contracts to the letter. He bought for cash, sold at a fair profit . . . guaranteed . . . and gave his customers entire satisfaction . . . adopted . . . the true principle by which great fortunes are gained—that of making money not by large profits from individual sales, few in number, but by small profits from a large and constantly growing number of customers. . . . His aim has been, as he says himself, not to see how much money he could make out of a single transaction, but how closely he could sell. To this he ascribes much of his prosperity, for, to use his own words, 'there are few people who understand that the expenses of running an increasing business do not increase as the business increases; consequently, the point to arrive at is a large volume of trade.' "

Tonk reports that Kimball "was a kind and forbearing employer during the short time I was employed by him and Mr. Bauer." He adds: "Mr. Kimball did all the selling; whether he had any outside salesman I was not informed. His musical talent was limited to the striking of a few chords; at least I do not recall that he ever did more in his endeavors to sell either pianos or organs. He was a man of few words, which must have been telling and convincing, from the fact that he seldom failed to make a sale to a real customer."

One aspect of his employer that baffled the young Tonk was his sense of humor. He writes:

"Mr. Kimball was fond of telling jokes, after which he would laugh in his peculiar way.

"He had one pronounced peculiarity: He would talk with you and laugh at some of his witticisms when, without warning, he would right-about-face and walk away, leaving you to laugh it out alone."

Kimball's own story of his first piano purchase, after the Grovesteen & Truslow instruments, shows the tough-minded but fair attitude with which he approached his new business:

"It was a good many years ago, when I was quite a young man. I had looked the field over and thought it would be a good thing to go into the piano business.

"I had a little money and I went on to New York. I didn't know anything about pianos then, and supposed you bought them like everything else—like wheat or pork—by the quantity.

"I called on a house, well known in those days . . . one of the oldest in the trade. After some dickering, I had made my bargain, and had my roll out to pay for the goods, when I said: 'Are you sure you are giving me your lowest prices? Are there not some cheaper pianos being made?'

" 'Oh, yes,' said the piano maker. 'The Fischers make cheaper pianos, but we wouldn't put our name on the trash they turn out! Why, they use green lumber!'

" 'I guess,' said I, as a thought struck me and I put my roll back into my pocket, 'that I'll think this thing over and come again in the morning.'

"I went straight back to my hotel, got a directory and hunted up the address of 'Fisher', a piano maker. Couldn't find it. Then I looked up Fischer and got it. That day I went up to the Fischer factory and met Mr. Fischer, the light haired one.

" 'Somebody told me,' said I, 'that you make cheaper pianos than anybody else, but that they are no good.'

" 'I think we make nice instruments,' replied Mr. Fischer, politely.

" 'Let me see some,' said I.

"So Mr. Fischer took me through the factory.

" 'Do you use green lumber?' I asked.

" 'No sir, we could not afford to,' was the quiet reply.

" 'By the bye,' said I, 'what kind of pianos do Messrs. ——— make?'—mentioning the name of the firm I had been to first.

" 'I understand that they make a very nice piano indeed,' said Mr. Fischer.

"That settled it. Fischer got my roll, and that purchase was the first of many more. I guess I must have bought over 1,000 Fischer pianos before I made other arrangements. During all that time I never had any trouble with any of their instruments, and I found them particularly fine, upright and good people to deal with."

The firm was J. & C. Fischer, established in St. John's Lane, New York City, in 1840 by John U. and Charles S. Fischer, descendants of a Vienese piano making family. Charles was "the light-haired one" to whom Kimball referred. The firm was absorbed years ago by the Aeolian American Corporation, which still manufactures a J. & C. Fischer piano.

5

**"He knew the true . . . value of a name
on a fall board."**

In November, 1897, on the occasion of the fortieth anniversary
of Kimball's entry into the American piano trade, the *Musical
Courier* described his impact as follows:

"Leaving aside the personal equation, it must be said that the
forty years of the Kimball prosperity embrace the period of the
greatest commercial and industrial development of Chicago and
the great West, and during these years, representing two scores, the
history of the piano trade of America was actually made.

"In 1857, when Mr. Kimball started business, all the great men
of the piano trade identified with its birth in this country were
busily engaged in it with the exception of Jonas Chickering, who
died in 1853. They have all passed away with the exception of Mr.
Chas. Fischer and Mr. James W. Vose. Mr. George Chickering be-
longs to a period somewhat later, although he is the only survivor
of the second Chickering generation. The second Steinway generation ended with the death of William Steinway a year ago next
Tuesday week. Mr. D. H. Baldwin, one of the pioneers of the
Western piano business, is among the living, being one of the most
robust and healthy men in it, and can be found daily at his desk.

"With Mr. Kimball and Mr. Baldwin the Western impetus really began. . . ."

Uncorking all its windy rhetoric, the *Music Trade Review* commented a few months later:

"The history of the Kimball house may be said to be the history of the modern West."

Enlarging still later upon Kimball's accomplishments, the *Musical Courier* accurately assessed the superbly energetic qualities of business enterprise that led him in the 1860s and 70s to become the chief among the musical instrument dealers and later the world's greatest piano manufacturer.

"No man that the piano business has produced," said the *Courier,* "saw more clearly than he did through the superficialities of the business of making and selling pianos. No man realized more astutely, more poignantly than he the fact that a piano was a piano no matter where made, no matter by whom made. He had, when he began making instruments, sold hundreds and thousands of Eastern made pianos, and he knew the merits—the intrinsic merits —of his great stock as few dealers know their wares. He knew the true, the actual value of a name on a fall board and all that was meant by the creation and maintenance of this super-value. He knew the cost of making, the cost of marketing, the profits of the manufacturer, the jobber and the retailer, and when, but a comparatively few years ago, he determined, after careful, matured thought, to start a piano factory of his own he entered the field equipped as no man before him had been, with an actual, accumulated knowledge of the business root and branch.

"It would be unjust to say that he did not make some errors in the beginning; he was perhaps over-sanguine, and he had learned by experience that pianos are made primarily to sell, and to sell to a public not over-particular as to what they buy. But it is justice to him to say that he quickly remedied his early errors and turned quickly into a method of construction that has redounded to the glory of his own name—to the credit of his own product.

The Kimball Story

"W. W. Kimball is by nature and by training an operator—not a speculator—an operator, a manipulator of means, a mover of men, or, to continue the alliteration, a creator of circumstances. Years and years ago, when he was merely a retail dealer in Chicago, he could not rest content with the limited transactions that came within the scope of that wonderful city, and he gradually took under his control vast territory adjacent to his headquarters for the representation of the several makes of pianos he then bought, so that he became the greatest jobber in musical instruments we have ever known."

These estimates of contemporary musical authorities must have been gratifying to the great manufacturer in his years of triumph, for they were the acknowledgment at last of the wisdom of the course he had pursued since his initial purchase of Fischer pianos in the late 1850s.

From the start Kimball determined to learn everything he could about the instruments he handled—the history of the piano, its development in America, the latest improvements in design, the manner in which pianos were made. The more he studied their development the more interested he became.

One thing was clear to him as he talked with piano men and sat up nights plowing through the literature of the trade: In some four centuries of evolution from the primitive clavichord, the piano had reached a high state of perfection. True there were refinements yet to be made, and Kimball's technicians and craftsmen in years to come would contribute their share of these, but the way to the future lay not in the drafting room but in the development of piano sales to the masses.

In this line of thinking, he was not alone. His view was typical of the early piano tycoons in the Middle West. They were business men, not craftsmen. Clifford C. Chickering of the Boston piano family, himself a Chicago piano manufacturer (Chickering Brothers) in the 1890s, commented on this point in a talk to the Chicago Piano Club in October, 1922:

"A very remarkable, significant and interesting fact concerning these pioneer members of our trade is that none of them were practical piano men. They were dependent on others to supervise the processes in connection with the construction of pianos. Consequently their knowledge of the instrument was necessarily superficial.

"Allowing my memory to run back over the history of the piano business, I do not recall a single instance where a big concern was organized and built up in a single generation by men who were practical in the piano line. The great successes, viewed from the standpoint of financial success, have been developed by men with keen business instincts and not by men with technical knowledge."

Nevertheless, as Kimball shopped in the 1850s and 60s for new pianos to add to his stock he went armed with an intimate knowledge of all that had gone into piano making to that day.

Already, he said in later years, he was dreaming of the day when he would manufacture pianos himself—the best that human ingenuity could produce, and at the lowest possible prices. He kept these points in mind, insisting upon quality from his suppliers but at a price that would enable him to get the widest possible distribution, the greatest possible volume of sales.

A realist, he was not a man to listen to the sort of sentimental hogwash used by some manufacturers of his day to justify outrageous prices. He dismissed as 98 per cent fiction most of the lofty claims of superiority based on Old World craftsmanship, or on supposedly secret acoustical theories of piano making. He believed, like Joseph P. Hale, who would become for a time in the 1870s one of his principal suppliers, that the prices charged by most piano makers were "disproportionate, fictitious, and fanciful" when compared with actual costs. Later, with his own tremendous factory, he would prove this was true.

It had required a space of many centuries for the basic principle of the pianoforte to evolve from the monochord, the single catgut string device invented by Pythagoras in 582 B.C., to the iron-bound, overstrung virtuoso instrument of the mid-19th century with its rich and noble crescendos of sound and tonal expressiveness.

From the 14th-century clavicytherium there had developed the first true prototype of the modern pianoforte, an instrument called a clavichord, with an independent soundboard and metal strings which were struck by a brass tangent. It was on such an instrument that Mozart composed his "Magic Flute" and other masterpieces.

Next had come the spinet or virginal, an instrument of louder tone produced by twanged strings, and then the harpsichord, an enlarged spinet with even greater volume.

After 1709, when the Italian inventor Bartolomeo Cristofori developed his *gravicembali col piano et forte,* there had been rapid progress. Cristofori wanted an instrument that could be played loud or soft by the touch of the fingers. This led him to design a new instrument, adapted from the dulcimer and embodying the principle of striking a hammer against strings to produce the desired effect. Several other inventors developed similar hammer actions at about the same time, but Cristofori was the first to develop a complete instrument of this type and is generally acknowledged to be the pianoforte's inventor.

In the latter part of the 18th century improvements came thick and fast. Johann Andreas Stein of Augsburg developed a sustaining pedal and won the praise of Mozart. John Broadwood of London built the first six-octave piano. The Parisian piano maker Sebastian Erard built a grand. In 1821 Erard perfected his double-escapement action, which let the hammer fall back part of the way from the strings while the key was held down. In 1824 the same maker built the first successful upright piano, although Matthias Muller of Vienna had tried it nearly a quarter of a century before. Alpheus Babcock of Boston pioneered the piano's greatest triumph—that of increasing the tension of the stringing—by inventing a full iron frame for the square piano in 1825. Another Bostonian, Jonas Chickering, improved on Babcock's invention in the 1830s and by 1843 had made the first grand piano with an iron frame cast or molded in one piece.

In New York the Steinways won widespread acclaim in 1855 for their overstrung square pianos. With skill and enterprise they had taken advantage of the principle of cross-stringing developed 30 years earlier and applied it to the full iron frame. By 1859 they had repeated this success with their grand pianos. In their overstrung scale the strings were arranged, fan-like, in two layers, with the treble strings below the bass. By lengthening the bridge they were able to obtain more tone color and a greater volume of sound from their soundboard.

The piano, by this time, had undergone practically every major improvement that it contains to this day.

Thus the scene was set for the entry of W. W. Kimball. The great age of the commercial development of the piano in America still lay ahead.

6

**"There is scarcely a hamlet in the West which has
not felt the touch of his gentle influence."**

IN THE florid 1880-style prose of his brother-in-law Albert G.
Cone, W. W. Kimball was a man entitled to the gratitude of a
considerable portion of mankind. For, by "placing within the
reach of the farmer on his prairie, the miner in his cabin, the
fisherman in his hut, the cultivated mechanic in his neat cottage in
the thriving town the most domestic and the most delightful of
instruments"—the reed organ—he had supplied "an influence
which refines his home, educates his children, and gladdens his
daily life like a constant ray of sunshine on his hearth."

"There is scarcely a hamlet in the West," Cone rhapsodized,
"which has not felt the touch of his gentle influence; and many a
home, into which the love of music has penetrated, is indebted to
him for the gratification of that love through the sweet-toned instruments which his active brain, and his shrewd and economical
management, have placed within its easy reach."

A chance breakfast table conversation had put Kimball into the
piano business, but it was more than mere chance that found him

turning in 1859 to the newly perfected melodeon, or cabinet organ—popularly known as the reed organ—for a larger volume of
sales.

Already the country was climbing out of the depression. In the
nation at large general business was still not back to normal, but
in Chicago lumber receipts were up, hog packing was booming,
and the decline in grain shipments and railway earnings had
slowed to a halt. The city was moving ahead: This was the year
when horse cars made their bow in State Street; Clark Street was
paved with wooden blocks. There was a new current of optimism
in the retail stores.

The depression notwithstanding, Kimball had managed to at-
tract a considerable trade with his gracious, courtly manners and
his confident salesmanship. In his first full year he had fared quite
as well, he reflected, as a beginning piano dealer might expect under the circumstances. His rental business was off to a thriving
start, and here and there he found a customer with the cash to buy.
The Fischer pianos were making friends, but in order to broaden
his sales possibilities Kimball had taken on some instruments from
a second supplier, the well-known Boston concern of Hallet, Davis
& Company. It was a connection that would endure for the next
thirty-six years, or until April, 1894, when the firm's Chicago retail
representation would be taken over, with the friendly consent of
all concerned, by Lyon & Healy. Established in 1835 as Brown &
Hallet, the Boston manufacturers were among the most respected
of the day. In the course of Kimball's association with them he
would sell more than 10,000 of their instruments to Chicago area
customers.

Still, as he analyzed his current position with characteristic thoroughness, there was one thing clear to Kimball on the eve of his
second anniversary in the piano trade: If he were going to make a
go of it, and get out of the real estate business altogether, he must
find a broader market than was afforded by the well-to-do customers now coming into his store. It was clear to him now that if

he depended solely on pianos his trade would be limited. A "polite" trade, they called it in those days, but limited. He was not reaching the man in modest circumstances. Even a cheap piano cost $200 to $300 in those days, with the prices for the fine instruments ranging up to $800 or more. The average man could scarcely afford one. On the other hand, the reed organ, "the piano's little country cousin," could be installed in a parlor for as little as $100.

The role that chance played in Kimball's long and profitable association with the reed organ was a happy coincidence of timing that destiny might seem to have arranged. For this homely instrument, like its fancier cousin the piano, was reaching its maturity in the United States at about the same time that Kimball arrived in Chicago and established his business. For some years the reed organ had been developing, and in time it would come to be the foremost rival of the piano. It was particularly favored in the small towns and on the farms because of its lower price.

The first practical American melodeon (there was a similar instrument in Europe known as the harmonium) originated in 1845 as the invention of one Josiah Bartlett of Concord, New Hampshire. There had been other experimental melodeons as long ago as the 1820s, but Bartlett's was the precursor of the commercial instrument as we know it. Inspired by a German accordeon which he happened to possess, Bartlett designed a larger instrument, about two feet long and a foot wide, to be held in the lap while the player worked a bellows with his left elbow and used both hands to play a set of push-button "keys." In its later versions the reeds were placed in a larger cabinet, before which the player sat, pumping the bellows with his feet. Piano-like keys eventually were substituted for the push buttons.

Bartlett's instrument contained only three octaves, or 22 reeds, but in subsequent development the Prescott Brothers of Concord, who operated a music store, increased the range to five octaves and designed a case. They called their instrument a "piano-style melodeon," since in form and appearance it was similar to the square piano. In later years it was to take the upright form, just as the piano became upright.

These early melodeons sold fairly well, but it was not until 1850 that the instrument really came into its own. In that year Jeremiah Carhart of the New York City firm of Carhart & Needham invented a device for exhausting air through the reeds instead of blowing it upon them. The improved tone quality that resulted brought a heavy increase in demand, and the manufacture of the reed organ was expanded tremendously. By the mid-1860s American plants were turning out 15,000 instruments a year, with Kimball's sales accounting for approximately a fourth of that volume.

Thus the Chicago newcomer rode the tide of an expanding interest in the reed organ, as he did with the overstrung, iron-framed piano. The organs he would purchase in 1859 and for some months to follow would sell very well until the outbreak of the Civil War. Then they would drop off sharply, to resume again in the spring of 1862, following the Government's issuance in February of $150 million in non-interest-bearing treasury notes, known popularly as "greenbacks."

As he made his decision to go after lower-priced sales in the reed organ field, Kimball's first thought naturally was of the instruments he had seen in the George A. Prince & Company stock at 83 Lake Street in 1857. The Prince people since that time had opened a new wholesale depot at 110 Lake, and Kimball hustled right over to discuss the prospects with Charles Prince and to pick out a small stock of instruments. Successful with these from the first, he turned as his business progressed to other makers for his supplies. Eventually he would manufacture reed organs of his own in the largest organ factory in America, beginning with the making of a few instruments in 1879 in the repair shops above his warerooms.

In 1862 Kimball advertised himself as the sole agent of the Alexander organ in Chicago. Among the other makes that he handled in this early reed organ trade were the Taylor & Farley; the widely popular Smith American, made by the Smith American Organ and

Piano Company of Boston; and the Shoninger, manufactured at New Haven, Connecticut, by Bernhard Shoninger. The Smith American was Kimball's leader all through the 1860s, and the Shoninger was a good second.

While Kimball's immediate aim in launching this branch of his trade was to supply music to thousands of homes where the piano was quite beyond the purse of the home maker, he also knew that the reed organ was in a sense a musical pioneer. Many of those who purchased organs were turned later into piano customers.

He also recognized from the beginning the great potential the reed organ held for sales to the smaller churches, the lodge halls, and the schools, for which it was ideally adapted. The churches especially were good prospects, since by the time Kimball began his business the Protestant denominations on the Western frontier had begun to relax their traditional prejudices against the use of musical instruments in the worship.

Most of the congregational singing throughout the first half of the 19th century had been without musical accompaniment. The Presbyterians were the last to turn from Psalm-singing to the more popular hymns and the swelling tones of the organ, but they at last joined the Methodists and the Baptists in recognizing the important contribution instrumental music had to make to the esthetic experience of the pioneer. In many a Western community the church organ became and remained for many years the only instrument available for serious music.

The 1860s were turbulent years in Chicago, a time marked both by patriotic fervor and vigorous expansion.

Politically, Kimball was a Republican, and he gave ardent support to the nomination in 1860 of Abraham Lincoln as his party's first presidential candidate. The convention was held in the wooden Wigwam at Lake and Market streets, on the edge of the downtown business district. From the outbreak of the tragic Civil War, Kimball devoted much of his time and energy, along with most of the city's businessmen, to the task of supplying the Union armies and backing their cause. A good friend of these days was the patriotic song writer, George F. Root, whose music publishing business was a tenant a few years later, along with Kimball, in Crosby's Opera House on Washington Street. It was Root who wrote the famous war song, "The Battle Cry of Freedom," and "Tramp, Tramp, Tramp," a favorite of the Union foot soldier. One of the great Northern leaders, Gen. Philip Sheridan, was in later years an intimate friend of the piano manufacturer.

Kimball's retail business prospered as the city around him prospered. Despite the war, there was no letup in the forward movement: Street railway systems spread out to the north, south, and west; the railroads did a profitable business in transporting soldiers and handling grain and livestock; the meat packing industry, spurred by war demands, became a major part of the economic life of the city; demands for other war necessities—wagons, uniforms, camp equipment, and an endless variety of items—brought an influx of new capital and the establishment of manufacturing and distribution facilities of many sorts. Chicago, as one writer put it, "became the paradise of workers and speculators."

When the increase in Kimball's sales and rental business forced his removal in 1862 from 99 South Clark to larger quarters at 142 Lake, he had already set in motion the plans for developing the West's first great wholesale trade in pianos and organs. The exact date of this advance to a new level of enterprise is not clear from the meager records available. One writer says merely that "he entered the wholesale field early in the 60s, and by 1864 had so well established himself in both wholesale and retail that he felt justified in opening warerooms in the Crosby Opera House, on Washington Street, then the center of trade in Chicago and the West." Another says, "From an early date Mr. Kimball had been doing a jobbing business as well as selling at retail. He controlled a string of agents in the Middle Western states, to whom he supplied pianos and organs, but principally organs."

In this connection, a writer in the "Encyclopaedia of Biography of Illinois" remarks, "The young merchant seemed to realize the necessity of patient waiting, and so rested content with a local trade, in the belief that the growing requirements of the country would in time call for the establishment of a wide agency system and wholesale traffic connections, with the larger opportunities thus implied. Nor did he miscalculate. In 1864 the wholesale trade in pianos had, through his individual effort, been established for the first time in Chicago, and the development of traffic became such as to justify his removal to the famous Crosby Opera House on Washington Street. Here he opened fine warerooms which became the center of the polite trade of the Northwest till the general conflagration of 1871."

The historian Andreas simply records that Kimball was the "first man to do a wholesale instrument business. It was he who inaugurated the installment plan, which has enabled so many families, without perceptible outlay, to purchase musical instruments."

7

"The silk hat gentry of the young and lusty city frequented the Kimball store."

A NEW ERA in the Chicago music trade began with W. W. Kimball's move into Uranus H. Crosby's splendid new "temple of the arts" on Washington Street, between State and Dearborn, in 1864, in advance of a formal opening and before the plaster was dry on the walls. This $700,000 opera house, art gallery, and office building sat on the north side of the street, where the Stop and Shop grocery now stands. It was a showplace that outdid anything Chicago had seen before. The first floor tenants included Kimball, with an elaborate stock of pianos and organs; the restaurant operator John Wright, whose establishment later became H. M. Kinsley's "celebrated and elegant confectionery, ice cream and dining establishment"; and the music publishing firm of Root & Cady.

Proudly Kimball subscribed for a full page announcement in Halpin's city directory for 1865 and proclaimed his new enterprise in confident terms: "Kimball's Piano Forte Warerooms, Removed

Kimball's elegant store (right) in Crosby's Opera House was a center of musical interest in the 1860s.
(Courtesy Chicago Historical Society.)

Early Chicago contemporaries of W. W. Kimball were (at top) Julius Bauer, left, and Hampton L. Story, and (at bottom) George W. Lyon, left, and P. J. Healy.

to 63 Washington Street, Chicago, In Crosby's Opera House. Wholesale Depot for Pianos, Organs and Melodeons. Constantly Receiving and Have On Hand the Largest and Best Assortment of First Class Pianos from the Celebrated Manufactures of F. C. Lighte & Co., J. & C. Fischer, J. Chickering, Hallet, Davis & Co., G. A. Miller & Co., Kurtzman & Hinze, and Other Boston and New York Manufacturers. Wholesale dealers will find it to their advantage to give us a call, as by greatly increased facilities, we are enabled to fill orders with dispatch. A liberal discount to clergymen, schools, etc. Persons in want of a Really First Class Piano will do well to call before purchasing elsewhere. Every Instrument Warranted for 5 Years. Pianos to Rent. Old Pianos taken in Exchange for New. Orders for tuning and repair promptly attended to."

Another advertisement, in the 1866 directory, boldly and simply conveyed to the reader an idea of the position of prominence in which the farm boy from Maine now stood:

"Address all letters W. W. Kimball, Chicago, Ill."

"The warerooms of W. W. Kimball in that musical center," says one writer, "were among the finest in land." His progress had been so swift, says another, "that these new warerooms were really something to talk about." He adds: "The silk hat gentry of the young and lusty city frequented the Kimball store, and it was not long before Mr. Kimball literally became one of them. Among his close friends were such men as Marshall Field, George M. Pullman, and John V. Farwell, whose names are also perpetuated in great business establishments."

His purpose to build a piano and organ business second to none was now firmly fixed, and he bent his every effort to the task. Promptly at 7 o'clock each morning he would show up as the store opened, making the rounds, greeting his clerks, tuners, and salesmen courteously, urging them to study better ways and means of performing their assignments, cheerfully offering suggestions on their individual problems, always encouraging them by kindly recognition of good work done. The hours were long, and many times it was 8 o'clock in the evening before Kimball shut his doors.

His business methods were simple, sound, and conservative. His office, said one music trade journal of the 1890s in a summary of the Kimball enterprise, "was the first to use solid journalizing; ledger forms in lease or installment record books, and to adopt a systematic averaging of installment paper." Everything was on a cash basis or for first-class secured paper, often at full list price, the same writer said. "Parties who wished to dicker had no chance to deal with him, and he turned them over to one of his employes, if they wished the trade, and required such employe to pay him the cost of the instrument sold."

As the profits mounted Kimball paid special attention to the requirements of his expanding wholesale business. With typical caution, he guarded against the possibility of losses by carefully selecting the agents who handled his goods. Most of this trade was handled by correspondence at the time and, since typewriters and stenographers were conveniences yet to come, Kimball personally handled much of it with letters in longhand.

It was in this period, long before he was to establish his organ and piano factories, that Kimball first branched out into the manufacturing field after purchasing a patent for casting iron screws and nuts. He saw in this process an opportunity to make a serviceable line of low-cost piano and organ stools, and for many years he carried on a profitable manufacture in this line.

Many years later, a Kimball contemporary, the late Hampton L. Story, who came to Chicago in 1866, described in the pages of the *Indicator,* a Chicago music trade publication, the atmosphere of business in these early days:

"We were feeling our way then in a great, almost limitless field. There was no such institution as the retail trade in the West in those days. Here in Chicago all the houses were jobbers as well as retailers—that is, we were willing to wholesale when we could, and it was a principal part of our business to establish sub-agencies through the Western states between Ohio and the Pacific coast.

The other jobbing centers besides Chicago were Cincinnati and St. Louis.

"Securing reliable agents was a still harder task then than now. Organs—which were everything in the trade, as pianos were far too expensive for any but the wealthy—cost a lot of money even at wholesale, and inexperienced merchants were cautious about accepting them even on consignment. My own method of working up wholesale trade was to start out on the road with a full line of goods, ship them to a promising town, set them up wherever I could and hold a sale; then after closing out a number of instruments at good prices go around to some druggist or furniture dealer, show him what I had done and get him to take over the remnant of the stock. Then on to another town. . . .

"Our territory was so wide and its trade possibilities so great that naturally there was no jealousy between us here in Chicago. I never saw a more friendly lot of competitors than the half dozen Chicago jobbers. We used to visit each other, talk over what we had done and consult as to plans. Such confidence would mean business suicide today, but you see each of us had as much business as he could well handle and knew where he could get more any time he wanted it, and there was no incentive to take mean advantage of the tips your competitor dropped."

Kimball was the dean of these early day dealers. The contemporary houses included Story & Camp, formed in 1868 when Hampton Story joined forces with Isaac N. Camp; Lyon & Healy (now Lyon-Healy), established in 1864 by George W. Lyon and Patrick J. Healy; Julius Bauer & Company, Root & Cady, and Alonzo Reed.

"The thing which worried all of us most," said Story, "was getting enough goods from the manufacturers, and at our conferences the talk drifted more often to that question than to any other. I remember distinctly several conversations I had with W. W. Kimball over the advisability of manufacturing a few organs of our own. Both of us were afraid of it at first, being doubtful whether the public would accept organs with 'Chicago' on them."

Story recalled that "the prices we got for organs are almost past belief." By this time the post-Civil War boom was in full swing, and prices were considerably advanced over the levels that prevailed when Kimball had first entered business. The cheapest style of reed organ, a plain little three-foot case with two sets of reeds, wholesaled at $87. And, Story added, "I don't think it was often sold at retail for less than $200." It was the custom of Kimball and his contemporaries to give discounts of 25 to 33 per cent from both wholesale and retail list prices. For a style of organ with three full sets of reeds they got from $25 to $35 more at wholesale, and about as much more for a fourth set of reeds. There were also other extra charges—$25 for couplers, $25 for tremolo, and $25 for sub-bass. Each of these features boosted the retail price by as much as $50 to $75.

The cases were usually of black walnut, with little ornamentation. An occasional one might be veneered with rosewood, but such exquisite instruments went only into the more elegant parlors and were charged for accordingly. Solid oak cabinets were used later, but mahogany was unknown. Story confessed that, while veneers were used, the manufacturers had not yet perfected the art of staining. There was also mechanical trouble to contend with, particularly with the stop action. In every case of complaint, Kimball made sure to put the instrument in proper order. He was building a reputation for such service that would be unexcelled in all the music business.

The pianos of the day were "all squares, all well made, and all high priced," Story recalled. "Cheap pianos were a thing unheard of; every maker built as thoroughly as he knew how, and that each succeeded in the matter of durability is at least attested to by the old remains standing around in our basements today. Our lowest wholesale price on pianos was $175, and the retailer never thought of taking a profit of less than $100. Often it was $300. Not many of the country dealers would stock pianos, and consequently our wholesale business in them was small. Persons who wanted pianos came to the larger cities to get them, and as the demand in the West was light the dealer had to control large territory."

An interesting aspect of piano selling, typical of the methods used by Kimball salesmen and the others in the days before newspaper advertisements were employed to lure customers into the stores, was described by Adam Schneider, another Chicago piano trade veteran, as follows:

"The successful man was the one who was willing to load a piano or organ on a wagon, drive into the country, unload his piano or organ at some farm house, and play and demonstrate it in the hope of making a sale. It was literally a matter of going into the highways and byways and compelling them to buy. In most cases, a piano or organ left in the parlor of a home eventually meant a sale."

George L. Hadley, a Kimball salesman and retired secretary of the firm, recalled in a talk the writer had with him in his Boston home in April, 1956, that it was sometimes the custom among these early day salesmen to rig a wagon wheel so that it would roll off the axle as the wagon passed a farmhouse. Pleading that he must get back to town for parts, the salesman would then enlist the family's aid in getting his piano or organ off the collapsed wagon and into the house for protection from the elements. Usually the request would be gladly granted. When the salesman returned to repair his wagon a day or so later, there was a good possibility that the housewife, practicing "Lead Kindly Light" or "Jesus, Lover of My Soul," would be so enamored of the new instrument that she would not permit it to be taken away.

The way in which Kimball went after the trade in the smaller communities is shown in a typical front-page newspaper advertisement which appeared in the Carlyle (Illinois) *Union Banner* of January 9, 1868. "LIGHTE'S PIANO TRIUMPHANT," the headline proclaimed. "Just received the First Premium At the Iowa and Illinois State Fairs, in competition with the most celebrated manu-

Evalyne M. Cone, "a most estimable lady," and W. W. Kimball, to whom she was married in June, 1865.

facturers." The notice carried the further advice: "Pianos sold on time. Payment received in installments. Second hand Pianos received in exchange for New." The advertisement also featured Smith's American Organs "for parlors, churches and lodges" and proclaimed them to be superior in "Great Fulness and Completeness of Tone, Expression and Elasticity of Touch." It added that 4,000 had been sold "within the year." Never missing a trick, Kimball solicited mail order sales, offering to send a circular, "giving prices and stiles of each instrument," to all who wrote in.

The prosperous young Kimball of the 1860s was not all business. His clientele at Crosby's Opera House included some of the city's wealthier and more important families. And with his affluence, his well-bred manners, his charm and good looks—he was clean shaven now except for a mustache—he fitted naturally and easily into their company. He was, his brother-in-law Cone assures us, "held in high esteem for his many endearing qualities" and was "an excellent conversationalist" who was known in the social circle as a man of "keen-pointed wit and the most delicate humor."

As such, he was destined to meet and eventually to marry, on June 22, 1865, a young woman who was in her brother's words "a most estimable lady, who is recognized as one of the chief ornaments of Chicago society." She was Evalyne M. Cone, the sister of Albert G. and Irving H. Cone and the daughter of Hubbell B. Cone, a pioneer lumber dealer who came to Chicago from Connecticut in 1849. The Cones first lived on Adams Street, near State Street, then at 413 South Clark Street, and later at 433. The elder Cone was at first an employe of Timothy J. Shilton & Company and later became a partner in the lumber firm of Cone & O'Brien.

After their marriage, the Kimballs lived for a short time at 611 South Wabash Avenue. They moved in 1867 to No. 594 on Wabash and in 1868 into a splendid home at 610 Michigan Avenue, in the heart of a fashionable residential district of the period.

51

Evalyne Kimball would in time become one of the great art patrons of Chicago history. At her death in 1921 she would leave to the Art Institute of Chicago one of the finest private collections of paintings in America, including Rembrandt's magnificent portrait of his father.

Her brother, Albert, entering Kimball's employ as an office boy on January 1, 1869, would become one of his ablest lieutenants, serving as his treasurer from the time of the W. W. Kimball Company's incorporation in 1882 until his death in 1900.

8

**"Mr. Cone was in the store . . . playing the Dead
March from 'Saul' on a dulcimer."**

I<small>T HAD BEEN</small> a mellow, pleasant Indian summer day for Chicago's
334,270 citizens: Sunday, October 8, 1871. A day of relaxation, an
almost perfect day in which the city dweller could rest and re-
plenish his strength for another week of activity. The busy and
prosperous city now extended from Fullerton Avenue on the
north to Thirty-ninth Street on the south; on the West Side the
street numbers stretched out, as a Chicagoan would put it, to the
"forty hundred" block.

Now the evening was almost over, and in countless homes across
the city the people were preparing for sleep. But few, if any, were
destined to sleep this night.

For at about 9:15 o'clock in a stable behind the home of one
Patrick O'Leary and his family at 137 De Koven Street, on the
West Side, the Great Chicago Fire of 1871 broke out. Legend has
it that Mrs. O'Leary's cow started the fire by kicking over a lighted
lamp when her mistress went to the house to get some salt for the
animal. All that is really known about its origin is that the O'Leary

The Kimball store in flames, 1871. *(Courtesy Chicago Historical Society.)*

drayman, "Peg Leg" Sullivan, first saw the flames and plunged into the barn to save one of Mrs. O'Leary's five calves at the cost of his eyebrows. After that he hobbled in panic down the unpaved street, spreading the alarm, "Fire! Fire! Fire!"

It so happened that only a few hours before, the members of the Little Giant fire company had finally put away their equipment after a seventeen hour battle with a fire that had broken out the evening before. It had destroyed some 20 acres of industrial and warehouse property in another West Side area, a half mile to the north, bounded by Adams, Van Buren, and Clinton streets and the Chicago River. Nevertheless, the weary firemen rushed forth again, heading for De Koven Street, where they found three barns, a paint shop, and a shed afire and the flames still spreading.

There was a brisk wind blowing out of the southwest, and the glowing coals and blazing timbers were caught up in the gusts to land on other wooden buildings, like tinder after the driest weather in the city's history.

The blaze spread from house to house, from store building to store building, to churches, to lumber mills, to factories. It was soon apparent that all Chicago, a city whose residential districts were made up largely of small wooden homes, was in peril of being totally destroyed. The flames swept swiftly northward toward the district burned out the evening before. Soon an area of the West Side three-quarters of a mile long and 150 square acres in extent was doomed. Blazing debris borne across the river by the wind fell into a hay barn of the Parmelee Omnibus and Stage Company at Jackson and Franklin streets and fed the raging blaze into the heart of the business district. The flames first forged into the La Salle Street area, then eastward toward Lake Michigan.

In his elegant new home at 610 South Michigan, W. W. Kimball was sitting in his Victorian parlor, talking with his wife at about the time "Peg Leg" Sullivan discovered the fire. They were discussing the scheduled grand opening on the following evening of the completely remodeled Crosby's Opera House. It had cost a whopping $80,000 to refurbish the magnificent "temple of the

55

arts," and Kimball, as a tenant of the Crosby building, had taken a personal interest in the effort. On Monday evening the famed Maestro Theodore Thomas would conduct a sold-out concert to open a new symphony season of brilliant promise.

The Kimballs' pleasant anticipation of what the Chicago *Tribune's* music editor had forecast as an evening "memorable in sight and sound" was soon interrupted by the alarm of fire. The music dealer's own story of the disastrous blaze and its aftermath is contained in an interview he gave to the Chicago *Daily Inter-Ocean* October 9, 1893.

Asked by a reporter to provide some reminiscences of the fire, Kimball replied:

"That reminds me of the story of the boy that got whipped; he did not care to brag about it. Still, looking back through the mists of twenty-two years, we can't complain of soreness, and even at the time we were too much rushed and heated to think about it. The only balm that we used was the encouragement of our friends, and enterprise did the rest.

"I do remember the night of the fire I started down the street allegro, with a pedal technique equal to the famous Dan O'Leary's. [Either the reporter or Kimball apparently was confused on this name; the real name of "Peg Leg" Sullivan, the O'Leary drayman, is variously given in the fire histories as Dan or Dennis.]

"Our store was in Crosby's Opera House, and people were rushing downstairs with all sorts of personal effects. Some tenants, who had a prejudice against carrying bundles, threw them out the windows. These objects that came by the air line frequently had the force of their fall broken by striking the crowd below . . . but everybody . . . was too busy to notice it.

"Mr. Cone was in the store when I got there, playing the dead march from 'Saul' on a dulcimer, which now reminds me of the melody that floats up and down the Midway Plaisance. [This is a reference to the Midway at the World's Columbian Exposition, then holding forth in Jackson Park.] He suggested that we get those pianos out, and as I felt as strong as Sandow we began business at once. I think we trundled seven grand pianos down the sidewalk a block and a half to the . . . northwest corner of Wabash Avenue and Washington Street. By that time the fire had entered the back door and had begun to wrap the furniture. I believe I gave vent to a few laconic remarks to the effect that I did not care whether school kept or not, and went home to take a rest. The next morning I thought of those pianos we had saved and went down to inspect them. A few hundreds of wires marked the spot where we had left them. So our labor had been in vain.

"When the cornices of the court fell they smashed the great skylight of our store, and the concussion of the air was so great that the immense plateglass window of the front was sympathetically smashed to smithereens. Among other pictures on the walls of the room were two medallions, 'Light' and 'Learning,' souvenirs of the great Sanitary Fair that I valued highly, and [I] had just succeeded in getting 'Morning' [*sic*] from her moorings when the crash came and knocked the picture out of my hands, and it went into the street as if shot from a catapult. I ruefully watched the fire, and, seeing a boy coming along, I bribed him to rush into the store and get that picture. In my after-excitement I dropped the precious picture, but, strange to say, Mr. Cone found it decorating a pile of rubbish on Wabash Avenue and brought it to my house, where it remains today the sole survivor of the store's stock.

"Of course our loss was heavy in the store, but the greater loss was in the rented pianos that were scattered all over the city, and a heavy percentage of them appeared to be in the path of the fire. We did not have much time to get blue; there was too much to be done. Our credit was good, and our first telegrams East were for needed stock; collections were prompt, and our country agents sent us plenty of money for the time being.

"I used the front of my Michigan Avenue residence for offices and the barn was utilized as a storeroom. This became the center of a new musical community. Root & Cady rented the house next door. Reed's Temple of Music pre-empted a riding gallery in the neighborhood, and Lyon & Healy located in a church at the corner of Sixteenth and Wabash Avenue. I remember I had a barrel of Kentucky copper distilled (spring water) in my barn aging, but after the boys had been in that neighborhood a week that barrel was a hollow mockery—age was no object in those days.

"When I was watching my store melt away a sympathetic friend passed, who kept a restaurant on Wabash Avenue.

" 'Hello! Burned out, eh?' said he. 'Well, you need not go hungry. Come down to my place whenever you feel the call.'

"An hour after, I met him on the run. He had just escaped from the ruins of his establishment without so much as saving a dishrag. While it was every man for himself in the excitement, a most remarkable undercurrent of unselfishness pervaded those days. Friends sprang up from every quarter who offered aid.

"One of the great mysteries is how help came so quickly. The whole nation appeared to reach a friendly hand toward Chicago.

"Among the cities east of us, Cleveland was the first to arrive with bread and raiment; among the cities south, Springfield perhaps took the lead on that memorable morning; then there were trains from Indianapolis and Cincinnati; and north, Milwaukee; indeed, from every point of the compass and every grade of life, help came, and the one aim seemed to be to do the utmost, in the speediest possible way for the miserable sufferers. Philadelphia, the city of brotherly love, showed its friendly spirits in ample gifts. Pittsburgh, city of iron, rained gold upon us. Boston, seat of all noble charities and beautiful accomplishments, lavished her thousands and gave her heartiest toil. Montreal, the American city of Canada, was glorious in her liberality. New York will never be forgotten for her liberal donation. When the late James Fisk, Jr. ordered the Erie cleared for the Chicago lightning relief train, sending seven carloads of provisions in unprecedented time, crowds of enthusiastic people assembled at the stations along the line and attempted to throw bundles on the train as it flew westward on its errand of mercy. The express train that followed the special from New York, it is estimated, had over $100,000 worth of goods sent through the same generous impulse."

A yellowed newspaper clipping in the Kimball archives, its source unknown but its content reading like a Kimball "reading notice" (advertisement) of the last century, quotes an unnamed "prominent musician" who supposedly watched Kimball and Cone wrestling their grand pianos down the street the night of the fire. It was probably written by Cone himself, since he wrote most of Kimball's advertising. His version of Kimball's "laconic remark" differs slightly from the piano titan's:

"I was watching the fearful progress of the fire near Crosby's. . . . The flames made such rapid progress that we were driven from the place where they had placed the piano[s]. We saw the Crosby succumb to the fury of the flames. I shall never forget Mr. Kimball's immovable face when he said, 'Well, I'm glad the darned thing has at last gone up,' and hurriedly turned to seek a place of safety. He at that moment, I honestly believe, was planning what he should do the next morning. I found him a few days after that in his Michigan Avenue residence, having turned it into salesrooms. I remember, being obliged to get to his office, his former billiard room, I had to pass through his parlor. He sat there, engrossed in business, calm as usual."

The rest of the account is an obvious sales pitch for Kimball's pianos and organs.

Dr. Florenz Ziegfeld, president of the Chicago Musical College and an intimate friend of Kimball, told the *Inter-Ocean* on the fire anniversary in 1893 that after the fire he went to Kimball's home and found the famous music dealer talking with Messrs. Root and Cady and other members of the music fraternity.

"They did not have much in the way of assets," he said, "except enterprise and a profound faith in Chicago."

It was faith indeed that Chicago needed on the smoke-blackened Tuesday morning of October 10, 1871, when the stricken city added up its terrible losses. More than 2,000 acres had been destroyed in the heart of the city. There were 90,000 people homeless, and 17,540 homes were in ruins. The property loss was an incredible $200 million. The known dead totaled 300, and there may have been many more.

One of the first men of whom W. W. Kimball thought as he looked at the ruins of his once proud store was Joseph P. Hale, the New York piano manufacturer with whom he had established a reliable buying connection the year before. Hale could give him quick action in replenishing his stock. About the time that Kimball was sending out his brave telegram, "Send me a stock of pianos and draw on me for what money you want," Hale himself was dispatching a wire to his beleaguered Chicago dealer.

"I telegraphed him to draw on me at sight for one hundred thousand dollars," Hale later recalled. "He answered that he thanked me, but would pull through without my aid!"

Joseph P. Hale is described by the piano historian, Alfred Dolge, as the father of the commercial piano in America. He at once has been more roundly praised and denounced than perhaps any other piano manufacturer in the world. He revolutionized the manufacture and distribution of pianos in America. At the same time he created the "stencil" piano—supplying an unlabeled piano to any dealer who might wish to stencil his name on it and, if he wished, pass himself off as the manufacturer. Stenciling itself was legal, but widespread abuse of the stencil privilege to mislead customers plagued the legitimate piano business for years.

A crockery salesman from Worcester, Massachusetts, Hale accumulated a capital of $35,000, went to New York City about 1870, and invested it in a piano factory. Determined to reduce the cost of pianos, he broke down the costs of plates, cases, actions, varnishes, other materials, and labor; bought at rock-bottom prices from specialists in the various fields of parts manufacture, and so managed his labor costs that he could sell his products at far below the prices of other manufacturers and still make a profit from volume sales. The old school of piano makers fought him every step of the way, but he forced his rivals in the end to develop their own low-cost production methods. His other innovation was to discard the agency system. He sold to anybody who put cash on the line.

Of these aspects of his efforts, Dolge wrote that Hale "had done splendid pioneer work in his sphere, to the benefit of the entire trade." He made it possible, Dolge added, "for the dealer, especially in the rapidly growing Western states, to market large numbers of pianos among the farmers, artisans, etc. . . . tenfold more than would have been possible if they had been restricted to the sale of high-class makes only."

A more skeptical writer of recent days, the music critic Arthur Loesser, concedes after a somewhat supercilious criticism of him in his book "Men, Women and Pianos," that "Hale did, in fact, perform a valuable service by producing a playable piano at a price that multitudes of people could afford." Loesser also notes that "some of the famed glamour-firms" bought parts from the very people who sold to Hale, and he names some well-known firms which were "suspected" of handling cheaper pianos that were really Hale instruments with a stencil.

All this to-do about the stencil was, of course, inspired chiefly by the older manufacturers against whom Hale was making inroads. In that day, as in this, the stencil was a legitimate business device only if used in such manner as not to deliberately conceal the facts about an instrument's origin. Properly employed, it enabled a manufacturer to market lines of pianos on which, for perfectly proper reasons, he might not want to use the company name. Again, it was considered proper for a dealer to have his name stenciled on an instrument if it had been made to the specifications that he supplied to the manufacturer.

Almost from the start of Hale's manufacturing, early in the 70s, Kimball employed him to make instruments to his own carefully drawn specifications. It was to a considerable degree the tremendous volume of business that Kimball gave him that enabled Hale to make more money than any other piano manufacturer of his day. This type of relationship with Hale and other piano makers was continued by the Chicagoan until he started his own piano manufacturing in the 80s. Eventually Kimball made every single component that went into his pianos.

The abuse of the stencil privilege became so widespread in the 90s that the Kimball company led a campaign against it. To safeguard its own dealers and customers, it decided shortly after the World's Columbian Exposition in 1893 to place the Kimball name on the iron frame of every instrument it manufactured.

9

"He has such an army of workers and such a brand of goods as to defy all competition."

BORN OF panic and depression, tempered in war and tested in the economic cross currents of the 1860s, the house of Kimball had come of age as the 70s began. It was the dominating force among the fifteen musical instrument dealers then operating in Chicago. But now, in 1871, after one October night of blazing fury, all that W. W. Kimball had dreamed of, all that he had built so carefully and well, lay in smouldering ruins.

It was a black moment in Kimball history. Yet before the 70s would pass there would come tremendous and exciting years—an immediate time ahead of immense progress, followed by another paralyzing panic; then a slow climb out of another depression as Kimball's wholesale business expanded under a new lieutenant shortly to join the home office staff; and, finally, the first bold steps into the field of manufacturing as the 70s faded into history and the 80s began.

It was a decade when the Kimball organization would gather its strength and resources—financial, material, and human—and make ready to launch the first of the great organ and piano factories in the West and thereby make the most significant single contribution to the golden age of American piano manufacture.

On the Wednesday morning following the great fire, Joseph Medill's Chicago *Tribune* gave ringing voice to the undefeated spirit of the city's leading businessmen with an editorial that proclaimed, "Chicago Shall Rise Again!" And W. W. Kimball's friend and fellow tenant, the music publisher George F. Root, offered his own melodic boost to their grim determination with a labored little song, "From the Ruins Our City Shall Rise!", whose lyrics were compounded of funereal gloom and fervent hope:

> "Ruins! Ruins! Far and wide
> From the river and lake to the prairie side
>   Dreary, Dreary the darkness falls
>   While autumn winds moan through blackened walls.
> But see! The bright rift in the cloud
>   And hear the great voice from the shore!
> Our city shall rise!
> Yes, she shall rise!
>   *Queen of the West once more!*"

A decade later Albert Cone reported that his brother-in-law's losses "were fully $100,000" when Crosby's Opera House went up in flames. The music merchant's own account of that tragic night suggests that nothing was rescued from his proud store except the beloved picture that was snatched off a rubbish heap by Cone. But the speed with which he rounded up a supply of instruments and got back into business would indicate that Kimball, as several writers have suggested, saved at least a part of the tremendous piano and organ stock. Indeed, the New York *Tribune*, in a glowing feature article on Kimball's career, stated in 1896 that "Mr. Kimball saved a portion of his stock; and, while suffering for the moment the depression which may be pardoned even a gallant man, he rallied with characteristic energy, and within twenty-four hours had resumed business in his home on Michigan Avenue."

The Chicago music trade journal, the *Indicator,* also noted that "a trunk filled with money, leases, notes and other valuable papers" was removed from the ruins, along with Kimball's safes, in which were locked all his rental and sales accounts. It painted a graphic picture of the anxious search for the latter in the smoking shambles of his Washington Street store.

Helping in the hunt were all the male members of Kimball's loyal staff—his clerks, tuners, salesmen, and draymen. Presumably they included old Matt Farley, the faithful piano mover who had been with Kimball since the early days on Lake Street, and Matt's cousin Phil, who had lately become an employe. They went to work in the opera house ruins, the *Indicator* said, "while the bricks were yet hot, so that they scorched their boots, digging away . . . so that tackle could be put around the safes and they could be hauled away to cool, for who could tell whether the records would be saved from that terrible heat?"

"They did come out legible," the account continued, "and Mr. Kimball, full of grit and energy, opened his office in the basement of his residence on Michigan Avenue, and had a force of builders rushing up a warehouse covering his lot, from his barn to his house, entering the salesroom through a window from his back parlor.

"His clerks were busy at once mailing circulars to all his agents, stating that the house was ready to fill orders promptly, shipping from the Eastern factories directly to the agents.

"The city papers had advertisements telling where W. W. Kimball's office was and of the clean, new goods he had to sell, and at prices to suit. For Mr. Kimball always believed in judicious advertising. One of his business axioms was: 'To have business, go where business is and use printer's ink.' He lived up to that axiom faithfully."

A part of the ample living space in the Kimball home was converted, at least for a time, into "a musical warehouse," while the owner directed all the varied activities of his staff from a desk in the big billiard room in the basement. "The mention of the billiard room," said the *Piano Trade Magazine* in 1947, "is evidence that Mr. Kimball had, even at that early age, moved into the top social circles of Chicago."

The shipping department was set up in the barn. The necessity for having to use this space where his blooded horses were stabled must have grieved Kimball very much, for he was a lover of horse flesh, and this meant that, for the present at least, the spirited team that drew his carriage would have to be boarded out at a neighboring livery stable. To supplement the barn space, his brother-in-law reported, he had the carpenters throw up some "hastily constructed sheds" at the rear of the residence.

No employe of Kimball's lost his job as a result of the blaze, but on the first day in the new location he called his staff together and suggested that they all take a temporary reduction in wages until the business could be re-established. Not a murmur of protest was heard.

Exactly how long the business was operated from the residence is not clear from a search through the available company records. Both Cone and Antonio de Anguera reported that it was "a few months," but there are evidences that the stay extended well into 1872. Among them is a receipt turned up in the Kimball files which is dated May 2, 1872, and which records in Kimball's hand the sale of a Kimball piano and stool for $435.

A removal from 610 Michigan was made sometime later that year when a lease was taken on another temporary headquarters, in a building on the northwest corner of Wabash Avenue and Thirteenth Street. It was "a big one-story barn of a place just put up," according to the De Anguera record. And here the business "fairly boomed." This was the year of the "epizootic," a peculiar disease that attacked horses, and Kimball's pianos and organs, like other merchandise, had to be moved about the city in wagons drawn by oxen and manpower. The wholesale trade was flourishing, and retail also showed surprising life, despite the out-of-the-way location.

As the rush of customers continued, Kimball restored the pay cuts with full back pay. At the same time he began to look about for permanent quarters among the new buildings springing up on the ashes of the downtown district. It was here he must return. A centrally located retail wareroom was a necessity. The quarters he needed turned up in a building just being erected on the southeast corner of State and Adams, where the Republic Building now stands. In the summer of 1873 the Kimball music house moved in, occupying elegant new warerooms at 205, 207, and 209 South State which had been especially outfitted to meet its needs. They were the finest piano warerooms in the country at the time, De Anguera reported.

To announce his return to the central business district, Kimball had the legend "W. W. Kimball Pianos and Organs, Cor. State and Adams Sts." stamped in bold red letters on the outside edge of the 1874 city directory.

A measure of his astonishing comeback after the fire is contained in a newspaper clipping of the day:

"W. W. Kimball's business in Chicago will amount during '73 to one million dollars, which is three times larger sales than any other piano house in America. His store is a beautiful stone front, four stories high, with basement, and one of the most beautiful structure[s] of new Chicago; the rent alone for which he pays twelve thousand dollars a year; his agents are in nearly every village in the north west of any size; he has such an army of workers and such a brand of goods as to defy all competition."

With such a tremendous new start, the Kimball business was not one to be taken wholly by surprise when a new financial panic swept the country in September, 1873. By now it had learned to live in the path and in the shadow of adversity, to yield to the savage blows when they came, to counter the milder ones, and to rebound with optimism and energy at the opportune time to regain and hold whatever ground might have been temporarily lost.

As one writer recorded it, Kimball "felt . . . that the panic was coming, and he prepared for it, drawing in his rented stock and holding a close rein on his outside agents. [He] was quick to foresee changed conditions in trade and to shape his business accordingly. He never deceived himself by carrying worthless assets, but ordered all such closed at once to loss, and he insisted that no inflation should enter into his inventories."

The bottom fell out on September 18, 1873, when the New York banking house of Jay Cooke, the financier regarded by many as the "pillar of the nation," shut its doors. Cooke had become over-involved in attempting to underwrite the Northern Pacific Railroad. The railroads were over-expanded. On the Western farms there had been an overproduction of crops. The nation's manufacturers and retailers took it on the chin along with the railroads and the banks. There were five bank failures in Chicago alone. And in the nation at large, 5,000 business failures were recorded by the end of the year.

A general scarcity of money and a lack of credit sent many another Chicago business house in that gloomy autumn to the wall. But Kimball was prepared to ride out the storm: His cash reserves were more than adequate and his obligations were few. Nevertheless he took a realistic view; his experience had been enough to tell him that Wilbur Fisk Storey, the bullish editor of the Chicago *Times,* was talking through his tall plug hat when he brashly proclaimed, "Except for a few old croakers who are always predicting a storm even under a clear sky, everybody now believes the panic is over and business is fast resuming its former activity."

Remembering the lessons he had learned in the panic of 1857, Kimball devoted his energies to stimulating his sales and to dreaming up new ways to turn the panic prices to his advantage. His retail salesmen were exhorted to even greater efforts; under his prodding some of them began to get out of the store, canvassing Chicagoans, door to door, for sales. In the field, especially in the sprawling Northwest, where new towns and villages continued to spring up in the footsteps of the pioneers, he directed his crew of agents to hunt out new markets, badgered the laggards with firm but kindly longhand letters, and rewarded the producers with bonuses. In the great manufacturing centers of the East, he kept up a steady pressure for lower, and still lower, prices to enable him to undersell his competitors. Volume and hard work. These were the two ingredients of the Kimball formula. With them he proposed to lick the long period of hard times that he guessed lay ahead.

His guess was right. "It took us about five and a half years to recover from the panic of 1873," he later recalled.

It was in these depression-ravaged years of the middle 70s that Albert G. Cone and Edwin Stapleton Conway, two future Kimball lieutenants who were to play all-important roles in the destiny of the organization, began to make their first forceful impressions upon the founder of the business. In the decade that followed, they would form with W. W. Kimball himself the great and closely knit triumvirate upon which the corporate enterprise of the W. W. Kimball Company was founded in 1882.

Cone was the less prepossessing of the two newcomers. He was first an office boy in 1869, then a clerk, next a bookkeeper, and, finally, treasurer of the Kimball company. A quiet man, he was content to remain in the background; nevertheless he became a powerful figure in company affairs and remained so until his death in 1900. For more than two decades he directed the company's advertising with skill and force, singing his brother-in-law's praises and becoming known throughout the music industry as one of the cleverest and most judicious practitioners of the advertiser's arts.

Conway, on the other hand, was a flamboyant figure, a bold and audacious country boy who made good in the big city as a super salesman in the piano's great age of ascendancy. For more than 40 years he was a dominating character in the music trade. He joined the organization in Chicago in 1876, heading the wholesale department, having served several years as an organ salesman in Minnesota and Wisconsin. He was secretary of the company from the time of its incorporation until 1905, when he became vice president.

It was in consultation with these two trusted associates, about whom we shall hear much more in the following chapters, that Kimball decided in 1878 the time had come at last to manufacture his own reed organs. He was emboldened in making this long-deferred decision by the moderate success enjoyed by the Burdett Organ Company, the pioneer among Chicago organ manufacturers. The Burdett factory was started in 1866 and turned out organs for Lyon & Healy until 1872, when it moved on to Erie, Pennsylvania.

E. B. Bartlett, a vice president of the Kimball company, recalled in 1923 that its first reed organ cases of Chicago origin were made by a group of furniture factories under contract to Kimball. The organ actions were built in the company's repair shops in 1879 above the State Street store. Within a few months, Kimball decided to call a temporary halt to this makeshift system while he worked with his staff to develop more permanent plans for large-scale organ manufacture.

In the meantime, he turned over his exacting specifications for the Kimball organ to John G. Earhuff, another Chicago manufacturer who started a factory on the North Side in 1876 and later moved on to St. Paul, Minnesota. The arrangement with Earhuff was continued until 1880. In that year Kimball rented the fifth floor of a building on Canal Street, between Van Buren and Jackson streets, assigned Jacob Hassler, one of his own organ experts, as superintendent, and began to turn out his first Kimball organs to be wholly made by his own men.

The sales steadily increased, and it soon became apparent that new and even larger quarters must be sought. They were found in 1881 in a big four-story building, formerly a basket factory, at Twenty-sixth and Rockwell streets. Around this original Kimball factory unit, which was at first taken under lease, there was destined to develop the largest piano and organ factory in the world.

Writing the copy for the first of the catalogs to be issued after the factory was established in 1881, Albert Cone recalled the circumstances that had led finally to this step. Before 1877, he said, Kimball "had simply furnished the capital and specifications for the manufacture of his instruments [organs] in Eastern cities. Since which time, until the present year, a large portion have been made in this city." He added:

"While the system worked admirably in some respects, it was not without its defects. Mr. Kimball's ambition was to make the best organ for the least money in America; and it was found, under the old arrangement, that too much of a margin was required by the contractor to make a first class instrument at a low price.

"A little study of the subject showed him that $3 or $4 per organ would be saved to the purchaser, by buying materials in large quantities. Becoming convinced that instruments could be more cheaply made in the West, where most of the lumber entering into their manufacture was close at hand, and prompted by a business-like desire to save the freight East on raw materials, as well as the return freight on the manufactured instrument, he . . . concluded to establish a factory in Chicago."

With the help of the ambitious and energetic Conway, Kimball also had launched in the latter part of the 70s a system of branch stores in important trade centers in the West. By 1881 there were established branches in Minneapolis, Kansas City; Grand Rapids, Michigan; Springfield, Rock Island, and Galesburg, in Illinois; Oshkosh, Wisconsin, and St. Joseph, Missouri. These stores were placed in the charge, Cone noted, of "the most competent salaried men in his employ, controlled from the home office." In addition, the house employed between 30 and 40 traveling salesmen who covered assigned territories and drew the best salaries paid by any house in the trade. Among the Kimball employes, Cone boasted, there were no less than 25 who had been with the organization from 15 to 25 years.

Sales of Kimball reed organs and pianos had reached the enormous total of 12,000 in 1880, and the goal for 1881 was 15,000 instruments. Cone, whose business it was to keep track of such things, assured his brother-in-law that the organization was doing a larger volume of business than any other house of its kind in the world.

10

"With a remarkable insight into human character,
he has surrounded himself with men who
idolize him."

In the Kimball archives there lies a yellowed newspaper clipping,
undated and unidentified, in which a reporter of the last century,
waxing poetic in praise of the company, pictured the Messrs. Cone
and Conway as the Damon and Pythias of the music trade.

"It often happens, unfortunately," he wrote in his windy, stilted
prose, "when two employes are elevated to proprietorships in a
large and flourishing concern, that a race for supremacy occurs in
which envy and jealousy are engendered, and a never-to-be-healed
rupture ensues. In the case of the two gentlemen of whom we
speak no feeling of this kind exists. . . . On the contrary, not a word
betokening the existence of discord . . . has ever been observed
during all the years that have elapsed since this modern Damon
and Pythias entered the W. W. Kimball Company as partners. . . .
In all matters . . . these gentlemen never fail to consult together,
and never allow the semblance of a jar or discord to come into
being. They thus illustrate the only methods upon which a great
mercantile establishment can be successfully managed. . . . The
foundation laid by Mr. Kimball has been well and solidly builded

upon, and the abundant success of the trio of State Street is assured."

Probably no other men in similar positions in the music trade were so successful in the piano's golden age, and so amply rewarded for able and intelligent service. Together, with its founder, who trained and developed their talents, they led the Kimball company through its great technical, artistic, and commercial triumphs in the last two decades of the 19th century.

Albert Gardner Cone, the son of the pioneer lumberman Hubbell Cone and the brother of Mrs. W. W. Kimball, was born in Chicago on September 30, 1852. The Cone residence, a comfortable frame cottage, was situated on Adams Street, about 200 feet west of the State Street corner on which the Fair store now stands. In the Chicago of that day this was one of the better residential areas.

An alert, ambitious, intelligent boy, Cone became a favorite of W. W. Kimball almost from the time the piano merchant met and married Albert's sister Evalyne. Some day, Kimball promised, when the lad was out of school, he would let him come to work in the piano store. On his sixteenth birthday, Albert Cone reminded his brother-in-law of that promise, and on January 1, 1869, he went to work in the piano and organ repair room at the rear of Kimball's store in Crosby's Opera House.

It was an unglamorous job to which he was first assigned—polishing the dusty pianos and ornate parlor organs in this crowded, strange-smelling room. It seemed far removed indeed from the elegant show space up front, where Kimball's well-mannered clerks waited on a busy trade, including the cream of Chicago society. But the boy had determined that he would learn the musical instrument business from the bottom up, and he eagerly set about performing the assorted tasks that normally befell an office boy or porter. Kimball kept an eye on his new employe and was quick to note his willingness to tackle any duty that came to hand—including the laborious job of boxing and unboxing reed organs—in order to play even the smallest part in helping the business grow.

Pleased by what he saw, Kimball passed the word on to his technical men to afford the young newcomer every opportunity to learn the practical side of the piano and organ trade—especially the tuning, repairing, and overhauling of instruments. A man named Jones was the chief organ technician at the time. He was an expert organ maker who had come West from Smith American in Boston. In his odd moments he helped young Cone take an old reed organ apart, piece by piece, and then stood by with assistance as Cone put it all together again. The piano tuner, W. H. Powers, with similar patience, instructed him in piano tuning and repair.

These lessons learned, the youth was called up front to the counting room. He served first as general utility clerk, later as confidential clerk and correspondent for his chief, then as bookkeeper for the business and finally as treasurer and financial ruler of all the company operations. He was a thorough worker and a master of detail. His greatest contribution to the music trade came in 1890, when he introduced the one-price system into piano retailing. The *Indicator* said of him: "Mr. Cone's ability and integrity are everywhere recognized. There is no man in the business life of this city who has a higher reputation for honesty or a cleaner record for fair and square dealing than he. This spirit has become a part of the Kimball warerooms, and his influence upon the salesmen of the house is of so salutary a character that under every circumstance every patron of the company is treated with marked consideration."

W. W. Kimball always prided himself on his judgment of human nature. His record demonstrates a superlatively keen ability to measure the qualifications of a man to handle a particular business task. In no case perhaps did he exhibit this skill more clearly than in his choice of the man who eventually became the first secretary and general superintendent of the Kimball company.

Edwin Stapleton Conway was born in McGillivray township, Ontario, near Toronto, Canada, on March 21, 1850, the son of

Patrick and Margaret Cotter Conway, who had emigrated in the early 40s from Oswego, New York. The Conways moved back to the United States in October, 1857, about the time that W. W. Kimball moved to Chicago from Iowa. They settled in Pepin, Wisconsin, for a time, and a few years later moved a short distance west to a farm near Lake City, Minnesota. Here the young Conway attended the public schools in winter and worked on the farm in summer.

At eighteen, a tall, powerful, rugged youth, he went off to Eau Claire, Wisconsin, to attend Wesleyan Seminary. While still a student there, in 1869, he became an agent for the Kimball organ in order to help meet his expenses. The sale of a few instruments to farm families, along with the tombstone orders he took for Bogart Brothers of Winona, Minnesota, and some part-time janitor work and sawing of wood on Saturdays, enabled him to get through a three-year course.

After leaving Wesleyan, he studied and worked for a time in the office of Dr. H. N. Rogers of Lake City, intending to become a surgeon.

Medicine's loss was Kimball's gain when one day in 1871 a man named H. A. French, an organ salesman and an old friend of the doctor's, called at the office and persuaded young Conway to part with his big silver watch in partial exchange for an organ.

Having suddenly found himself in possession of a reed organ for which he had no use, he determined to get back at least the cost of the timepiece, and promptly went out and sold the instrument. The ease with which this sale was consummated and the lure of further commissions such as he had made at Wesleyan found him writing again to his old Chicago source for the latest agent's prices. Kimball looked up his record and, finding it good, appointed Conway to be his Minnesota agent for piano and organ sales. The young man promptly took off for the rural areas, where he soon was doing a brisk business selling organs and an occasional piano to farm families.

In 1872 the appointment was extended to include Wisconsin,

and the summer found Conway in West Eau Claire, where he met up once more with the salesman who had taken his watch in trade the year before. This meeting produced an unusual but short-lived business agreement in which the firm of French & Conway was set up to engage in "General Music Business and the establishing of agencies," as stipulated in an "article of agreement" drawn up in Conway's hand and signed by both parties on July 1.

A clue to Conway's future as an acute bargainer and an able business man was boldly spelled out in the following peculiar clause, which constituted "Sec. 2nd of Article IV" of the agreement: "If either of the parties hereto desires to invest capital in the business which cannot at the moment be balanced by the other party the delinquent party shall allow and pay interest at the rate of ten per cent per annum on one-half the amount so invested commencing at the date such capital is invested."

Full of high energy and winning talk, Conway ran up a sales record in the depression years of the mid-70s that registered impressively in Chicago, where Kimball still kept a close eye on the figures. As he watched Conway's progress the feeling grew within him that here was a real comer—exactly the sort of salesman he had been looking for to head the growing wholesale operations.

"A natural-born salesman," Kimball chuckled one day as he reviewed a new batch of Conway orders with his brother-in-law. "Fresh from the farm himself, with the manure still on his heels. This man Conway knows the people on the farms and in the small towns out there. He's one of them, Albert. This is the kind of man I want to handle my trade in the field."

Thus it was that at Kimball's call Conway moved to Chicago in 1876 to take over as head of the wholesale department. Settling in suburban Oak Park with his wife, the former Sarah Judson Rogers, a Wisconsin girl whom he had wed on Christmas Day, 1871, he brought up three children—a daughter Sybil, who became Mrs. Philip A. Munro, and two sons, Earle E. and Carle C., Kimball salesmen in their day, and in time the owners of their own piano factory in faraway Boston.

Through the years E. S. Conway became not only a leader in the music trade but an active force in the civic affairs of his own community and of Chicago itself. For many years he was a leading spirit in the Chicago Association of Commerce, serving it in various capacities, including a four-year term as vice president. An advocate of waterways and an authority on freight traffic, he served as vice president of the Lakes-to-the-Gulf Deep Waterways Association. As a widely popular figure in Republican circles in both state and nation, he repeatedly declined the support of political friends and prominent citizens who urged him to become a candidate for United States senator from Illinois.

Upon his death in 1919, the Chicago *Evening Post* said: "Mr. Conway was a self-made man in all that the term implies. He was . . . worth $50,000 before he stopped carrying his lunch to the office.

"Character, personality, sentiment and honesty were the keynotes of his life. He harped upon these virtues at every opportunity and held them up as beacon lights to young men. He believed in giving the other fellow a leg up and playing his cards on the table."

E. S. Conway believed with Albert G. Cone that the first requisite for service to a business enterprise is loyalty. "Without loyalty all along the line," he once said, "no business can be successful, and this loyalty is an impossibility, unless the controlling heads are democratic, sympathetic, social and broad."

These then were the two loyal and perceptive personalities whom Kimball had made his allies as the 70s ended and the 80s— the great years of company expansion—began. *Freund's Musical Weekly* would later comment, "With a remarkable insight into human character, which he appears to read while running, he [Kimball] has surrounded himself with men who idolize him. He is assisted in his ventures by brainy men whom he selected with customary discretion, and his judgment in that respect never plays him false."

11

"I must manufacture my goods or go out of business."

THE BIRTH of the W. W. Kimball Company as a corporate organization is first formally recorded in a license issued by the Illinois Secretary of State on July 8, 1882, to William W. Kimball, Edwin S. Conway, and Albert G. Cone. It empowered them as commissioners "to open books for subscription to the capital stock of said company." The object of the corporation was to be "the manufacture and sale of musical instruments." The location, Chicago. Duration, 99 years. The capital stock was fixed at $600,000—6,000 shares at a par value of $100 a share.

E. B. Bartlett, who joined the Kimball organization on October 1, 1880, recalled many years later that the notice of such a move was sent around to Kimball's employes on July 1.

"At that time," said Bartlett, "Mr. Kimball established the policy which has been adhered to since of giving an opportunity to members of the organization to acquire a financial interest in the business."

Only Conway and Cone were included, with Kimball, however, in the list of original subscribers submitted in the "Report of the 3 Commissioners" filed with the Secretary of State that July 10. Of the 6,000 shares, Kimball was recorded with holdings of 5,996, valued at $599,600. Conway and Cone were recorded with one share each at $100. The two remaining subscribers, with one share each, were W. C. D. Grannis, a former wholesale grocer who became president of the Union National Bank in the year Kimball incorporated, and Joseph L. McKittrick, an attorney with the firm of Ayer & Kales. Neither Grannis nor McKittrick ever assumed an active role in the business; they served only as directors and as advisers in financial and legal matters through the early years.

The three commissioners set the first meeting of subscribers for 9:30 A.M. Thursday, July 20, for the purpose of electing directors. Kimball was chosen temporary chairman and McKittrick temporary secretary as they sat down with Conway and Grannis in the executive office at 207 South State. Cone was unable to attend because he was home with a cold. All five of the subscribers were elected directors of the corporation for one-year terms.

A state "Certificate of Organization" was issued on July 21, and on July 26 recorder's certificate No. 410,488 was filed in the Illinois Book of Corporations.

A director's meeting followed next on August 3, when Kimball was chosen president, Conway was elected general superintendent and secretary and Cone was named treasurer. (There was no vice presidency in the company setup until January 11, 1898.) This second meeting also brought the adoption of the by-laws.

On August 14, Kimball offered to sell to the newly-formed company his "property and assets and entire business of manufacturing and dealing in musical instruments" for $600,000 in full paid

79

capital stock. To support this offer, he submitted a balance sheet, as of July 1, 1882, which testified to the enormous strides he had made to date. It follows, just as it appears in the company's original records:

RESOURCES

Bills receivable	$420,813.00
Accounts receivable	192,418.32
Merchandise inventory in store and in transit	50,470.75
Instruments rental	12,376.00
Stock in factory—manufactured and in process of manufacture	46,687.22
Machinery in factory and expenditures in fitting up factory, including dry kiln	20,551.97
Newport Lumber investment	14,650.26
Cash	12,907.61
Store and office fixtures	2,062.00
Suspense	2,500.00
Total Resources	$775,437.13

LIABILITIES

Bills payable	$117,413.84	
Accounts payable	40,712.97	$158,126.81
Present worth		$617,310.32

The transfer was consummated on August 17, and Kimball signed a receipt for 5,996 shares of stock and $400 in cash as full payment for the property and assets as set forth in his balance sheet.

Kimball's decision to incorporate was a direct outgrowth of his entry into reed organ manufacture in the latter part of the 70s. All through that decade, as Hampton Story's memoir has indicated, he had toyed with the idea of producing his own instruments. It was not alone a matter of economies on freight rates and materials. The Chicago jobbers were having great difficulty in getting enough organs from the Eastern manufacturers to supply their demands. And despite Kimball's longtime record of enormous sales of Smith American and Shoninger organs, there were certain

First factory (top, left) was occupied in 1881. Piano plant was added in 1887. By the early 1900s, Kimball's Chicago factory (center) was "world's largest" of its kind. New home office and factory (bottom) is in Melrose Park, Illinois.

The company turned to the walnut forests of Arkansas for top-grade wood for piano and reed organ manufacture. Artist's sketch shows saw mill and lumber yard operations at Newport, Arkansas, in 1880s.

basic specifications for his instruments that he could not seem to persuade their manufacturers to meet. These related particularly to mechanical improvements developed by his own technical men and stylistic modifications and alterations in cases, by which he sought to meet the taste of his Western trade. Already a few of the Eastern organ manufacturers were dropping by the wayside, and some said the trade was beginning to die. But Kimball had tremendous faith in the future of the reed organ in the West and he laid the failures that had occurred to a lack of progressiveness.

"I must manufacture my goods or go out of business," he told Cone and Conway.

Chicago, he felt, was the logical center for the manufacture and wholesaling of musical instruments. But even after this decision was made, most of his Chicago associates viewed the proposed venture with skepticism. "Chimerical" and "utopian" were the terms they used. They still believed that Western-made reed organs could not be sold successfully, and more than one business man warned him he might be risking everything he had.

But, as the *Indicator* reported, "Mr. Kimball decided there was nothing in the way of enterprise but a foolish prejudice, and he shrewdly surmised that a reduction in prices would banish any supercilious objections on the part of the buying public, while for the sneers of his Eastern competitors he cared not a straw."

The move into the original factory at Twenty-sixth and Rockwell was completed on May 1, 1881, more than a year before the incorporation. The location was on a western fork of the Chicago River's south branch known locally as Mud Lake, and it was here that the earliest factory employes used to swim and fish for catfish along the tree-shaded banks. The property consisted, as Bartlett set it down, of "one building, 80 by 240 feet on the ground floor and four stories high, and a detached engine room." A fifth floor was added in 1890, bringing the total floor area of Factory A, as it was termed, to 96,000 square feet.

The *Indicator* described the new organ plant in 1883 as "doubtless the largest of its kind in the world." The machinery, it said, was the most extensive and complete for its purpose in existence. Motive power was supplied by a 250-horsepower Corliss engine, which also had steam connections to a dry kiln, where the lumber used in manufacturing instruments was seasoned and dried.

In the summer of 1881, still looking ahead, Kimball sent Conway off to the South in search of lumber supplies for the new operation. Such a source was located at Newport, Arkansas, and a lease was obtained on a fine walnut forest and extensive sawmills, where timber could be prepared in precisely the shapes and grades needed in the production of fine instruments. This operational division was organized as the Newport Lumber Company in August, 1881, and Conway was named president and general superintendent. It was this project that was represented in the $14,650.26 "Newport Lumber investment" listed in the Kimball balance sheet of 1882.

Preparing a new Kimball catalog for 1882, Cone wrote that the factory "is supplied with all the improved machinery known to the trade; is superintended by men of long and varied experience in the process of manufacturing these favorite instruments; and employs, all told, a force of about 150 men—many of them graduates of the largest and most extensive factories in the country. At present [the winter of 1881] the factory turns out 80 to 100 finished instruments every week. Even this large production does not supply the enormous demand, and preparations are making to increase output by one-half. The workmanship put into these instruments is simply unexcelled. With his abundant capital, Mr. Kimball is able to buy for cash and consequently at the best possible advantage."

Besides obtaining the best materials at minimum cost and employing the best help obtainable, Cone boasted, the manufacturer had, by adopting a system of paying all his workmen "stated salaries instead of paying them by the piece," removed all the possible incentives or reasons for them to slight their work. The savings on freight and materials in a business as large as Kimball's, he added, amounted "to a fortune earned every year." Finally, he claimed that all these things "have enabled Kimball to attain the great object he had in view, viz: the manufacture in Chicago for the least money of the best organ that has ever been produced in the American market."

The catalog prices, the customer was reminded, "are those for which our instruments can be sold in the most distant markets—where large expenses are incurred for transportation." A considerable discount would be allowed upon instruments sold in the Chicago warerooms, in the various branch houses, or through regularly appointed agents.

All the instruments were guaranteed as follows:

WARRANTY

This certifies, That Style——— No. ———, of our manufacture, is in every respect a FIRST-CLASS INSTRUMENT: that the materials used in its construction are of THE BEST QUALITY, the wood THOROUGHLY SEASONED, and that all the work is FINISHED IN THE BEST AND MOST SKILLFUL MANNER. And we do hereby warrant it for FIVE YEARS from date against failure of any part, except such as may be caused by accident, misuse, or neglect. This Warranty does not include the tuning of the instrument.

Chicago, Ill. ⸺⸺⸺⸺⸺⸺⸺⸺⸺⸺⸺⸺

⸺⸺⸺⸺⸺⸺⸺⸺⸺⸺⸺⸺⸺

The prices of the first organs from Kimball's own factory ranged from $175, for a nine-stop instrument with a case five feet seven inches high, four feet four inches wide, and two feet deep, to $435, for the Cymbella Organ King, a superior quality instrument of thirteen stops—"six sets of reeds of two and a half octaves each and one set of sub-brass reeds." This massive, 400-pound (when crated)

An ornate Kimball reed organ of the 1880s of a type widely popular in parlors and churches of small-town America. This hand-carved model had French walnut panels and stood five feet four inches. Kimball led world in reed organ making.

instrument was six feet six inches high, four feet long and two feet four inches deep. It possessed, so the catalog said, "a magnificent chime of bells and useful book closets, together with many other valuable improvements." The music desk could be turned down to form a convenient writing desk. For a somewhat higher price the instrument could be "richly ornamented" in black and gold. Its music desk could, if the buyer desired, be "magnificently inlaid with a variety of colored woods."

Not forgetting the smaller churches, the house also manufactured two "powerful organs," at $275 and $300, which were said to be well adapted for churches and Sunday schools. The finish on all sides, so the catalog said, was "so arranged as to form no objection to the performance when facing the congregation or company."

The housewife was the particular target of such parlor organ features as the Safety Pedal, "so arranged as to be closed when not in use, protecting the interior of the instrument from mice—the greatest enemy of an organ," and "our patent book closets, which are conveniently placed on either side of the pedals and provided with lock and key."

Never overlooking a trick, Cone also devoted three pages of the catalog to testimonials. One of the letters was from a Professor James O'Connor of Denver, Colorado. It was dated July, 1881, and O'Connor testified as follows:

"Your organs seem to stand the test of our extreme and changeable climate better than any instruments on the market. I purchased one of your smaller styles last summer, which was taken apart and 'packed' across the Continental Divide on mules, and it arrived in perfect condition, and continues to remain so."

The catalog also advertised Hallet & Davis and Emerson pianos, as well as Kimballs, the latter ranging in list price from $485, for the No. 1 square grand of seven octaves, to $650, for a cabinet grand of seven and one-third octaves. An upright piano of seven octaves, four feet three inches tall, five feet wide and two feet three and one-half inches deep, was listed at $500.

The square grand, typical of the lower-priced instruments of the day, was described as follows: "double veneered rosewood case, front round corners, heavy serpentine moulding, full iron frame, French repeating action, with over dampers, carved legs and pedal. . . ." It was six feet four inches long and three feet two inches wide.

This early effort of Cone's must have been a catalog with plenty of what the advertising man of today would call "sell." For on July 9, 1883, after its blandishments had been at work for a year, W. W. Kimball, acting on a resolution of the first annual company meeting on July 2, declared a dividend for the fiscal year ended July 1, 1883, of sixteen per cent on the $600,000 capital stock. This amounted to $96,000. The surplus was $2,106.35.

12

"He turned intuitively to the human resources within the family as he strengthened the sinews of the organization."

As Albert Cone and E. S. Conway were advancing into the executive realm of W. W. Kimball's growing organization, there were two other men, somewhat younger, moving into the lower echelons who were destined for even greater responsibilities far in the company's future. Both were nephews of the manufacturer. Both would prove themselves over the years to be men of exceptional ability in their respective fields. And after Kimball's death in 1904, each in his time would serve as president of the company. As such they would become important links in the retention of family control over the business through its first century.

There is no way of knowing today whether all this was by accident or design. But those who have credited Kimball with an uncanny ability to look into the future are perhaps entitled to suggest, as did a latter-day company officer, that "the old man turned intuitively to the human resources within the family as he strengthened the sinews of his organization for its greatest period of expansion."

First of the two nephews to arrive on the scene was Curtis Nathaniel Kimball, the strapping six-foot three-inch son of David Williams and Sarah Moore Kimball of Mitchell County, Iowa, who reached Chicago in 1879. The second, coming in 1883 from the old home country at Rumford, Oxford County, Maine, was Wallace W. Lufkin, the son of Merritt Newell and Lucy Kimball Lufkin, a sister of W. W. and David.

Through all the years of progress since he had left northeastern Iowa, Kimball had remained in continuing contact, both by letter and personal visit, with his younger brother and his growing family. David by now was a prosperous farmer and a leader in the rural community where he had pioneered. The *Indicator* later recorded that "Mr. Kimball visited Chicago frequently in his early days and met many members of the local piano trade," and another Chicago trade paper, the *Presto,* reported that David indeed "was also to some extent a member of the 'trade.' He then sold organs in a desultory way, and in his neighborhood of Iowa, instruments sold by him are still quite plentiful. . . . All through the country . . . may be found Shoninger organs and the old Smith American[s] that were sold by Mr. Kimball in those comparatively early days of the Western trade."

Both David and Sarah were leading spirits in the religious affairs of their community, and in 1866 Sarah became the secretary of a union Sunday school organized by the women of the neighborhood farms. The Kimballs were charter members of the Wentworth Congregational Church, which was organized on October 30, 1868, with the Rev. G. S. Martin as the first pastor.

David also participated actively in civic affairs and was a member of the first school board in his community. A lifelong Republican, he was the first person to be elected to the full Mitchell County assessor's office when it was created in the winter of 1856-57, and he served until this office was abolished by law and the duties reverted to the township assessors.

Of the five children of David and Sarah, Curtis was an only son, born on June 4, 1862. From infancy he had been a favorite of his Chicago uncle, who took note on his infrequent visits to the Iowa farm of the boy's alert and intelligent nature and of the strength of character that was apparent even in his teens. Just as Albert

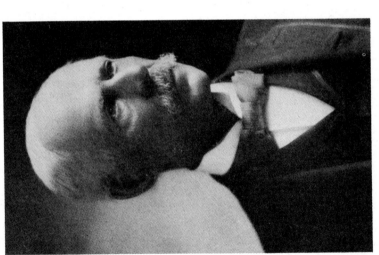

W. W.'s brother David (left) went west, settled in Iowa. At right: Edwin S. Conway in the 1890s.

Cone had done before him, young Curtis Kimball let it be known that some day he would like to go to work selling pianos and organs for the Chicago music house. And in anticipation of that day, his father had seen to it that as a schoolboy he got a thorough grounding in arithmetic, penmanship and other skills that might be beneficial in a commercial career. A willing and able worker on the farm, Curt helped with the plowing and the other chores, developing in the process a powerful, muscular physique.

Now at seventeen he was in Chicago, bent on a business career. As the boy eased his awkward frame into a chair in the Kimball offices, his Uncle Wallace turned from the papers on his rolltop desk and beamed a welcome.

"Well, Curt," he smiled, "you're looking fine. We're glad to have you with us."

Then, after the mutual exchange of pleasantries and news of the family, he outlined a training course for the hopeful young salesman:

"Everybody starts at the bottom in this business. You can't sell pianos or organs unless you know what you're selling. We'll start you off in the repair room. Then you can come down to Cone's office and learn bookkeeping and collections. After that Conway will show you the ropes on the road. In the meantime, son, you'd better take a business course to get the hang of the way we do things around here."

And so it was that C. N., as everybody soon called the newcomer, enrolled in the Bryant & Stratton Business College, 81 State Street, that had flourished in Chicago since 1856. Under the tutelage of Cone and Conway, he soon learned the routine of the Kimball offices, handling many of the longhand letters to dealers and agents in the Western territory. Typical of the correspondence with which he labored in this period are three letters which have been preserved from the files of William B. "Billy" Roberts, one of Conway's field representatives and later the manager of the Kansas City branch office.

One, dated October 2, 1880, and addressed to Roberts at Fort Dodge, Iowa, concerned an itinerant salesman who was misrepresenting himself as a Kimball man. "We have a man by the name of *D. J. Brook* at Sandwich, Ills.," wrote the company, *"but not a Brooks on our books, much less in Iowa. Tell your customers to buy a #22 K. O. [Kimball organ] for $70.00 from him & that you will take it off their hands & pay them for [the] trouble. We know no way to stop the mouth of a liar; if we did we would care for this case. Such fellows are to be pitied more than blamed, as they are short lived!"

Another note to Roberts, dated April 23, 1881, and marked "Confidential," dealt with another trouble maker, this time within the organization. "Mr. [name omitted]," it said, "has been knocked about from house to house, and being very anxious to secure a *permanent position,* is trying hard to get [a] position of 'Organ Inspector.' He came back telling us your organs were not in *fine tune,* and may have said much more to you. Now, Mr. R., we ship 25 to 30 *every day* and strange to say this is the *only complaint* of any being out of tune. Not doubting your word at all, it seems strange. However, we will exercise great care in future and endeavor to send goods that will please, and when you can do so, leave all selections to us, and the writer will personally see you get a 'square deal.' "

Still another letter, addressed to Roberts at Ottumwa, Iowa, and dated August 4, 1882, concerned the representative's assignment to close out the accounts of certain stores, over which the home office always exercised a close check. It said: "Your letter in regard to [dealer's name omitted] rec'd. If you have got their account down to one old Piano and a couple of organs, doubtless ere this they are closed out. Now for one more hard job. You have done well in Ottumwa and the minute you get that cleaned up we want you to take the enclosed letters and statements to [name of branch store omitted] and go at once to Sioux City and close out the stock he has got on hand. We do not wish him any longer on salary under any circumstances. [He] is a good boy, strictly honest, and might do well if put on a small contract and let work on our August 1st rates with a $600 or $800 balance and work on commission. This we would be pleased to have him do, and if he will consent to doing so, put him on contract, close out the stock down to $500 or $600 and turn the balance over to him and let him go ahead. But if he declines to do either and says he must have a salary or quit, then stay right with him until the last Dollar is closed out and close up the agency. [He] has worked for us a couple of years on salary and during the whole time, we have just succeeded in getting cost for the goods, and we have got tired of it. . . ."

After several years of mastering such ins and outs of the business in the home office, young Curtis was sent out on the road under Conway's supervision. For many years he was one of the company's top salesmen, covering the Kimball territory in Iowa, Minnesota, North Dakota, and South Dakota. He returned finally to the home office and a vice presidency of the company in 1898.

It was on one of the road trips through the Northwest that Curtis met the young teacher of elocution and dramatic art who became his bride on November 3, 1894. She was Miss Fannie C. B. Hadley of Chicopee Falls, Massachusetts, a member of the teaching staff at the Moorhead (Minnesota) state teachers college and a roommate of Curtis' sister Isabel Moore Kimball. A year younger than Curtis, Isabel had gone to Moorhead to teach art. She lived with Miss Hadley in an old boarding house at Fargo, North Dakota, across the Red River of the North from Moorhead.

Three years after their marriage, C. N. would be instrumental in inducing his wife's brother, George Louis Hadley, a onetime professional bicycle rider, to join the Kimball office staff in Chicago. As with most new employes, young Hadley spent his first few months after coming to work in October, 1897, learning the office routine. Then, in 1898, when C. N. became a permanent member of the Chicago executive staff, Conway sent George on the road, assigning him to the exact Northwest territory that Curtis Kimball had traveled for so many years. In 1914 Hadley would return to Chicago and become secretary of the company and manager of 22 branch stores.

When Wallace W. Lufkin reached Chicago in the spring of 1883 he was twenty-three and "with scarcely sufficient funds to sustain him for two days." A reserved and diffident young man, he stayed away from the office of his well-to-do uncle for several weeks, first obtaining a job as a brick layer so that he could get some new clothes. A sensitive youth, he wanted to avoid the appearance of being one of W. W. Kimball's "poor relations" from the sticks. All the money that he had earned as a farm boy in Maine had gone into helping the family get along. He often spoke in later years of the difficulties of grubbing a living out of the stony New England farm land.

The Lufkin farm at Rumford adjoined the old Kimball homestead, and it was here that Wallace was born on September 11, 1859, one of six children of M. Newell and Lucy A. Kimball Lufkin. One of his two brothers was George B., born September 13, 1874, who would follow him to Chicago upon the death of W. W. Kimball in 1904 and become in time superintendent of the factories and later vice president of the company.

In the genealogical record kept by George's wife, Sara Eaton Lufkin, and in Babson's "History of Gloucester, Mass.," the Lufkins are described as an old New England family which may be traced back to Dedham, England. There is, says Babson, a record of a Hugh Lufkin at Salem, Massachusetts, in 1654, but the earliest known ancestor of the Lufkins of Rumford seems to have been one Thomas, who settled in a "remote section, near the Ipswich (now Essex) line" in Massachusetts, probably a few years before he received, on December 16, 1679, "six acres of upland above Deacon Haskell's saw mill."

The grandfather of Wallace and George was the Rev. Joseph Lufkin, who married Loruhamah A. Kimball, a sister of W. W. Kimball's father David. It thus appears that M. Newell Lufkin and Lucy A. Kimball, the sister of W. W. and David W., were first cousins. In this connection, the Sara E. Lufkin manuscript record of the family says that Lucy was born on June 1, 1834, the daughter of David W. and Lucy Wheeler Kimball; on the other hand, the Kimball family record, as taken from Morrison and Sharples' "History of the Kimball Family in America," lists only eleven children from that union, and Lucy A. is not included. If she was indeed a sister of the manufacturer, as the families believe, then Wallace and George Lufkin were Kimball's second cousins as well as his nephews.

As a youth Wallace Lufkin left the farm in winters to take employment in the lumber camps of Maine, and the rugged work of felling trees and carrying out the other logging operations developed within him an extraordinary physical strength. One spring after having spent the winter in a lumber camp, it is said that he came out of the forest with $500, most of which he spent for materials with which he rebuilt the Lufkin farmhouse with his own hands.

When he finally showed up at W. W. Kimball's State and Adams streets store to seek employment in the summer of 1883, there was a joyful hour of talk about the old home country in Maine.

Kimball was all ears as young Lufkin reported on the latest news from home. Sadly he listened as his nephew described in vivid detail the harrowing night the old Kimball homestead burned to the ground in 1880, two years before the death of Lucy Wheeler Kimball.

"All that was saved," said Lufkin wryly, "was the dinner bell and the custard pie."

Appraising the muscular young newcomer, W. W. gave him his usual indoctrination lecture about the importance of learning the business from the ground up. Then he said:

"We've got a lot of work at the organ factory for a strong young man like you, Wallace. We're turning out 40 organs a day—more than any other organ company in the country. I'll give you a note to the foreman. Go out and see what you can find to do."

The Kimball Story

In time the young lumberjack would put to the company's advantage all the expert knowledge of hardwoods he had gained in long experience in the green forests of Maine. It was know-how that would be extremely important in the purchase of materials for the great organ manufactory and the piano plant still to be built. At Lufkin's death 62 years afterward a Chicago lumberman would say: "W. W. Lufkin knew more about lumber than any man I ever knew."

It was a thrilling scene that greeted Mr. Kimball's nephew as he arrived at the humming factory that day in 1883. The building itself, said Cone's catalog description of that year, looked "like a smith-shop of the primeval giants, as well as a mighty art mill and laboratory of ideas."

The first man to greet him was old George B. Demes, the foreman of the mill room on the first floor and the man who supervised the installation of the factory machinery in 1881, when Kimball took over the massive building from Eugene D. Fisk, the basket manufacturer. The Demes family, incidentally, has been represented in the factory since the beginning. George B. Demes' son George Jr. went to work there at age fifteen on March 11, 1886, rose through the various factory divisions to a foremanship and retired in 1946. And his son, Ray, joined the factory force in 1934 to continue in the family tradition, and is now an expert piano tuner and regulator.

Young Lufkin took everything in with amazement as Demes escorted him on a quick tour through the vast plant. The first two floors were a whirl of action as the great Corliss engine turned the shining wheels and propelled the glittering arms of half a hundred machines. The lathes and great mechanical saws sang noisily as hundreds of artists and mechanics worked on 3,000 Kimball organs in simultaneous production. The third floor was a busy workshop of skilled wood craftsmen and cabinet makers, and on the fourth floor were the action men and tuners.

Little did W. W. Lufkin dream how many memorable decades

these factory walls would hold within them the major hopes and triumphs of his life.

The young man's first assignments at the factory were in the stool and bench department that was newly established that summer. Some time before, said a writer that year in the *Indicator,* "the intuitive mind of the management" had seen that the enormous amount of waste material accumulating in the factory might be utilized in producing a practical piano stool "at a price which would defy opportunities for competition." The Kimball factory thus was producing "some of the finest stools on the market," shipping extensively to Chickering & Sons of New York, Hallet & Davis and the Emerson Piano Company of Boston, and James Bellak's Sons of Philadelphia. The production by 1889 totaled 2,000 to 3,000 stools a month.

Late in the summer of 1883, the report from the factory was that Wallace Lufkin was "making out real well." W. W. Kimball and his wife Evalyne were preparing at the time to close up all except the servant quarters in their fashionable new home at 1641 Michigan Avenue, where they had moved three years before, and set off on their fourth trip to Europe. They planned to travel this time in Austria and France.

It was a well-earned rest for the manufacturer, a chance to get away from the daily rush of business, the complexities of the new factory operations, the nagging pressure of sales and collections. The business was running along smoothly with Cone and Conway in command. Now for a time he would relax and have the opportunity to consider in the calm and quiet atmosphere of an ocean voyage and the museum visits that would follow the broader aspects of his thriving trade which still demanded answers. Foremost in his mind was the still-to-be-decided question of what to do about piano manufacture and when and how the newly organized company would move on a large scale into this unexplored field.

98

Already there had been a few experimental piano models produced in the organ repair shops above the retail warerooms in the downtown store.

"The first pianos—about two dozen—were not very satisfactory," the younger George Demes recalled in 1956. "They didn't have a very good tone, and you couldn't tune them, my father said."

As Demes remembers it, the first Kimball scale was drawn by a German piano maker named Becker who was employed at the organ plant. He was, says Demes, more often drunk than sober.

"Sometimes," he recalls, "this old gentleman would turn up missing, and we would start a search of the factory. More often than not we would find him sleeping off a spree in an empty packing box in the shipping department." Every time a saloonkeeper on nearby Blue Island Avenue would kick the bucket, Becker would shake his head sadly and sigh, "Another bill paid."

The results of the earliest piano experiments were not such as to encourage Kimball to proceed. But Conway and Cone had both been urging "the Governor," as they now had begun to call him, to put up a piano factory almost from the time the organ plant was started two years before. As he hesitated, he nevertheless recognized that the time for such a decision was approaching. With the advent of the Joseph P. Hale pianos, which ceased to be featured in Kimball's line after 1880, there had been a great rush by various manufacturers to copy the New Yorker's revolutionary piano-making methods and exploit the lower-priced market. The competition was getting tougher all the time. And it would get tougher. Already C. A. Smith was all set to start C. A. Smith & Company, later Smith & Barnes, the first Chicago factory to turn out pianos for the general wholesale trade, and to produce his first 250 instruments in 1884.

As Kimball, in a moment of resolution, had commented to his friend Robert B. Gregory, later president of Lyon & Healy, "When the business begins to get good, the other fellow comes along and takes it away. Consequently I am going to make my own pianos."

13

"If he starts a piano factory in Chicago . . . he will
become a more formidable rival than ever."

THE YEARS 1884 and 1885 were satisfactory if not spectacular for
the Kimball company, despite the economic dislocations caused by
the panic of May, 1884, and the slump that followed. The Repub-
licans ran James G. Blaine for President against Grover Cleveland
in the campaign that gave rise to the cry, "Rum, Romanism and
Rebellion," with Cleveland winning in the greatest outpouring of
votes ever cast to that date. In Chicago, the nation's first skyscraper,
the 10-story Home Insurance Building, was erected in 1884, and in
the following year Kimball's friend Potter Palmer built himself a
North Side mansion.

In 1884 the Kimball company declared a dividend of 20 per
cent, amounting to $120,000, and in 1885, the dividend was 14
per cent. Kimball credited the satisfactory showing not alone to
his own careful management, but to the loyalty and continued
enthusiasm of his staff.

In the latter year also, W. W. Lufkin had so made his mark in
the huge Kimball organ plant that he was placed in overall charge
of factory operations. From the start, George L. Hadley recalled in

1956, Lufkin was "absolute ruler" of the factory. Ultimately he would be known in the music trade for having personally supervised the building of more organs and pianos than any other man in history. In his long span of factory duty he would likewise purchase more materials for such manufacture than any other single man.

An examination of his early factory cost sheets discloses the meticulous way in which Lufkin figured to the fraction of a cent every item of material and labor that went into his uncle's instruments. A typical entry for one of the early reed organ styles broke down these costs as follows: "Lumber, $5.6133; machine work, $5.1560; cabinet, $4.0450; finishing, $3.5626; action—bellows, $1.7780; fly finishing, $1.0413; stop, $ .8925; reed, $5.8632; key, $2.0467; getting out action stock, $ .07; tremolo, $ .2250; coupler, $ .50; tuning, $3.60; regulating, $ .12; mirror, 14 x 20, $1.05; cleaning & trimming, $ .1550; packing box, $1.50; packing labor, $ .08; general expense, $4.00; general help, $ .50. Total, $41.7986."

It was Lufkin who set the pattern for the accuracy with which the company kept track of costs from its earliest days of manufacture. His planning thus played a vital part in enabling it over the years to meet the crises with confidence when they came. Typical was the action of Kimball in reducing prices when the panic struck in 1893, as illustrated by the wholesale price list of February 15 and what happened to it.

The reduction at the top and bottom price levels on the list will suffice as examples. The style 159 solid satin walnut reed organ, with a factory cost of $22, bore a wholesale price of $40, reduced to $37.50 on October 1, when Lufkin refigured the cost and discovered it to be $20.87. The style 459 walnut or oak chapel organ, with a factory cost of $47, and wholesaling in February at $108, was reduced on October 1 to $76 at wholesale when Lufkin's revised cost sheets showed an actual factory expense of only $41.51.

Lufkin's careful accounting methods were introduced into the piano division also after its establishment in 1888.

At the annual meeting of the Kimball directors on January 10, 1886, Lufkin was elevated to the board, replacing J. L. McKittrick, who had become an attorney for the Chicago & North Western Railway. At this meeting, it may be noted in passing, a seventeen per cent dividend was declared for the six months ending January 1. It was not until the company by-laws were rewritten in 1898 that Lufkin was formally included in the executive group as general superintendent of the Kimball company, assuming a title held until that time by E. S. Conway.

The experimental manufacture of pianos continued on a small scale through 1885 and 1886, although, as E. B. Bartlett later reported, "the Governor" still "was not very enthusiastic about it, fearing he was too advanced in years to shoulder the added responsibility of manufacturing pianos."

As the new Kimball pianos continued to make an occasional appearance, the news spread alarums throughout the trade. A tocsin was sounded on February 27, 1886, by the hostile New York publication *Music Trade Free Press* in a shrill editorial blast entitled "The Kimball System":

"Every house of any prominence in this country is supposed to have a certain system of doing business, or, at any rate, a systematic way of doing things. But probably none has got their business systematized to a greater degree than the W. W. Kimball Company of Chicago.

"In the first place, there is W. W. Kimball himself, a sharp, shrewd man, a keen observer, and a thorough organizer. Then there are his assistants, Conway, Coon and Northrup [*sic*]. [The last two references were to Albert Cone and John W. Northrop, a Kimball man later associated with the Emerson Piano Company.]

"His field of operations extends throughout the entire Northwest, and his little army of workers are scattered over this vast area of territory. No general ever marshaled his men or held them under greater subjection [*sic*] than does W. W. Kimball. Everything is subservient to the Kimball system. They have their field days, with their tactics, which are issued from headquarters. They march and counter-march, and go through all the various evolutions with the regularity of clockwork, and so thoroughly are these men controlled by the general and his aides-de-camp that whenever they come in contact with the agent of an Eastern manufacturer, and it behooves them to attack him, the latter gets so completely vanquished that when the Eastern manufacturer comes to look up his man, he finds nothing but the 'footprints in the sands of time,' where the Kimball army passed along.

"So thoroughly imbued have a great many Eastern manufacturers become with this idea that when their representatives start out on the road they give them strict injunctions not to sell to any agent who buys of W. W. Kimball. Manufacturers may not be aware of this fact, but it is nevertheless the truth that the strongest competitor the Eastern organ manufacturers have today is the W. W. Kimball Company of Chicago. Not so much on account of the goods they manufacture, as of their thorough organization and the large capital at their disposal. The theory on which a Kimball man works is that if other people's goods will sell in any place, no matter whether large or small, his will sell also. Consequently he goes to a place imbued with this idea. He offers his wares to whatever agents happen to be in the place. If the agents refuse to buy of him, he hires a store, has a car load of organs and pianos sent to him from Chicago, and then advertises, largely in the local press, gets up an excitement, sells off what goods he has at a fair profit, and by so doing gluts the market with goods in that section; and then moves on. If the agents in any place give him an order he lets them alone, and thus it is that we have often heard agents say they bought Kimball organs just to keep him away, or, in other words, so that they would be let alone.

"When Kimball gets hold of a good agent, he don't [*sic*] try to cramp him, and sell him only such goods as he is able to pay for—cash down. He looks him over well and says, 'Here is a good man to work for the Kimball system, if we can only once get him under control,' so they tell him to go ahead and sell all the organs he can and never mind about paying for them. The agent does so and the first thing he knows, he owes Kimball twelve or fifteen thousand dollars. Then one of Kimball's aides swoops down on him and gathers in whatever he happens to have in the way of bills receivable and then lets the account run to a higher figure, when he takes a mortgage on everything the man owns, and makes him keeper for W. W. Kimball, and thus the man becomes a member of the Kimball system and looses [sic] his own identity.

"The W. W. Kimball system today is to the music trade what the Standard Oil Company is to the oil trade, and if he starts a piano factory in Chicago, as has been reported, he will become a more formidable rival than ever."

This attack with its distortions was typical of others that were to appear, especially in the trade publications of the East, for at least a decade after Kimball began his own piano manufacture. They were encouraged by Kimball's manufacturing rivals in the East. As we shall see in a subsequent chapter, the Chicago trade papers and the more honest New York papers defended the "Kimball methods," which for some years created industry-wide debate as the East-West rivalry was intensified. But in the end, the most savage of the attackers, including the *Music Trade Free Press* and the *Musical Courier,* would concede that Kimball's only real offense was the development of the greatest manufacturing and selling organization in the history of the music trade.

The *Music Trade Free Press,* notwithstanding its 1886 article, unctuously editorialized on April 1, 1893: "Possibly not in any industry in the world has there been a firm that have shown a more progressive and enterprising spirit than the W. W. Kimball Company. Since they first embarked in business the energy they displayed has been the admiration of all unprejudiced minds. They pushed their instruments to the front in such manner that none but men of the greatest calibre could do."

And the *Musical Courier* confessed on March 25, 1896: "The Kimball method is just the same as any other commercial method in or out of the piano trade. It is an intelligent effort to sell pianos; make as consistent a profit as is commensurate with prevailing trade necessities; sell as many pianos as possible; get as much cash money or as high a percentage of cash as can be gotten, and do all this irrespective of the feelings or consideration of competitors. . . . Does not the above apply to any house in the trade? . . . There is only one point of difference between the Kimball methods and the methods of the other firms and that is this: The other houses are not prepared, not organized, to conduct their affairs on the Kimball plan; the moment any other piano house finds itself able to follow the Kimball methods it will so follow them, but that will take some time, judging from the condition or the individual disposition of the firms or the peculiarly limited horizon their views cover in many instances."

Whatever W. W. Kimball was thinking in the winter of 1886, he kept his friends and rivals in the Chicago music field guessing. As Harry Freund, the trade paper editor, later recalled, "he only smiled that inscrutable smile" and answered all inquiries about the possibility of his entering the manufacturing business with the remark: "The 'boys' think we ought to run up a few more walls, put in a wheel or two and a saw, and turn out a piano now and then."

Already he had begun to import a nucleus of highly skilled European-trained piano technicians, hiring them away from the large, long-established Eastern factories to whom he would soon become a hated competitor. And, though he never tipped his hand, he had abandoned the early piano models and had the scales for his first factory upright piano drawn by the chief designer for one of the most distinguished houses in America. From the first he determined to confine his manufacture to uprights and grands, since he looked upon the square piano as too cumbersome, too clumsy and ungraceful in appearance, and too expensive in quantity of material involved in its manufacture to justify production. With his Chicago trade the square had long since become unfashionable and quite limited in demand.

The year 1887 was an important one for two reasons: Early in the year "the Governor" called in Lufkin from the factory and instructed him secretly to start erecting a new building which would be used as a piano plant. It was to be five stories high, with a ground floor area of 80 by 240 feet, and would adjoin the organ factory. And later in the year the downtown offices and warerooms were removed from State and Adams streets to even larger quarters in a six-story building, massive for that day, at State and Jackson streets.

14

"You've done it, Governor! The tone of this piano is marvelous in every respect."

"THERE WAS great joy in the organization," E. B. Bartlett recalled, when it became known early in 1887 that a piano factory was under way at last. It was scheduled for occupancy on the following January 1, and as the construction neared completion W. W. Kimball authorized his factory manager to order sufficient materials for building the first 200 pianos at the new factory.

A writer in the *Music Trade Review* reported that year that the decision to begin manufacture had "caused much talk among the trade and considerable anxiety on the part of some manufacturers." He added:

"I asked Mr. Kimball if he has as yet made any pianos and he said he had not, but had some under way which would soon be finished, and when they were he should not hesitate to have them undergo critical examination. One thing is sure that Mr. Kimball means business, and there is no better proof of this than to note the anxiety of certain manufacturers. These manufacturers have already gone so far as to buy up a certain self-styled trade paper, and through its columns have already begun a course of tirade upon Mr. Kimball and the piano he proposes to make, which is sickening for any honest person to read. It would show a little more common sense to wait until the child is born and then its color can be ascertained with some accuracy. However, these attacks of the scurrilous sheet to which I allude will do Mr. Kimball no harm. He is far too sensible to answer these slurs but will go steadily forward, and, I will venture to state positively, manufacture his pianos and readily sell them without the aid of that sheet or the manufacturers who are putting up the cash to run it in such a nefarious way."

The "child" was born in the spring of 1888, and it was a proud moment for W. W. Lufkin when he was able at last to ring up his uncle on the single private telephone line that connected the plant and the general offices and inform him that the first lot of Kimball pianos was ready for inspection.

It was a proud day also for the great manufacturer and his companions, Cone and Conway and their friend, the eminent concert pianist Emil Liebling, as the purple-liveried Kimball coachman tooled his spirited team of horses down Blue Island Avenue toward the factory and the first demonstration.

The first finished lot of Kimballs were style 4 uprights, a favorite of both the company and its customers in the early years. It was a piano of "seven and one-third octaves; three strings and agraffe." The handsome walnut case was plain but dignified. It featured a swinging music desk and a rolling fallboard. The piano stood four feet eight and one-half inches high and was five feet five and one-half inches wide and two feet four and one-half inches deep.

To Kimball it seemed as though Lufkin and his factory staff had outdone themselves in creating the first Kimball pianos—row on row of shining instruments that would do credit to any parlor. But what most profoundly concerned the little gathering at the factory was what would be the critical reaction of Liebling, an influential and powerful figure in the world of musicians.

Peter Tapper, the general foreman of the piano department, led the way through a maze of instruments in various stages of manufacture and finally to an area of the floor that had been cleared for the demonstration of piano No. 1. He prefaced the ceremonies with a little talk, delivered in a thick German accent. Tapper, who later left Kimball's employ to manufacture pianos on his own, was an able piano maker, trained in some of the most celebrated factories overseas. His brother at the time was a superintendent for the Bechsteins in Berlin.

"Gentlemen," he said, "here it is. Our first Kimball-manufactured piano. We have used only the highest grade of material in making it, and all the labor has been closely watched over every step of the way by Mr. Guricke [a onetime employe of the Bechsteins and of the Steinway factory in Hamburg], the superintendent of our action department, and myself. We believe it is a piano that will compare favorably with anything on the market."

"And now, Mr. Liebling," said Kimball, as Tapper finished, "you as an artist are the best qualified man among us to judge whether Mr. Lufkin and Mr. Tapper and Mr. Guricke have merely produced another piece of machinery or whether the Kimball piano also has a soul. We await your verdict with interest."

There was the scraping of a few piano benches on the heavy board floor as the little company of auditors settled back to listen, and then a dramatic silence as Liebling sat down and swept his fingers with a flourish along the gleaming ivory keyboard.

For this first trial he selected from his prodigious memory a medley of three German dances by Beethoven, in his own arrangement, the difficult "Tre Sonetti di Petrarca" by Liszt, and a spirited Chopin mazurka.

And as he finished the final number, he turned to face Kimball, and his smile and the expression in his eyes told the manufacturer and the rest of Liebling's hearers everything they had waited breathlessly to know.

"It's a superb instrument!" he beamed. "The equal of anything I have ever heard or seen in America, and better than most of

109

those made in Europe. You've done it, Governor! The tone of this piano is marvelous in every respect—in richness, in power, in delicacy, in precision, in articulation, in everything that makes a piano great."

In that same year, the records show, the instrument that Emil Liebling played—Kimball No. 1—was shipped out to Ann Arbor, Michigan, on July 5, 1888, for delivery to E. F. Greenwood, one of the company's wholesale agents on the road and later manager of its big branch store in Detroit. It was purchased from Greenwood by Lou H. Clement of Ann Arbor, who was reported in the 90s to have sold it to a clubhouse when he moved on to West Virginia. George L. Hadley recalled in 1956 that about twenty years ago he heard that it was still in use in the music department of the University of Michigan. Its ultimate fate is not known.

The production of the Kimball piano had reached 500 by the end of 1888.

Meanwhile, Albert Cone continued to promote the Kimball organ, rolling off hundreds of reading notices in his fine longhand. He delighted in extolling the virtues of the organ, which remained his favorite instrument, and in this period produced one of his minor masterpieces of high-flown prose, captioned "Music for a World":

"Wherever musical taste is introduced it is accompanied by the Kimball organ. The quaint old chapels of New England, the cosy farm houses of the sons of the Pilgrim fathers, the school house of our oldest settlements, the homesteads of the western highlands and prairies, the faraway mountain homes of the land of the gold and the fruitful farms around the Golden Gate, the plantations of the South, the Canadian farm and the city mansion of the Old Dominion are all enlivened by the music of the Kimball organ. From its factory with its unceasing hum of machinery; its capacity of forty organs a day incapable of meeting the ever-increasing demand, the Kimball organ is distributed all over the world by agencies numbering over a thousand. Invading the territory of the

Famous Style 4, first of the Kimball pianos (1888) is shown at top. At center is "small" parlor grand (1891). At bottom is "push-up" piano player cabinet in position before a Kimball upright. This was a forerunner of the player piano.

By covered wagon and iron horse products of the Kimball reed organ and piano
factory went out to the nation. Photo at bottom shows a factory group of 1880s.

organ-producing localities of olden time, it has its emporiums in Boston and throughout the East, even securing men as its representatives who have hitherto represented the Estey in Brattleboro, and Shoninger in New Haven. In London, Glasgow and Dublin a Kimball agent is as easily found as in Chicago. The regions of the Norsemen are not neglected, for an agent at Christiana attends to Sweden, Denmark and Norway. France will be supplied from an agency established in Paris; instruments are shipped to China, New Zealand and the isles of the Southern Archipelago, while from Chicago as the great centre of the trade, every railroad bears its carloads, and the lakes their boat freight of the Kimball organ to every point where a church is found, a missionary station established, a school house is built or music is appreciated. The existence of such a factory in Chicago tells a truthful story of the wonderful progress of this city, not merely as the granary and abattoir of the civilized world, but as the great Western centre of those humanizing influences whose capstone is music."

The Chicago *Herald,* commenting in 1888 upon the completion of the piano factory, recalled the "protracted incipiency" of piano and organ manufacturing as a Chicago industry. It noted that until Kimball had started his organ factory seven years before, the supply of these instruments for Chicago and the West had come largely from New York and New England manufacturers. It observed also that in addition to serving "the larger part of the Western, Southern and Northwestern trade," the Kimball factory was also supplying a "very large proportion of the best traffic of South America, Australia, New Zealand and Europe." Kimball's development of this trade, it added, had been "a bold venture against the law and logic of American mercantile development" and its success "one of the business surprises of the century."

The new piano factory contained fifteen rooms, each 80 feet square. It was connected with the organ plant, still only four stories high, by a covered bridge, or chute, of the type that was used to link the entire network of factory buildings later erected on the site. The organ plant's twelve rooms were of a size similar to those in the piano plant, so that the total floorage was 172,800 square feet. In addition to the two main structures, there was an outside system of accessory buildings—dry kilns, sheds, storage rooms, and engine and boiler houses—spread over two full blocks of grounds totaling seven acres. The main buildings were heated by steam and lighted electrically. Both were equipped with the latest ventilating systems and with automatic sprinklers for fire protection. A company booklet reported that the factories were "equipped throughout with every kind of machinery that has yet been invented for advancing, improving, expediting and economizing this, the finest and most delicate of the great mechanical industries."

On the east side of the factory layout lay the Chicago River stub, and on the west a private branch railway track. The *Herald's* correspondent, on a visit to the site with other newsmen in the spring of 1888, commented that "the significance of these two lateral boundaries, connecting the premises directly with the rail system of the continent and the shipping waters of the globe, was instantly and intuitively recognized by the entire party."

One of the features that impressed the visiting newsman "was that of the stupendous quantities of cabinet lumber—from the company's own mills—and seen in the various processes of unloading into the yards, transfer to the mammoth dry kilns of a capacity of 15,000 feet dried lumber a day, and the transfer thence to the great storage sheds from which the supplies of the machine room are drawn."

This 20,000 square-foot room, where the lumber was cut, was preparing the material not only for the new Kimball pianos but for a vast organ production which had reached 240 instruments, and sometimes more, a week in 1888.

"We are not yet fully running on pianos," Lufkin told the *Herald's* man. "Only thirty a week. The number will be increased soon, however, to fifty a week."

As the company's directors met on January 23, 1888, the balance sheet showed a profit of $127,077.88, and a twenty per cent dividend was declared, the balance of the profit being placed in the surplus account. In view of the expansion of the manufacturing interests, Secretary Conway introduced a resolution, which was approved, calling for a meeting on the following February 28 to discuss increasing the company's capital stock to $1,000,000. By this time the individual stock holdings were: Kimball, 5,348 shares; Conway, 300; Cone, 300; Grannis, one; and Lufkin, 50.

The stockholders on the same date approved the purchase by Kimball of the organ factory and the land surrounding it, which had been under lease up to now. They also formally approved the erection of the piano factory.

An increase in the capital stock to $1,000,000, or 10,000 shares, was unanimously approved in February, and when the directors next met, on January 14, 1889, Kimball had increased his holdings to 7,948 shares and Conway and Cone to 1,000 each. The balance sheet showed a profit of $178,651.31 for 1888, but in view of the heavy expenditures made that year in getting the piano factory rolling it was decided to omit a dividend and place the earnings in the surplus account. (An error in the balance sheet of January 1, 1889, was later discovered, increasing the profit for 1888 by $15,-074.36. This amount was added to the surplus account at the 1890 annual meeting.)

Kimball's progress through this period set the pace for his contemporaries. Writing in *Harper's Monthly* for May, 1888, in a series of "Studies of the Great West," the noted journalist Charles Dudley Warner expressed his surprise at the growth of the Chicago musical instrument trade.

"Chicago," he said, "is not only the largest reed organ market in the world, but . . . more organs are manufactured here than in any other city in Europe or America. The sales in 1887 were $2,000,000, an increase over 1886 of $500,000." The organ output was 30,750, up 5,645 over 1886. The piano sales, Warner reported, amounted to about $2,600,000, a gain of $300,000. And the W. W. Kimball Company took note of his comments with the statement that "fully one-eighth of all the organs produced in the United States are now produced within it." The new piano factory, it added, would be in full production by summer. As it entered the field there were a dozen other Chicago piano factories going, the more prominent being Julius Bauer & Company, Bush & Gerts Piano Company, and C. A. Smith & Company.

In 1889 the Chicago music industries turned out 60,000 pianos and organs, of which ten per cent was the product of the Kimball factories. There were 500 workers employed in the two plants, and production was up to 50 organs a day and 50 pianos a week. The company's net gain for 1889, as reported at the 1890 annual meeting, was $186,728.80, out of which a dividend of $100,000 was paid, the balance being placed in the surplus account.

In 1890, when the *Music Trade Free Press* sent a reporter to the factory, Lufkin reported to him that he was shipping twelve pianos a day and soon would be shipping a hundred a week. There were 1,200 pianos in progress and four million square feet of lumber on hand. The factory force in peak periods was up to 600.

The move into the new office building and warerooms at State and Jackson in 1887 provided the company with an aggregate traffic floorage of nearly 60,000 square feet. The building consisted of two stores, with a frontage of 80 feet and a depth of 160 feet. The main warerooms and business offices were on the main floor, and on the second floor the first "Kimball Hall" was established. The *Indicator* reported that this concert room, a plush one for its time, "is a spacious apartment of exceptionally excellent acoustic properties and has a seating capacity of five hundred." It added: "It is devoted to concerts and piano recitals and other musical events, and has become a popular and fashionable resort of those who find enjoyment in listening to sweet harmonies environed with chaste and elegant surroundings. Paintings by eminent artists adorn its walls and add to the sense of the artistic and beautiful that involuntarily establishes itself in the mind of the visitor."

The rear portion of the third floor was used for the Kimball repair shops, while on other floors of the building there were stored numerous boxed instruments of all the organ and piano manufac-turers Kimball represented, including Chickering, Hallet & Davis and Emerson.

These extensive quarters, Albert Cone boasted in a reading no-tice inserted in the advertising columns of the newspapers of the day, corresponded "in commanding magnitude with the manufac-tory" and were "unapproached by any other similar establishment in existence." In these extensive quarters, boasting "the largest show room in the world," the Kimball force could "at a moment's notice exhibit 300 pianos and samples of 50 styles of organs, which as sold are replaced, a constant ingress and egress of instruments being constantly going on." The salesmen, the notice further as-serted, "are ever at work exhibiting, explaining and testing the various organs and pianos, and the sales may be said to be per-petual, half a dozen instruments being frequently disposed of with as much celerity as common articles of groceries or dry goods."

At the rear of the corner wareroom were the general offices where, the company said in a booklet prepared for the trade, "a business aggregating several million dollars annually is trans-acted, which is equal in volume to that of many of the larger Chi-cago national banks and requires as large a force of clerks to handle it."

Helping to pay the rent on the new building were numerous studios on the upper floors which were occupied by leading teach-ers and other musicians. Among these was the famous pianist Emil Liebling, who in time would help Kimball to break down much of the resistance in the East to his Chicago-manufactured pianos.

15

Adelina Patti: "It gives me great pleasure to testify to the merits of the new Kimball piano."

As the 1880s drew to a close, the W. W. Kimball Company was on the eve of its greatest decade—a period when the "New Scale Kimball Piano" won the acclaim of some of the world's most famous artists and went on with the Kimball organs to sweep the musical instruments awards list at the World's Columbian Exposition; when Marc A. Blumenberg and his *Musical Courier* rose in venomous violence against the piano's fantastic successes, and then later recanted; when the company ventured with brilliant success into pipe organ manufacture; when the company's production and profits reached heights never before achieved in the history of the American music trades.

The 1890s were indeed an exciting period of progress, and Albert G. Cone closed out the 80s and set the pace for the decade to follow with what must have seemed to him like an innocent enough exploitation of an artist endorsement for the pianos rolling off the production line under W. W. Lufkin's supervision.

The artist was the great soprano Adelina Patti, a perennial

favorite of Chicago music lovers since the time in 1853 when she had first appeared at the age of twelve in the music hall of the old Tremont House, a "delicate, pale-faced, dark-browed child with glossy hair hanging in two long braids down her back, dressed in rose-colored silk, pink stockings and pantalettes."

Cone was an old hand at the practice—an ancient and honorable one in the piano-making world—of obtaining endorsements from outstanding musical figures. It was a custom that had originated in Europe, where Beethoven, Liszt, Chopin, Haydn, and many another man of genius had lent his name to such exploitation. In the late 80s Cone had worked with Hallet & Davis in obtaining such sales-making help from Liszt, the composer Johann Strauss, Franz Abt, and other Europeans, while in Chicago he had won the cooperation of visiting artists, as well as such local celebrities as Emil Liebling and Dr. Florenz Ziegfeld, founder in 1867 of the Chicago Musical College, of which W. W. Kimball was a director.

Perhaps no other manufacturer of the day spent so much money or exerted so much effort on its artist endorsements as did the New York firm of Steinway & Sons. Their efforts reached fantastic heights in 1872, when, as Arthur Loesser has reported in "Men, Women and Pianos," William Steinway guaranteed the great pianist Anton Rubinstein a $40,000 contract—200 concerts at $200 apiece—to use the Steinway piano exclusively on his American tour. In later years the Polish pianist Ignace Jan Paderewski is said to have had similarly lucrative arrangements with the Steinways.

Cone's exploit, which was to cause so much furor in the early 90s, was to obtain the endorsement of Adelina Patti for the new Kimball piano and publish it widely in the trade and to the buying public. This noted prima donna had long been considered a Steinway artist, and on January 4, 1882, she had signed an endorsement of that maker's pianos that was featured widely in the Steinway advertising.

The Kimball endorsement came on December 16, 1889, following Patti's appearance with the tenor Francisco Tamagno and other members of the Grand Italian Opera Company in the first session of opera at Chicago's famous Auditorium Theatre.

A glittering assemblage turned out on the evening of December 9, when Patti, for a fee of $4,200, stood on the Auditorium stage at the dedication and sang "Home, Sweet Home." In the audience was the President of the United States, Benjamin Harrison. Among the boxholders were George M. Pullman, the sleeping car magnate; the Marshall Fields and the E. Mandels of department store fame; R. T. Crane, the founder of the Crane Company, and his wife; and the W. W. Kimballs.

In the Kimball party on this notable evening was a newcomer to Chicago society, Miss Evaline Kimball of Rumford, Maine, a niece of the manufacturer and daughter of his brother, Virgil D., who had remained on the family farm when W. W. struck out on his own. Miss Kimball had come to Chicago to visit her wealthy uncle and his wife and had remained to live in their home as a companion to Mrs. Kimball, who was attracted by her beauty and charm.

At the end of the opera engagement, the Kimball treasurer made a wholesale raid on the Patti-Tamagno company, emerging with testimonials for the new piano from all its members of any musical consequence.

The Patti endorsement read: "It gives me great pleasure to testify to the merits of the New Kimball Piano. It has a wonderfully sweet and sympathetic tone and supports the voice in a most satisfactory manner."

And Tamagno wrote: "I have never used a piano that has afforded me more genuine satisfaction, and believe that you have attained an excellence which cannot fail to give your instruments a worldwide reputation."

Cone promptly put the enthusiastic endorsements into the next Kimball catalog, along with similar praises from other musical contemporaries, among them Mme. Albani, Giuseppe del Puente, Lillian Nordica, Minnie Hauk, Lilli Lehmann, Max Alvary, Mme.

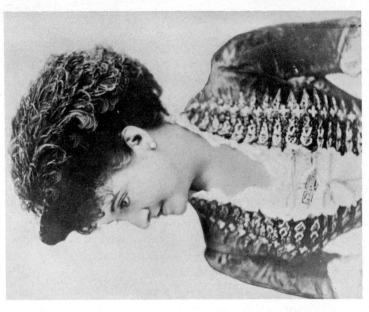

Arrow points to Adelina Patti's signature endorsing the Kimball piano. This instrument is still on display in Kimball showrooms. Photograph of the Italian star at right is from files of the Chicago *Daily News*.

Fursch-Madi, Emil Fischer, Arditi, Galassi, Mme. Clementine de Vere Sapio, Julius Perotti, W. C. E. Seeboeck, Charles Kunkel, Hans Balatka, P. S. Gilmore, Luigi Ravelli, Giovanni Perugini, Paul Kalisch, Sophie Traubman, Conrad Behrens, Sarasate, A. de Novellis, Frederic Archer, and numerous others.

In 1890 Patti presented to the company the Kimball instrument she used on her American tour of 1888-89. It was a studio upright with walnut case, the 3,463rd piano to be manufactured in the big factory at Twenty-sixth and Rockwell. When one of the company officers asked for her autograph, the great prima donna replied by scratching "Adelina Patti-Nicolini" on the music rack with her diamond ring. The name, having been engraved deeper into the wood, is still visible; it has been inspected by thousands of visitors to the company's Chicago showrooms. "Patti is gone," said the Chicago *Daily News* in a special feature article on the piano in 1939, "but her piano, except for the age-stained ivory, still looks like it did the day she autographed it, and it still plays the tones she heard half a century ago."

The Patti endorsement turned out to be a sensation in the musical world of the 90s, although she was distinguished for her voice and not her piano playing. "Musical artists," the *Piano Trade Magazine* has said, "began to sit up and take notice of the Kimball piano, to the consternation of some Eastern piano manufacturers who, in those days, thought they should wear armor against the arrows of the savages when they visited Chicago."

Reaction in the East was immediate, and for several years afterward the *Musical Courier* and its editor, Marc A. Blumenberg, attacked "the so-called Patti letter," insinuating that it was a forgery "as no one has ever seen the original." Blumenberg further charged that the company could not show the original of Dr. Ziegfeld's endorsement. That both these charges were baseless was evidenced by the continued association of Patti and Ziegfeld with the Kimball instruments over many years.

Patti, as a matter of fact, reinforced her testimonial on several later occasions. In the course of a long interview published by the

The Kimball Story

Chicago *Evening Post* on February 2, 1892, she described Craig-y-Nos Castle, her picturesque forty-room home in the Swansea Valley at Ystradgyplais, R. S. O., Breckonshire, South Wales, and said: "Oh, yes. I must not forget one thing. I have something in my castle that ought to give satisfaction to you Chicagoans. It is a W. W. Kimball grand piano, and it is a beauty, too." Upon the publication of which, the *Indicator* remarked: "Mr. Blumenberg will please read and then fall in a fit." And on July 28, 1897, she wrote to Mr. Kimball from Craig-y-Nos to acknowledge the safe arrival of a Kimball baby grand piano: "It is, indeed, a beautiful piano and has an exquisite tone. It has already been greatly admired by many connoisseurs who are all united in pronouncing it to be a *chef d'oeuvre.*"

Blumenberg's attack on the Patti and Ziegfeld letters was part and parcel of an unremitting war he waged against the Kimball company, as well as certain other piano manufacturers and artists, throughout the 90s.

As the editor-in-chief of the *Musical Courier,* Blumenberg was in the position to exercise a powerful influence over anything in the world of music, and he chose to turn this power against those who refused to pay him tribute.

A talented, sensitive man of undoubted musical instinct and ability, Marc Blumenberg was born in Baltimore, Maryland, on May 21, 1851, the son of a merchant. He was brought up in a musical atmosphere and in the 80s went to New York City, where he bought an interest in a small paper called the *Musical Courier and Dramatic Weekly*. The dramatic department was dropped shortly after he took over.

The story of his blackmailing attacks on the Kimball company has never been adequately told. There is, for example, not the barest mention of it in Loesser's supposedly thorough account of American piano history.

That certain unidentified but powerful Eastern competitors of Kimball were behind the Blumenberg attacks was generally acknowledged by respectable music trade publications of the 90s.

123

The New York publication *Music Trades* in December, 1898, aired the whole dismal mess in a series of articles by Milton Weil, business manager of the paper, and John C. Freund, its editor. Weil reported that Kimball had for years been paying thousands of dollars to Blumenberg, who had "steadily defamed him." Freund commented: "He should have added that Mr. Kimball paid blackmail, under protest, that he is paying today under protest, that he regards the payment as the most shameful act of his whole life and that he never would have paid a dollar had he not found that his competitors were willing to use 'organized blackmail' in an effort to crush him, when, had they had any self-respect they would have thrown aside such a weapon with contempt. Mr. Kimball has not paid tribute because of Mr. Blumenberg's attacks, but because of the shameless use to which these attacks were put by his competitors and their representatives."

The *Musical Courier's* attack on the testimonials Cone had obtained from the Grand Italian Opera Company charged Kimball with "paying certain Chicago daily papers large sums to make Mrs. Patti-Nicollini [*sic*], Tamagno and the other stars of the organization say pleasant things about the Kimball piano." It added that "what a reporter says Mr. Kimball says Patti says is to be taken with a great big grain of salt, epsom preferred."

Blumenberg also took occasion to ridicule a two-hundred-pound floral piece the Kimball company had presented to Patti at an appearance in Omaha, Nebraska, through its Omaha dealer, A. Hospe Jr. He charged that "as a sort of offset to the Kimball piano which he furnishes Patti, [Kimball] also sends with it a floral offering which is carted from place to place accompanied by press notices. . . ." And he added: "Mr. Hospe writes us that the statement made by the Chickering agents in Omaha to the effect that Kimball also supplied Nicollini with a tub of Chicago spaghetti per day is not founded in fact. He would also have us to know that when Patti 'scratched' the Kimball upright she did not do so in anger, and that where the gumwood showed through the two coats of varnish he [*sic*] filled in the lines of the 'well-known signature' with red ink, so that some people think that it is really, truly mahogany." The reference to two coats of varnish over gumwood was typical of Blumenberg's attempts to discredit the Kimball pianos as instruments made of inferior material. (Actually the Patti piano was of walnut, as we have already noted.)

In the *Courier's* issue of September 30, 1891, Blumenberg concocted a satirical report from one "Harvey Hayseed" concerning the demise of one "Jared Diggs, Esq., late of Pilltown, N.Y.," a dealer in "Wimball" pianos. In an obvious slap at the Kimball installment payment system, the Hayseed report ascribed to the mythical Diggs "the great honor of having introduced the installment plan, and by that I mean the installment plan at its very worst, for toward the last he was giving away (in addition to himself) large lamps full of oil, with every Wimball piano. . . . So, you see, when you take into consideration that he bought the Wimball —a low grade instrument—for $88.67, wholesale, he could well afford to give away books, stools, lamps, mangles, pumps, prayer books, heifers, even cradles and safety pins, and what not."

Correspondent "Hayseed" also reported finding a lot of "Wimball" endorsements, "all in Diggs' handwriting." It quoted one, dated "Charlestown Jail, Mass., January 31, 1890" and addressed to "My Dear Mr. Wimball." The letter read: "In reply to your favor of the 16th hasten willingly—gladly—to write to you that in my opinion your gumwood upright Style 16½ B, is the best instrument I have ever played upon since my immurement within these hospitable prison walls. (I have had no other piano, though.) For rendering that touching melody that I am so fond of, 'I Butchered My Aunt with An Axe,' the Wimball piano is simply unapproachable, and I assure you—even promise you (of course this must be kept strictly private)—I will use your wires as pick locks when I make my next effort to escape." It was signed, "Yours repentantly, Jesse Pomeroy (Sec), the Boy Murderer (aged 32)."

The Patti endorsement came in for ridicule in another letter, dated "Ygdrasili, Lllewellen Parg, Whales, G. B." It read: "Dear, Dear Mr. Wimball—Yes, it *is* true. I have dyed my hair black again.

Nick is well; so is the parrot. I sing with Abbey. Ask Alfred all about it. In paste, OYSTER PATTY."

A New York letter from "Clambake Harry"—presumably Harry Freund of *Freund's Musical Weekly*—said, "I won't call your piano the 'Monarch of Grands' for less than $10, cash in advance." (The Kimball grand piano was introduced in the spring of 1891.) Still another, this from Chicago and signed "L. O. Sox"—obviously O. L. Fox, publisher of the *Indicator*—said "Look here! I've had a h——ll of a time about the 'Monarch' business. My rent is due and the printer is raising a row. You know what to do."

A week before, the *Courier* had printed a long article from its Chicago correspondent, J. D. Hammond, which consisted mainly of an attack on Kimball. After noting that a strike was in progress at the piano factory of W. H. Bush & Company, Hammond went on to report that a most interesting aspect of the Chicago trade was the way in which other piano firms, by continuing to handle stenciled pianos, were unwittingly aiding the Kimball company.

"The foundation of Kimball's fortune," said the *Courier* man, "was laid by the stencil in the days when there existed no antagonism to that feature of the piano trade. Today the Kimball house parades as an opponent of the stencil and makes its greatest hit in the retail warerooms in Chicago with this assumed virtue, for in selling at wholesale Kimball has stenciled his pianos and organs and is probably doing so now. But in the retail Chicago warerooms the stencil piano is abominated by the Kimball salesmen, and the way they do make sales and kill the sales of competitors by denouncing the stencil would make the editors of the stencil music trade press of this country blue in the face with anger if they knew it. Well, we'll tell them and everyone else."

The facts were, as the writer conceded in the same dispatch, that "every customer who starts out undecided and looks up the matter will find the statement of the Kimball salesman confirmed." None of the instruments mentioned—the "Geo. W. Lyon," the "Twichell" (sold by J. O. Twichell, a onetime Kimball employe), the "Adam Schaaf," or the "Camp" piano—was manufactured by the man whose name it bore. What the *Courier* really resented was Kimball's success in outselling his Chicago competitors. Hammond lamented that since September 1 Lyon & Healy had sold only six pianos a day.

The report included another attack on Kimball testimonial methods as an "intellectual bunco game." It charged that Dr. Ziegfeld and others who endorsed the Kimball grand when it was introduced at a Kimball Hall reception that spring were "entrapped, caged and, with the aid of the editor of Kimball's Chicago music trade paper, committed to this Kimball grand without knowing anything about the execution of the scheme of which they became the victims." It added:

"With the aid of such testimonials and the cooperation of a Chicago music trade paper, backed up by the whole New York music trade press, with the sole exception of this paper, Kimball pianos, costing about $100, are sold in competition with the whole line of pianos, beginning with those that bring $600 to $800 at retail and ending with pianos that cost $200 and less at retail."

It was, of course, a typical *Courier* falsehood to imply that the *Indicator* was "Kimball's Chicago music trade paper." It was an independent publication, established by Fox in 1879, and the forerunner of today's *Piano Trade Magazine*.

Blumenberg was not content with these lines of attack, however. In another article in the September 30 issue he charged that the New York City piano action house which was supplying Kimball was requiring New York piano makers to pay 10 to 30 per cent more for actions than Kimball paid for them.

In the midst of these malicious onslaughts, the *Courier's* editor sought, as he confessed, to demonstrate that his paper was "conducted upon conviction into which prejudice does not enter" by printing a contribution from one E. P. Hawkins lauding the Kimball organization. Within the course of this remarkably ecstatic document Mr. Hawkins managed to refer to W. W. Kimball as "the Napoleon of the musical instrument industry" and "the Nestor of piano and organ manufacturing in the West."

John C. Freund's *Music Trades* took note on November 7, 1891, of the *Courier's* "nearly three years" of attacks on the Chicagoan and in an open letter reviewed Kimball's personal and business life. Freund then concluded:

"You stand today with your three score years and more, one of the most sincerely respected and honored men not only of your great city, but of the entire music trades of this country.

"You can afford to despise the attacks made upon you. And when men ask you whether a testimonial you publish is genuine, you can point to the record of your life and smile!"

And on February 13, 1892, following the Patti interview with the Chicago *Evening Post*, Freund wrote that "the *Musical Courier* owes Mr. Kimball an apology."

But Blumenberg never apologized and the attacks continued intermittently throughout a great part of the decade.

16

"They must undoubtedly serve to give the pipe organ a new mission in musical art."

BIG THINKING had brought the new Kimball piano a swift and successful start, but still bigger thinking and bigger achievements lay ahead. The habit of thinking big was well established in every rank of the W. W. Kimball Company long before the advent of its first uprights in 1888. This was true, despite the close control the founder personally exercised over the company's affairs until the eve of his death in 1904. And it remains true today as the organization faces its second hundred years.

Kimball believed profoundly, as do those who have followed him in leadership, that the first requisite for the success of a business is that all employes must work with one another to get the corporate job done; and he recognized that to win such loyal interest it is necessary to develop within the various members of a business a sense of their individual importance in its operation. No company can progress without ideas, and Kimball encouraged suggestions not only from his closely knit executive group but from all the employes—from the shipping clerk to the piano tuner, from the retail salesman to the traveler in the field.

One of the idea men to whom the Governor gave rein in this period was Albert G. Cone, who was pressing a one-man fight against the total absence of any piano and organ pricing policy in the Chicago retail houses. It was a generally accepted trade practice in those days to try to sell the piano or organ customer an instrument regardless of what the price tag said. Price cutting was rampant. Unless a customer was shrewd, the average retail piano store was a mystery and a trap. Cone believed ardently that this was demoralizing to the music trade, and he set out in 1888 to try to put an end to it.

Backed by the suave and courteous Edgar C. Smith, the manager of the Kimball retail warerooms and a Kimball employe since the late 70s, he outlined his one-price proposal to the skeptical Governor and persuaded him at last to give it a fair trial.

"When its success seemed a matter of doubt," wrote the *Indicator's* editor, "Mr. Cone, whose foresight in the matter was certainly a tribute to his business sense, fought for it through thick and thin. The trade did not approve it. Even those near to him in business questioned its wisdom. One of the best known local dealers declared that failure would surely follow in its wake. Finally Mr. Cone triumphed and the arguments he advanced, based on the solid premise that good business principles, honestly and faithfully observed, would win in the end, carried the day."

After the company publicly proclaimed its one-price policy in 1888, the rest of the Chicago trade gradually followed, beginning in 1890. By the middle of the decade it was an established policy in all the stores.

In the same manner, Kimball attentively listened when E. S. Conway, Cone, and Smith began to urge him in 1889 to make new arrangements to handle the rapidly expanding business. Already the retail store at State and Jackson streets was proving inadequate.

And W. W. Lufkin at the factory was thinking big also—asking for more space to keep abreast of the demands imposed by Conway's free-wheeling sales staff.

The plans for a further expansion were laid that year when Kimball signed a contract with the builder Hulburd Dunlevy to erect a new Kimball Building on Wabash Avenue, near the southwest corner of Wabash Avenue and Jackson Street. At the same time he authorized the addition in 1890 of a fifth floor to the piano factory and the erection of a five-story connecting link between that plant and the old reed organ factory.

Big thinking also was occupying Conway when he repeatedly stressed to the Governor the importance of expanding the piano line at the top and the bottom. His salesmen needed a grand piano to compete with Steinway and other leaders for the top quality trade, and they were calling for a Kimball-made instrument in the lowest-priced field to compete with the stencil trade. Such musical friends of the company as Dr. Ziegfeld and Liebling were all for a Kimball grand, and Lufkin was instructed to set his best piano men to work. At the same time the Governor began to look around for a suitable name other than his own which he could apply to a lower-priced piano while reserving the Kimball name for the best of the instruments. He found it in the name "Hinze," the rights to which he acquired from Carl Hinze, who was associated with the Rice-Hinze Piano Company, later Rice-Macy, until 1890. The Hinze name would continue to be featured on certain lower-priced instruments of Kimball origin until it was finally abandoned by the company in 1949.

The first of the Kimball grand pianos was introduced on Tuesday evening, April 26, 1891. It was also an auspicious time in the company's history for another reason: It was the occasion of the formal dedication ceremonies for the new Kimball Building at 243-253 Wabash Avenue.

Seven stories tall, the structure cost "somewhere in the neighborhood of $140,000." The ground rent was $26,000 a year. It was one of the largest buildings of the day to be devoted entirely to musical instruments.

Every item in its design was especially considered with a view to meeting the needs and wishes of the Kimball company. Six large plate glass windows and two doors were spread across the eighty-foot frontage of the main floor wareroom and general offices. All the walls were deadened throughout the building, and the double floors were cement-filled and provided with air chambers to confine sound. On the second floor was Kimball Hall, with a pipe organ and 700 permanent opera chairs. On the five upper floors were "upwards of seventy" studio rooms, which were quickly rented to artists and musicians.

The reception on the evening of the dedication was the one that Marc Blumenberg's *Musical Courier* denounced a short time later as an "entrapment" of W. W. Kimball's distinguished guests. Nothing could have been farther from the truth, for it had been widely reported in the Chicago musical world that the formal opening of the building with its magnificent Kimball Hall would mark the debut of Kimball's new grand piano.

News of it had long ago leaked out of the factory, where Peter Tapper had drawn up the first scale and supervised the manufacture. The first model turned out to be somewhat less than a success because there wasn't a tuner in the place who could get it in tune, George B. Demes Jr. recalled recently. William Heintzmann, a member of the Canadian piano making family who had come down from Toronto to work for Kimball, finally was given the job of perfecting the instrument. Demes recalls that he helped Heintzmann to voice the new grand in one of the big sound-proofed factory rooms.

The initial effort was a "small" parlor grand, six feet four inches long, of seven and one-third octaves. The big concert grand was yet to come.

Among the musicians who inspected the shining new ebony instrument and sat down to finger its keyboard at the Kimball Hall reception were Ziegfeld and Liebling; the noted Dutch pianist August Hyllested, W. C. E. Seeboeck, Louis Falk, the conductor Hans Balatka and his pianist son Christian. The *Evening Post* reported that "nothing was heard on all sides except praise for this notable Chicago production." Frederick Root, another of the musicians attending, was pleased that "Chicago can boom something else besides packing houses and real estate."

One of the big thinkers among the newcomers to the organ division in 1890 was Frederic W. Hedgeland, the first of a distinguished group of organ makers who were to make the name of Kimball a worldwide symbol of excellence in pipe organ building.

"A singularly modest and unassuming young man," Hedgeland was the son of an English organ builder. Born in London, he came to the United States in 1883, going first to St. Paul, Minnesota, where he was engaged for a time in the business of repairing pipe organs. When he reached Chicago he was only 23, but he proudly reported to W. W. Lufkin that he had already built several successful organs in St. Paul.

For one so young, this seemed hardly credible, but when the young man fished in his pockets and pulled out a set of his newest organ specifications, the factory manager took a second look and promptly hired him. The plans, which were still unfinished, were those of a portable pipe organ. Here, thought Lufkin, is a man with ideas. He decided to encourage Hedgeland to go ahead and experiment in the well-equipped Kimball factory.

When Lufkin reported that day to downtown headquarters, he imediately headed for his uncle's office to tell him about his new organ maker. The Governor was delighted. Along with other manufacturers, Kimball had long since recognized that there was a special gap to be filled between the largest size of reed organ then manufactured and the bulky, expensive stationary pipe organ. Up to now neither he nor any of his competitors had been able to develop a satisfactory compromise.

133

What he wanted was an instrument that would be powerful enough to rival the pipe organ in variety, beauty, and volume of tone yet reasonable in price, small enough to be boxed and shipped anywhere, in tune and ready for use, and capable of being installed without the services of an expert.

As was the usual procedure when something big came up, Kimball called on Conway and Cone to come into the conference and listen to Lufkin's evaluation of the Hedgeland designs.

Essentially a piano man, Conway was not inclined to great enthusiasm over the prospect of a portable instrument. The pipe organ with its numerous and fantastic mechanical refinements was an expensive item to manufacture, since it usually was made to the customer's own specifications. Many times a manufacturer would lose money by underestimating a complicated job. Still, Conway conceded, a portable pipe organ, made in standard sizes, would have considerable sales possibilities among the smaller churches, with lodges, and as concert hall installations. And it would spread the fame of the Kimball name to advantage.

Cone, who favored organs over pianos anyway, was highly enthusiastic over the potential importance of the pipe organ as a prestige instrument for the company.

All were agreed that young Mr. Hedgeland should be given a free hand. Perhaps he could really evolve a practical portable instrument. At least he was the kind of big thinker the company liked to have around.

Less than a year after Hedgeland went to work at the factory his tinkering bore its first fruit in what the company described as a "triumph of mechanical ingenuity in the service of religion and art." The Chicago *Inter-Ocean* of November 22, 1891, broke the news of Hedgeland's new portable pipe organ with a headline that read: "A NEW ORGAN. A Successful Test of a New Invention at Kimball Hall." That was more than two weeks before the first patents were granted on the new instrument—Numbers 464,936 and 464,937, issued on December 8, 1891. A long series of further patents, covering the numerous innovations developed by Hedgeland and other Kimball craftsmen, were issued in 1892 and for several years afterward as the instrument was perfected.

The November demonstration was a private one held in Kimball Hall with Harrison M. Wild, popular organist of Chicago's Unity Church, at the console. Emil Liebling played a piano accompaniment to demonstrate the musical effect of such a combination.

This first of the portables was little larger than an upright piano, but "was equal," said the *Inter-Ocean,* "to a fair-sized church organ in appointment. Its full, round tones were highly appreciated."

Just before Christmas, it made its first public appearance in Chicago at the dedication of St. Cecilia's Church, Forty-fifth and Atlantic streets. The *Catholic Home* of December 23 reported that the Hedgeland invention "was pronounced a success by all who heard it."

With this auspicious start, the company placed the first three models on exhibit in its Wabash Avenue warerooms and set out to drum up the church trade: "The Clergy and all others interested are kindly invited to call and inspect them, whether desiring to purchase or not."

All three instruments, it said, were "so compact as to pass through an ordinary door." The first style had one bank of keys; the second was similar, with pedal bass added; and the third and largest had two manuals, with pedal bass and twelve stops, including mechanical accessories.

Two years later the Kimball portable was the only instrument in the field to win an award at the World's Columbian Exposition, the judges describing it as "meeting a long felt want" and "entitled to the highest award." One of the judges was Dr. Hugh A. Clarke, professor of music at the University of Pennsylvania, who promptly ordered one of the instruments sent to him in Philadelphia.

The special features of the portable which enabled it to be shipped and installed almost anywhere with ease were its detachable keyboard, which permitted it to pass through a doorway; a

135

pipe clutch and rack, which held the pipes firmly in place during transportation, and a pedal action constructed so that the pedal keyboard could be removed for shipment without disturbing the action.

Other features included a blow lever, which was applicable at either end of the organ; a wind chest with two wind pressures and a tubular pneumatic action, insuring quick repetition; a bellows—"the heavy pressure bellows being inside the lighter, rendering the tone of the organ unusually firm and heavy"—and a pneumatic draw-stop action.

Among the church musicians who assisted the company in perfecting the early portables was C. E. Reynolds, organist and choirmaster at Chicago's Church of the Ascension, La Salle and Elm streets. For ten years Reynolds had been the organist at the famous St. James Episcopal Church in Chicago, and he expressed surprise when he found the scale of the Kimball instrument the same as that of the large three-manual organ at St. James'. The wind pressure was steady, he reported to the company, and the tubular pneumatic action "satisfies every demand."

P. C. Lutkin, director of the music department at Northwestern University in suburban Evanston, joined Pennsylvania's Clarke among the musical educators endorsing the new organ. "It is certainly more substantially built and more satisfactory in every way than most pipe organs costing twice the amount and occupying twice the space," he wrote on August 9, 1894, after the university had acquired one.

In the fall of 1894 the Chicago musical paper, the *Presto,* warned the pipe organ trade in general that "if there is an idea that this branch of the trade is slumbering, they will soon awake to their error. . . . From present indications Chicago is destined to figure conspicuously as a pipe organ center, and the influence of the Kimball will play no small part in this result." It was hinting broadly that, having perfected the portable, the company would move shortly into large scale pipe organ manufacture.

The *Presto* paid its tribute to the organ in one of its "Presto Ballads," an illustrated weekly feature built around the products of its advertisers:

> Seated one day at the organ
>   I was filled with a great surprise
> At the wonderful wealth of music
>   And the beauty that met my eyes;
> For the organ was rich and dainty,
>   With pipes of matchless grace,
> And I marveled that so much volume
>   Could come from so small a case.
> In the music of that organ
>   The long "Lost Chord" was found,
> And the "Grand Amen" was lifted
>   In the glory of the sound;
> It flowed in tones of grandeur
>   From out of the flowing case,
> As the sweet tones mixed and blended
>   With the surge of the pedal base [*sic*],
> I had played on many organs,
>   From giants to smallest type.
> But till now I had never listened
>   To the tone of a perfect pipe;
> And my eyes soon wandered downward,
>   From the pipes to the gleaming space
> Where the name dispelled my wonder—
>   'TWAS A KIMBALL PORTABLE CASE!

The *Music Trade Review* of New York City best summarized the Kimball accomplishment on May 24, 1893, in an article which hailed the company for having succeeded where others had failed in condensing the best qualities of the pipe organ and putting it into portable form "so that its beauties might penetrate into the homes of the people." The editor had visited the Chicago showrooms and inspected the pipe organ line.

"They must undoubtedly serve," he wrote, "to give the pipe organ a new mission in musical art.

"The wonderfully effective way in which the inventors of the Kimball portable pipe organ have adjusted the pipes, economized the wind chest, and disposed of the various actions may be comprehended somewhat from the dimensions and general specifications of style 4. Thus, within a case of six feet eight inches in height, six feet in length, and three feet six inches deep, they give the appended range of tone effects, independent of the open diapason (eight-foot tone) of five octaves c. c. to c. Specifically the other stops consist of a dulciana cornet (cornopean) of forty-nine pipes (eight-foot tone) inclosed in the great organ; gamba (eight foot), forty-nine pipes, and flute (four foot), sixty-one pipes, enclosed in the swell; also, a pedal range consisting of twenty-seven notes open diapason and bourdon of the same range, both sixteen-foot tones. Besides those stops there are the following mechanical movements: Swell to great coupler, and super octave coupler, pedal to manual coupler, and a balanced swell pedal and two wind indicators.

"Organists and organ builders will ask wonderingly how it is done?

"To this imaginary inquiry we answer: Examine the twelve or more patents taken out for features of originality in these organs by the W. W. Kimball Company since December, 1891, or else go and examine the structural features of these instruments. Either examination will reveal evidences of the earnest desire of that enterprising Chicago house to produce an organ with some bona fide claim to the honors of originality and popular usefulness.

"Have they succeeded? Yes!

". . . . They have invented, designed, and introduced an organ which anticipates almost every possible feature looked for in an instrument of this character."

17

The Prairie Avenue chateau. "One is easily convinced that Kimball paid a million to build it."

WITH THE beginning of the gay 90s, it was almost inevitable that the prospering founder of the Kimball company should gravitate to fashionable Prairie Avenue, "the most expensive street in America west of Fifth Avenue." Stretching for blocks along the Illinois Central and Michigan Central right-of-way on the Near South Side, this genteel residential "street of the stately few" was lined with the homes of literally dozens of Chicago's millionaires. Here lived many of William Wallace Kimball's most intimate friends, among them the merchant prince Marshall Field and the sleeping car baron George M. Pullman, with whom the piano manufacturer lunched almost daily at the "millionaire's table" in the exclusive Chicago Club.

Field lived at 1905 Prairie in a red-brick, French-style mansion built in 1876 by the noted architect Richard Morris Hunt. Pullman's mansardic palace of brownstone was a block and a half north at 1729 Prairie. It was from Pullman that Kimball acquired, in 1890, a large building lot half a block south on the southeast corner of Prairie Avenue and Eighteenth Street, directly across the street from J. J. Glessner's magnificent Romanesque residence at 1800 Prairie.

Upon Pullman's recommendation, W. W. and Evalyne Kimball decided upon the young architect Solon Spencer Beman, pupil of Upjohn and designer of the Pullman Building, as the man who should prepare the plans for the new home they would occupy for the rest of their lives.

Their three-story mansion, completed in 1892, was built of gray Bedford stone and modeled after the 12th-century Chateau de Josselin in Brittany. It has been called Chicago's finest example of French chateau style of architecutre. With all its magnificence it was not so large a home as Field's or Pullman's, but it still endures today as a landmark of the classic tradition and an aristocratic symbol of the glory that once was Prairie Avenue.

John Drury described it in the Chicago *Daily News* of May 19, 1939, in an article that later became a chapter in his book, "Old Chicago Houses":

"This style is known as the pepper-pot chateau, probably because of the many large and small turrets, topped by spires, which are an outstanding characteristic of the roof of such a dwelling. . . . The stonework over the arched entrance is highly ornamental.

"The top story is characterized by numerous turrets, gables, balconies and stone chimneys, as well as ornamental iron work. There are many windows at each floor level, some of them of curved glass and others leaded. An oriel window protrudes from the north facade. Along the front of the house is a high fence of iron grill work.

"If the exterior of the Kimball house is impressive and ornamental, the interior is no less attractive to the eye of the observer. . . . The ceilings are beamed and the walls paneled in oak and mahogany. There are onyx fireplaces in some of the rooms. The bathrooms are tiled from floor to ceiling and the washbowls are of onyx. A staircase of intricately carved wood leads to the second floor."

Top: W. W. Kimball's Prairie Avenue home. (Photo courtesy Chicago *Daily News*.)
Bottom: Ridgewood, the home of C. N. Kimball. (From "Upland, Vale and Grove.")

A contemporary view of the Kimball residence was published in *Musical Age* in the 90s under the heading "A Piano Magnate's Home." It said in part:

"The exquisite taste of Mrs. Kimball and her skill as an entertainer have made that lady very prominent and popular in society life. Her receptions are famous among the events of uncommon delight, and the accumulation of the treasures of travel which fill her pretty rooms is the envy of many who have seen them. The Kimball home is the perfection of architectural beauty. Mrs. Kimball admires the massive style of furniture, and her library, in which she spends most of her time, is grand in its severe simplicity. The walls are wainscoted half way to the ceiling with mahogany, and above that is red canvas. A huge writing table stands in the center of the room. The window-seats are covered with tan leather, and the chairs are substantial and handsome. The large hall, which is used as a reception room, is furnished in a lighter style, as is the drawing room, into which it opens. The polished floors are covered with Eastern rugs, the walls and ceilings are entirely of polished wood, a magnificent piece of tapestry hangs on the staircase landing, fine old paintings are on the walls, and much handsome china in the way of vases, jars, etc., lightens the appearance of the room. In the hall above, glimpses are caught of the large pipe organ, and a beautiful piece of embroidery is thrown carelessly across the railing of the stair. Mrs. Kimball has a passion for old books and rugs."

Just how much all this magnificence cost Kimball nobody knows, but Drury wrote that he was said to have spent a million dollars on its design and construction, and added: "Looking at it today, seeing its solidity, its majestic interior, its richly paneled halls and parlors, one is easily convicted that Kimball paid a million to build it." It is more likely, as the Chicago *Tribune's* Charles Collins suggested in the column "A Line o' Type or Two" in 1943, that the million dollar figure included the furnishings.

As "chatelaine of the great stone mansion," Mrs. Kimball made it the showplace for her priceless Chinese and Japanese vases, bowls, and figurines, and for her magnificent collection of paintings, which became the property of the Art Institute of Chicago following her death in June, 1921. This collection, much of which was assembled after Mr. Kimball's death in 1904, is noted especially for Rembrandt's famous 1630 portrait of his father ("Portrait of Harmen Gerritsz van Rijn," by Rembrandt van Rijn), acquired in 1913 at a cost of $110,000, and for its brilliant examples of English paintings. For many years it was exhibited in a special Kimball Gallery.

"It is odd today to pause in passing and reflect upon how much Chicago itself has changed," wrote Eleanor Jewett, the art critic of the Chicago *Tribune* on August 9, 1942. "Prairie Avenue and those numbered streets which were the fashionable residence quarters of a half century ago are in quite different circumstances today. Meanwhile, the paintings which Mrs. Kimball was most instrumental in collecting are carrying on, both for her and her husband and for the Chicago of another era."

In 1905, Miss Jewett reported, Mrs. Kimball purchased Emile van Marcke's "Cattle in Hilly Country," and in 1912 she added the fine "Wooded Landscape" of Meindert Hobbema to the collection. Three years later, Sir Joshua Reynolds' beautiful "Lady Sarah Bunbury Sacrificing to the Graces" became an outstanding acquisition. The collection also contains John Constable's dark, romantic "Stoke-by-Nayland," an English countryside scene described by the *Tribune's* critic as "the finest Constable in existence," and J. M. W. Turner's "Dutch Fishing Boats," the only important work of that artist in the Institute. "In it," wrote Miss Jewett, "is all the enchanting color for which Turner won worldwide recognition. A Turner sunset is still something more than a manner of speech. Those who know the depth and scope of Turner's palette visualize a sky flaming with a hundred drifting, harmonizing colors. Skies and ships were the two subjects on which Turner built his reputation."

Also included in the collection were two paintings by Thomas Gainsborough, the famed "The Countess of Bristol" and the less

143

pretentious landscape "The Skirts of the Wood." Another noted item is Sir Thomas Lawrence's "Portrait of Mrs. Wolff," which "shows to what an engaging extent a casual pose, set off by a dashing color combination, can enhance the beauty of a lovely woman."

Other outstanding works in the collection are listed by the Art Institute as follows: Jacob Van Ruisdael's "Waterfall Near a Castle," Jean-Baptiste Camille Corot's "Les Baigneuses a l'Enfant," Virgilio Diaz de la Pena's "The Pond in the Woods," Jean-Francois Millet's "The Bather" and "The Keeper of the Herd," Richard Wilson's "Italian Landscape," George Romney's "Lady Francis Russell," Sir Henry Raeburn's "Dr. Welch Tennent," John Jackson's "Portrait of John Jackson" and "Portrait of an English Gentleman," George Frederick Watts' "Joseph Joachim" and "Time, Death and Judgment," Gabriel Dante Rossetti's "Beata Beatrix," and Benjamin West's "Troilus and Cressida."

The mansion that once housed these treasures was purchased from Mrs. Kimball's estate in 1924 by approximately 100 Chicago architects who put up $1,000 each to buy it. They acted upon the promise of the millionaire Glessner that he would leave his own home to them at his death provided they would occupy the Kimball home and protect him against undesirable neighbors. (When Glessner died the architects decided, however, that one white elephant was enough, and returned the Glessner home to his estate.) The Kimball residence was maintained until 1937 as a professional headquarters for the Chicago chapter of the American Institute of Architects, the Illinois Society of Architects, and the Architects Club of Chicago. Although Drury omitted the incident from "Old Chicago Houses," he recently told the writer that he learned on unimpeachable authority that the gang leader Al Capone attempted to buy the fortress-like mansion in the late 20s. True to their pledge to Glessner, the architects turned him down cold.

When these groups abandoned the Kimball mansion in 1937, it was leased by their Architects Realty Trust to the Elizabeth Hull School, a private institution for backward children, which finally bought it in 1943. The purchase price for the onetime "million dollar" mansion was $8,ooo. Since then it has changed hands again. Air-conditioned and remodeled by its present occupants, a publishing house which issues the trade magazines *Institutions* and *Domestic Engineering,* the mansion with its stately grandeur remains a Chicago landmark.

As a center of refinement and culture, the Kimball home on Prairie Avenue was in its heyday a fitting answer to the foppish New York social leader Samuel Ward McAllister, who taunted Chicago in the 90s by looking down his long nose and sneering at "the sharp character of Chicago magnates," whose "growth has been too rapid for them to acquire both wealth and culture." The old Kimball residence is a noble monument to the rare good taste of Kimball and his wife, and, as a onetime associate lately remarked, "an impressive example of the thoroughness that has marked the building of everything his name bore, from castles to ivory keyboards."

18

"And if my congregation don't like it they can go to hell."

THE William Wallace Kimball of the latter years, the onetime Maine boy who had risen to become merchant, manufacturer, and millionaire, was almost a legendary symbol of success in the American music trade.

In the business and social worlds his commanding figure attracted attention wherever he appeared—striding through his splendid warerooms on Wabash Avenue's "Music Row," chatting at noontime with Marshall Field or others of his friends as they sat on the huge sofa opposite the entrance to the library of the Chicago Club, riding with Mrs. Kimball in their spacious, high-built Stanhope carriage down Prairie Avenue, or tending to rural chores at the Kimballs' beautiful summer residence at Beverly Farms, in Essex County, Massachusetts.

Among his employes, he was beloved for his generous spirit and his "infinite jest and humor," although his great natural reserve often led the less well-acquainted among them to hold him somewhat in awe.

Kimball had grown old gracefully. In the early 80s his brother-in-law, Albert Cone, had written: "Although on the shady side of 50, he bears his age well. In person he is tall, somewhat sparely built, with a peculiarly striking presence. His face, once seen, is not easily forgotten. It is stamped with the impress of intense energy and power—a face that would be almost severe, were it not happily relieved by a mouth which may be said to enjoy a chronic disposition to break out into a smile. His forehead is large and high, and his eyes set deep back in his head, several undoubted signs of a large executive ability." Now in the 1890s he was, as George L. Hadley recalls, "actually ministerial in appearance, more than six feet tall and bearing his lithesome frame with such dignity that his carriage could be described as really imperial."

His fair complexion seemed to grow more and more colorful, his once brown hair more silken and silver white, and his large, impressive steel-blue eyes more brilliant.

His morning arrivals at the Kimball Building at 8:30 and his afternoon departures at 4:30 were daily events, and his punctuality, year in and year out, impressed the office staff, as did his close attention to every detail of his business long after most men in his position would have left things to their subordinates.

Typical was the letter he dictated to his nephew W. W. Lufkin at the factory on October 18, 1900, four years before his death. With his customary formality, he addressed it "Dear Sir," and went on: "The inclosed line referring to the pins in the bass of the piano, that are near lag bolts, would probably come under the head of Rice's department. We used to have some trouble with these bass pins near the lag bolt, as they had a way of using some kind of an oily substance on the bit in the boring. Would you kindly look this thing up and have it placed in the proper direction, and see that there is nothing going on that should not. Referring to the tuning department, I should fancy that it would be cheap and a good investment to have another tuning; at least when pianos go out in car load lots, they should all be tuned to a uniform pitch. Sincerely yours, w. w. KIMBALL."

147

In his employment of personnel, Kimball was acute but fair-minded. C. C. Chickering once recalled that in 1892 the Governor considered hiring him to utilize his technical experience as a member of the Boston piano making family. "He finally decided the combination would be ill-advised and instead of coming out and saying so, as most men would, he told me a story. He said, 'I am a lover of fine horses and I have bought and owned quite a number of them; some of them were young and promised to be great, others were old and had formerly been great, and in consulting with my hostler as to the purchase of another fine animal, he gave me the following advice: "Mr. Kimball, you have been buying has-beens and going-to-bes. I would suggest that you get one that is." ' And he left me wondering at the time just what he meant, but it dawned upon me shortly that in the Governor's opinion, I had not yet arrived."

One day a prospective country dealer inadvertently got past the home-office staff and into Mr. Kimball's inner office, where the manufacturer greeted him and made him feel at home. Appraising his visitor as a shrewd customer, he quoted the wholesale price of a certain reed organ style by saying, "The cash price is $80. If purchased on time, we bill it at $64." The baffled dealer asked Kimball to repeat what he had said, and was quoted the same figures again. Finally he asked why the cash price was higher than the time price, and Kimball quickly replied, "You see, when a dealer pays cash we get it all. But when we sell on time and don't get fully paid, we don't lose as much." The joke paved the way to a long-enduring and successful dealership.

Another agent, a bachelor, showed up one day when everybody was occupied, George Hadley recalls, and, finding no one to talk with except Kimball, he applied directly to him for a Kimball agency. Extolling his own good qualities, he assured the manufacturer that he did not smoke, drink, or use profanity. Kimball, a non-smoker himself and a man who took wine or champagne only on state occasions, listened quietly to all this self-praise and finally said, "Well, young man, you paint rather an attractive picture of yourself, but there is always a 'must' somewhere and you must be a very devil with the women!" And time indeed proved that he was.

Although Kimball played scarcely a note, he had an ear for music. Over the years he learned much from his own technicians and musician friends about the qualities of tone in the instruments he manufactured. He resented the claims of European piano makers, particularly the German manufacturers, that their instruments, while not so "loud" as American pianos, were superior in tone quality.

"The first requisite of a piano," he contended, "is power. What you want is a hand of steel in a glove of velvet. . . .

"Take the human voice. Can you get a magnificent, full tone out of a thin, weak voice? But if you have a good, strong, resonant voice to start with, then you can regulate and modify it at your will. To get a good, full tone out of a piano, you must have the resources in the piano itself. There is no depth to the German pianos, especially to their uprights. They are thin and shallow. The American piano has depth. There is something to it, and, consequently, you can get something out of it. What you get out of it must, of course, depend largely on the skill of the player."

There are numerous stories in the Kimball canon about the low-priced Hinze piano that the company manufactured for many years.

James V. Sill, who retired in 1952 as vice-president and general manager, recalls that a country dealer one day suggested to Kimball, "You take that Hinze piano and put down on the fallboard 'Made by W. W. Kimball' and I can sell it." To which the manufacturer replied, "No, I won't do that. If I did that, that Dutchman would get all my business."

Another of the Hinze stories is told by Carle C. Conway, a son of E. S. Conway and now the emeritus chairman of the board of the Continental Can Company and chief of its executive committee. After graduation from Yale, young Conway went to work in the Kimball retail wareroom in Chicago. He was Number 4 in the informal hierarchy of floor salesmen. One day, just as his turn came to wait on a lady customer, it was his misfortune that the Governor should emerge from his second-floor office and stroll down the stairs to the retail floor. Young Conway's selling effort proved to be a failure, and as the customer walked out the Governor approached him and gently asked, "What's the trouble, Mr. Conway?"

"She wanted a second-hand piano, and we have no second-hand pianos here, Governor."

"We don't?" Kimball replied. Then he walked slowly over to a $195 Hinze that was sitting nearby, lifted a polished shoe and scratched the sole of it roughly along the shining surface of the Hinze. "What's the matter with this one for a second-hand piano?"

Kimball smiled at the flustered salesman and walked away. It was the Governor's way of impressing him with the fact that there was more than one way to sell pianos. The lesson apparently stuck, for Carle Conway eventually became one of the top Kimball salesmen of his day.

Another time during Conway's apprenticeship, a sailor off a tramp ship bound for China came in with $150 and asked for a second-hand piano. Called out of his office to help, the Governor sold him a lowly Biddle, a cheap New York-made instrument that happened to be the only piano in stock that could be sold in that price range. A year later, Conway recalls with a chuckle, the whole store was astonished when the sailor walked back in, demanding to see Kimball.

"Remember that piano you sold me to take out to China last year," he said. "Best damned piano I ever saw. The only piano in China the keys won't stick on. Can I get another one?"

One day a customer came into the store and asked, "Do you keep pianos here?" Before any of the salesmen could answer, Kimball shot back, "No, we sell pianos here. The fellows down the street keep them!"

D. A. Clippinger, a music teacher who had rented studios in the company buildings since the 80s, wrote in 1915 that in his young days he was mortally afraid of his famous landlord, though greatly admiring him. "He always impressed me as a man who could not be tampered with," said Clippinger, "consequently I never tried it. I recall going up in the elevator one day with him. On the way up, he said, 'Is it going to rain?' 'Yes, sir,' I replied. 'Glad to know it,' he said. 'I thought you might like it,' I answered. Neither one cracked a smile." It was the most serious and the longest conversation he ever had with him.

One of Kimball's good friends in the Chicago trade was the bold and handsome John V. Steger, who founded the Steger & Sons Piano Manufacturing Company in 1879. One day in the late 90s as the two rivals met on the street, Kimball joshingly remarked:

"Steger, the probability is that the next man to pass away in the trade will be either you or I." Steger indicated his disagreement and the Governor continued, "Yes, either you or I. And I think it ought to be you."

"How so?" asked Steger.

"Well," said Kimball, "I think *we*"—and he pointed to himself —"can get along better without *you* than without *us*."

Then, telling Steger to be a good boy, Kimball stepped briskly down the street.

His jocular attitude toward the possibility of his dying continued to the end. In his last illness he was visited by Carle Conway, who recalls that the Governor nodded toward the window and the Prairie Avenue home of his good friend, the undertaker C. H. Jordan: "See that fellow over there. He's just waiting for me to kick off. But I'll outlive the old buzzard yet."

In his latter years, he was respected and loved as the wise and kindly elder statesman of the music trade. O. L. Fox's *Indicator* said in 1896:

"Today he knows the results and the producing factors for losses or gains in his great business just as thoroughly as he did twenty years ago. Mr. Kimball never carries his business home with him. He is a man of pure life and gentle impulse; of kindly humor and sturdy character; a man upon whom one can rely and feel that one is resting on a rock. The years have brought him a deeper in-

151

sight into men and their methods, and have softened his nature. Today in the fullness of his business life he is the ideal employer, the model business man, the noble-hearted friend and associate.

"How much better life would be for the living if there were more men like William Wallace Kimball in this wicked world!"

A difficult man to pin down, Kimball often was a problem for the music journalists. "It is about as easy," said a reporter for *Music Trades Review,* "for a newspaper man to extract juice out of a stone as persuade Mr. W. W. Kimball to express an opinion on music trade affairs. Mr. Kimball is an admirable raconteur; he can be jocose, facetious, and irrelevant, but woe betide the scribe who takes him seriously." The reporter had caught the Governor as he was returning to Chicago by way of New York City after a five-week stay in southern Florida, where the Kimballs often spent part of their winters. After sparring with the newsman over several questions about the trade, he said with a twinkle in his eyes, "Now, I think if you'll go back to your desk and draw on your imagination, the general result of this interview will be just as satisfactory as if I were to cogitate and draw on my feeble intellect. . . . Good day." And the *Musical Times'* reporter, after a long interview, went back to his office prepared to write a column on Mr. Kimball's views. When he tried to do it, he confessed, he couldn't locate a solitary fact.

The *American Art Journal,* when it could find nothing else to say after Kimball paid a visit to New York, simply reported that "William Wallace Kimball has been spending the past few days in New York, looking after the birds." The manufacturer would often stroll down Fifth Avenue and stop at Madison Square Park to feed the sparrows and sit sunning himself on the park benches. The *Journal's* reporter, for lack of anything else to report, once conjured up a story to the effect that "it was the sweet singing of these feathered creatures in the tall pine trees of his native woods of Maine that first led him to form the resolution that he would some day manufacture and transfer the natural scales of the songsters to a keyboard that would charm the heart of mankind."

Asked the secret of his success, Kimball had enigmatically told the reporter:

"Fearlessness of competitors and reverence for the birds."

George Hadley recalled that when going abroad in later years Mr. and Mrs. Kimball usually would stop over in New York City for several days before sailing on their regular trips to Baden-Baden, the popular German health resort of that period. C. C. Dunbar, chief accountant in the home office, used to go East with them to arrange their transportation matters, which included the shipment of their favorite bay mares and their carriages, sent on from Chicago. It was also his duty to arrange steamship reservations for their coachman and footman.

On one of these stopovers Dunbar was with Kimball when he dropped into his favorite hat store on Fifth Avenue, to purchase a tall silk hat before sailing. Because of his dignified bearing, the manufacturer was often mistaken for a clergyman. After making his hat selection on this occasion, he solemnly asked the salesman if a discount from the regular ten dollar price would be allowed to the clergy. Assured that there would be a two dollar allowance, he proffered a ten dollar bill.

Accepting the change and stepping toward the door, the Governor paused and looked in a mirror as he adjusted his topper. Whereupon the salesman rushed forward to inquire if everything was satisfactory.

"Yes, indeed, my good man," he replied, turning his head from side to side and eyeing his purchase. "And if my congregation don't like it, they can go to hell!"

Then, while the salesman stood blinking, Kimball buttoned his long ulster tightly, pulled his hat down rakishly, and swept out of the store to chuckle with Dunbar over the incident.

As head bookkeeper, Dunbar was also called upon to handle the Governor's personal finances. His employer enjoyed a quiet evening of poker with his well-to-do neighbors, and at least once a week the accountant would be called to his office immediately upon his morning arrival. There the piano maker would stand before his great desk, extracting what looked like innumerable tiny green pellets from his trousers pockets. They were dollar bills, rolled tightly into little balls. Dunbar later said that he never in his life saw anyone else so able to compress so much money into so small a space.

Perhaps nothing speaks more eloquently of the personal devotion of Kimball's friends and associates than a group of remarkable letters received in the year of his final illness.

Carle Conway wrote, "As I told you some months ago, since childhood I have had your sterling character held up to me as an example to admire and to follow. I can truthfully say that from my earliest recollection I have always had my ambition turned in the direction of becoming a strong Kimball man. Permit me to thank you from the bottom of my heart for the many favors and kindnesses you have granted and shown me since my connection with the Kimball company."

Edgar C. Smith wrote, "Twenty-five years we have been together —since my boyhood—and I strongly hope these happy relations may continue for many years to come. With my love and very best wishes."

W. H. Cotter, a field agent to whom Kimball had mailed a personal check for $1,000, wrote to E. S. Conway in acknowledgment, "I was very much affected. Not that the gift was given, or that the amount was so extremely generous, but the spirit that prompted the same is what almost made me shed tears. Words cannot express my gratitude, for not only this very generous remembrance from dear Mr. Kimball, but for the many kindly words spoken, and his many kindly acts towards me in the past. Won't you convey to him my love? Say to him that he has always had my highest respect. I hope and trust he will fully recover. . . ."

The scholarly E. R. Blanchard, the company's treasurer from 1920 to 1934, wrote, "I am deeply sensible of your goodness in remembering me during your illness, as well as the constant kindness and consideration you have shown me. I have thought of you many times, every day while you have been away from us, always hoping you would be with us again for many years. Please accept my heartfelt thanks and my love."

The devotion of the men who surrounded him was one of the marvels of the music trade. In October, 1894, following one of Kimball's European trips, in which he had visited Schwalbach, Hamburg, Aix [-les-Bains], Paris, and London, Editor Fox of the *Indicator* dropped into the company offices and glimpsed two huge vases of American Beauty roses on the Governor's desk.

The roses, he wrote, "were a gentle reminder that those about the establishment were glad to have him home again. It may be said here that Mr. Kimball's unvarying kindness and liberality in dealing with his employes have endeared him to everyone, from the office boy to those associated with him in the corporation. No employer in Chicago stands higher in the esteem of those about him than does Mr. Kimball, nor is there one for whom his work-men would more gladly make sacrifices. . . .

"It is, perhaps, somewhat due to this harmony of interest and effort that this leading house occupies so overshadowing a position in the trade. . . ."

Taking note of the Kimball-Conway-Cone triumvirate, the editor of the *Indicator* remarked that in the twenty-five-year association "there has not been a word spoken to interfere with the pleasant relations existing among the gentlemen; not a single harsh word; a remarkable fact indeed, when one stops to think how much friction there is and how much wear and tear upon the nerves in doing business in this highly competitive age." He concluded: "It is this perfect agreement that has largely helped to make this company one of the greatest of its kind in the universe."

Kimball's closest approach to a clash with E. S. Conway occurred one day, according to the old timers, when the manager of the Newport Lumber Company in Arkansas sent up an expense account which included an item: "$7 for whisky for the mule." Conway, who was president of the subsidiary, wanted to approve the item; Kimball didn't. The Governor won.

Conway's own testimony in 1896 was eloquent in respect to the esteem in which the Governor was held:

"I tell you that W. W. Kimball is one of the grandest men living. He knows how to bring out of a man everything there is in him. He knows how to win his affection and how to keep it. . . . There is not a man in Mr. Kimball's employ or that has ever been in his employ that is not loyal to him and to his interests. Mr. Kimball's character permeates the whole fabric and it is the secret of the success of the W. W. Kimball Company."

Indeed, the loyalty that William Wallace Kimball inspired appears to live on among the "Kimball men" within and without the company more than sixty years after Conway spoke those words. So, at least, is the evidence encountered in gathering the material for this 100-year record.

19

"For having attained the highest standard of excellence in all branches of their manufacture."

T HE Kimball company's great achievement of the 90s—the sweeping victory at Chicago's World's Columbian Exposition of 1893 in which it captured the highest awards for pianos, reed organs, and portable pipe organs and, in addition, an exclusive award for general display of musical instruments—was not won without difficulties.

It was a triumph of artistic excellence that was opposed every step of the way by rival manufacturers and by Marc A. Blumenberg, the blackmailing editor of the powerful *Musical Courier*.

The year 1893 started auspiciously, without any hint of the financial calamity—the seventeenth panic since 1790—that would strike the country before 1894 rolled around. December, 1892, had been a tremendous month for sales, the best in the company's history; and on the following January 11, the stockholders voted to increase the company's stock from $1,000,000 to $1,200,000 to repay a $200,000 indebtedness to its founder. Up to that time the division of financial interest among the three principals had been: Kimball, 7,900 shares, and E. S. Conway and Albert G. Cone, 1,000 shares each. Curtis N. Kimball, who in 1891 had replaced the banker W. C. D. Grannis on the board of directors, held 50 shares.

Profits had been high. In 1890 a quarterly dividend system was inaugurated, the declarations for the year totaling 10 per cent, or $100,000. The balance of the earnings, totaling $81,896.87, was placed in the surplus account, to be joined in January, 1892, by a whopping $235,000 after payment of dividends totaling $90,000, or nine per cent.

As the year began, all Chicago was agog over the city's grandiose plans for the celebration with a great world's fair of the 400th anniversary of Columbus' discovery of America in 1492. The fair buildings on the Jackson Park and Midway Plaisance site on the South Side were dedicated in 1892, but the exposition itself was postponed until 1893 because the city had got too late a start on the planning. Much larger than any other ever held up to then, the great fair was formally opened on the damp, rainy day of May 1, 1893, and continued until October 31.

The musical instruments exhibit was held in the famed Section I of the liberal arts department, which occupied the southeast end of the mammoth 30.5-acre Manufactures Building, up to that time the largest building ever put under roof in the history of the world. It attracted more visitors than any other exhibit at the fair, excepting the fine arts gallery.

Fifty-eight piano, and piano and organ manufacturers were represented, exhibiting 50 grand pianos, 260 uprights, and 176 organs, including the new Kimball portable pipe organ.

Almost from the start the exhibit was plagued by friction and internecine warfare. Virtually all the important American piano and organ manufacturers at first announced their support and contributed to the funds for the fair. But as plans went forward, jealousies and rivalries inevitably asserted themselves, particularly with respect to the selection of the committee on awards.

An act of Congress, passed in April, 1890, provided that the Na-

Dr. Florenz Ziegfeld (left) and Emil Liebling were musical associates of Kimball. Ziegfeld was a target of the manufacturer's World's Fair foes. Pianist Liebling made concert tours to push Kimball's sales.

tional Commission of the World's Columbian Exposition should "appoint all judges and examiners for the Exposition and award all premiums, if any." The commission in turn appointed John Boyd Thacher to be chairman of the Board of Awards. It was his responsibility to select a panel of judges which would meet the approval of the various musical instrument manufacturers and submit their names to the commission to be finally acted upon.

As had been expected, some of the prospective exhibitors protested against awards of any kind, and among the small group of malcontents were such Eastern piano houses as Steinway & Sons; the Weber Piano Company, successors to Albert Weber; Decker & Son; and George Steck & Company. All these manufacturers, along with William Knabe & Company of Baltimore and certain others, decided to boycott the fair. They were joined by a group of European exhibitors.

The reasons they offered were various, but the principal one was a suspicion, aided and encouraged by the notorious Blumenberg, that undue influence would be exercised in the selection of the awards jury in order to slant as many diplomas and medals as possible in the direction of the Chicago manufacturers.

All through the spring and summer, Thacher wrestled with the onerous task of satisfying the clashing factions. Almost daily he was confronted with recommendations of suitable jury material, but no matter what move he made he was met with opposition from one or the other quarter.

The Steinways and their allies were particularly aroused by the report that Dr. Florenz Ziegfeld, the president of the Chicago Musical College, would be one of the members of the piano and organ award committee. After all, wasn't W. W. Kimball a member of Ziegfeld's board of directors? Rumor soon had it in these circles that the Kimball company already was assured "first prize."

Kimball himself felt called upon in February to issue a blanket denial that he had in any manner sought to influence or predispose the selection of the judges. *Music Trades* commented that this statement was hardly worth his while, since it changed nobody's mind. It added: "An unconscious prepossession exists in his favor, and he cannot be held responsible for that, for it is his just due as a business man and a gentleman."

In the meantime the company went ahead with its preparations for the fair. It had appointed 32-year-old Irving L. Holt, its general agent for central Illinois with headquarters at Joliet, to be *chargé d'affaires* at the Kimball exhibit. Widely acquainted in the music trade, the Vermont-born Holt had been one of Conway's top hustlers since joining the company at Webster City, Iowa, on April 5, 1880. In October, 1886, he had been assigned to the Illinois territory.

With his great handlebar mustache, his high-standing collar and white cravat, and a great linen handkerchief billowing from the breast pocket of his well-tailored jacket, he was an impressive, even dashing figure on the exposition floor.

Poor John Boyd Thacher's perplexities were not in the least relieved on March 26, when the Chicago *Herald* reported from its correspondent in Denver, Colorado, that the president of Knight & Campbell Music Company, the big Denver outlet for Kimball, had predicted the Chicago-made piano would win the fair's top award over all the Easterners.

It was an innocent suggestion, born of dealer enthusiasm, but *Freund's Musical Weekly,* the normally friendly New York trade paper, hopped on it to ask, "Oh, Mr. Campbell, Mr. Campbell, where is your canny Scotch caution? How can you say that your money is ready to go up on Kimball securing the prize? Are you in his confidence so deep, so far and so friendly?"

Blumenberg's brash *Musical Courier* did not hesitate to charge, under a big scare headline reading "KIMBALL HAS GOT IT," that everything had been arranged for Kimball. It was this, the *Musical Times* reported in an 1895 review of the fair, that led the Steinways and their Eastern colleagues to begin "a stampede to the outside." The *Times* added that "behind every bush the other makers seemed to see lurking in the shadow the form of 'Kimball.' The entire world's fair, according to their unreasoning views and statements, was intended for the exaltation of 'Kimball.' Cool-headed men . . . seemed carried away before the storm of prejudice."

The majority of the exhibitors who had signed up—including such famous houses as Chickering & Sons, Sohmer & Company, Julius Bauer, Mason & Hamlin, and Hardman, Peck & Company—deplored the withdrawals and expressed complete confidence in the rectitude and fairness of purpose of Thacher and the exposition authorities.

Nevertheless the clamor persisted. According to the *Times,* "More or less every candidate proposed for the judgeship was declared to be a 'Kimball' man, until a reflecting person had but to stop and think to discover that, if the Kimball Co. had really secured, by monetary consideration, the services of all the candidates proposed for the office of judge, they must have more money invested in that way than they had in their legitimate business of piano manufacturing."

In the midst of all this furor, Marcus Aurelius Blumenberg himself announced as a candidate for judge.

"Great Scott!" exclaimed the *Times* in its reminiscent account. "That meant it was going to cost just about $4,000,000 to get the gentleman with the classical praenomen to direct his regal gaze toward an instrument. The popular idea was that Marc was going around followed by an attendant with a large sack, and if the exhibitor did not contribute satisfactorily to the contents of the sack—and there was only one opinion as to what the sack contained—woe be to the unfortunate instrument of the recalcitrant. It was doomed to oblivion—no mention would it get—and those who did get awards would have the excellence of their products measured entirely by the magnitude of their contribution to the sack."

Blumenberg later withdrew his candidacy, after having received the unenthusiastic support of most of the music trade "because," said the *Times,* "they were afraid of him." Incidentally, the publication *Music Trades* later disclosed that the Kimball company was determined to bar him as a judge and had instructed its counsel that if Blumenberg were chosen he should immediately be arrested "in an action based on the many libelous articles he had published against them."

Working persistently behind the scenes to smooth the ruffled feathers of exhibitors was the Columbian Music Trade Association, formed early in May with W. D. Hutton of Hardman, Peck & Company as chairman. P. J. Healy of Lyon & Healy and E. S. Conway of the Kimball company were named to the finance committee and, together with the veteran Isaac N. Camp of Estey & Camp, Chicago organ dealers, helped to erase the differences. With the exception of the French, all the foreign exhibitors returned.

Wherever the tall form of Conway appeared on the exhibition floor, he was besieged by questioners. A handsome figure with closely curling black hair, a luxuriant mustache, a dark, shrewd, pleasant face, and a hearty handshake, he succeeded in convincing all the exhibitors who remained loyal to the fair that in the Kimball company they had a formidable rival but never an unfair one. A man who helped him in these efforts was the small, quiet-spoken John W. Reed, son of Alonzo Reed, the founder of A. Reed & Sons, a pioneer Chicago manufacturer.

In the midst of the summer, on July 7, the Kimball company tossed a fancy reception at Kimball Hall to host the women's section of the Musical Congress being held at the Art Institute as an annex to the fair. Standing in the reception line were Mrs. George B. Carpenter, Mrs. Clarence Eddy, the Misses Katharine Fisk and Amy Fay, L. G. Gottschalk, and Emil Liebling. In the huge company of guests were the great conductor Theodore Thomas, musical director for the fair, the Potter Palmers, the Harry Gordon Selfridges, the E. S. Drakes, Florenz Ziegfeld Jr., Evaline Kimball (now calling herself Eva, in the fashion of the Governor's wife), and—smiling his supercilious best—the inevitable Marc Blumenberg, an old hand at "free loading."

The harassed John Boyd Thacher finally announced his commission-approved panel of piano and organ jurors on August 13— and promptly was subjected to another unprincipled attack by Blumenberg.

The six jurors were a representative and distinguished company, all of them well known in the music world, and all of unassailable reputation, in the opinion of the overwhelming majority of exhibitors.

From Russia, Thacher had chosen the celebrated composer V. J. Hlavac (pronounced Glavatch), professor at the Royal Music School in St. Petersburg. Previously Hlavac had been a musical instruments judge at the Paris Exposition of 1889 and at the Antwerp Exposition of 1893.

The other European representative was Max Schiedmayer, a German musician and member of the distinguished Stuttgart piano making firm Schiedmayer Pianofabrik.

The American members were Dr. Ziegfeld, George Steck, Dr. Hugh A. Clarke, professor of music at the University of Pennsylvania, and E. P. Carpenter.

The elderly, full-bearded Steck, a German-born New Yorker, was a scale-drawer of international renown. The concert grands he had turned out after establishing George Steck & Company had won the praise of Richard Wagner, among others. He had retired in 1887 from the company that bore his name, and it pained him now to see his company unrepresented in the Chicago exposition. Carpenter was an organ maker who had retired some years before from the E. P. Carpenter Company of Brattleboro, Vermont, which he established in 1850.

Persuaded as Blumenberg was that the jury was loaded, he could easily have turned his fire on Steck, since the New Yorker was a good friend of W. W. Kimball. On a stopover in Chicago in October, 1892, Steck had heard Emil Liebling play the Kimball parlor grand and then said of it, "The piano sounds beautiful. It has a flute-like tone that is very fine. The scale is even and accurate all through, which produces a high quality of tone." But the *Courier's* cunning editor well knew that an attack on this beloved veteran was unthinkable.

Instead Blumenberg turned a senseless last-ditch blast at Carpenter. This prompted the exhibitors on September 2 to address an indignant letter to Thacher, protesting the *Courier's* attack and declaring their "utmost confidence in Mr. Carpenter's honesty, integrity, and impartiality" and in that of all the other members of the jury.

Abstaining was the Chase Brothers Piano Company, a small manufacturer from Muskegon, Michigan, which filed suit in Federal Court on September 7 and got an injunction against the judges to restrain them from making public the results of their deliberations. It was not until September 26 that the strain on the exhibitors was relieved when the court ordered the injunction dissolved.

Thacher immediately published the awards to checkmate further litigation. Virtually every exhibitor could take comfort in the results for, as the Chicago *Tribune* commented two weeks later, the "unusual generosity" of all the fair's juries in passing out sundry honors all summer long had left it "a matter of doubt whether they have not awarded more diplomas and medals than Congress has provided." The authorized total was 50,000 awards.

There was no doubt in the musical instrument section, however, concerning the significance of the Kimball awards which, as the *Musical Times* pointed out, were couched in superlative terms in each of its three special exhibits—pianos, reed organs, and pipe organs—and were the only awards so phrased. In addition, the company received, but did not immediately publicize, a special "Award for General Display," which stated, "This firm deserves the greatest commendation for the superlative merit and variety of exhibits, and also for having attained the highest standard of excellence in all branches of their manufacture."

In the award to the Kimball piano, the judges cited the following specific points:

"First.—The tone quality, which is full, round, sympathetic, and musical. Second.—The duration and singing quality of the tone are remarkable. Third.—The scale is even and free from breaks. Fourth.—The action is first-class in every respect. Fifth.—The touch is easy, elastic and prompt in response, admitting of the most rapid repetition. Sixth.—The materials and construction give evidence

165

of extreme care in their selection and workmanship and are all of the highest class. The designs of the cases are of great artistic excellence and are finished in the most perfect manner."

The *Musical Times* took note that the reference to the "remarkable" tone was the only instance of such a superlative in the award list for pianos.

Kimball's reed organ likewise won the highest commendation in the following terms: "For superior construction, distinguished by the high grade materials employed, originality and first-class finish. Their tone, touch and action leave nothing to be desired."

The award to the portable pipe organ was an unmistakable triumph: "The article admirably fulfills the requirements of a first-class portable pipe organ and marks a decided advance in the art. It meets a long-felt want, and for its superlative excellence in every detail merits the highest commendation."

Thacher posted the award winners on the 26th, right after the court ruling, and on the following morning complete typewritten copies of all the reports were made available to the exhibitors. Before nightfall of September 27 Albert Cone had put into the mail to all Kimball dealers and salesmen large circulars giving the text of the judges' reports. That afternoon he sent telegrams ahead to herald the news. On the morning after that, the company took quarter-page advertisements in all the leading Chicago newspapers to advertise the overwhelming victory scored by the Kimball instruments.

Cagily, Cone withheld the news of the general award until April, 1894, when the *Presto's* souvenir book of the fair published its text. This enabled him to exploit this award in the trade journals all through the 90s, long after the excitement of the individual honors had ended.

Meanwhile, Judges Hlavac and Schiedmayer had gone back to New York City, en route to Europe in advance of the announcements. There they let loose twin blasts at Blumenberg and the *Courier* in an interview published in *Music Trades* on September 16.

"Such a paper like the *Musical Courier*," said the Stuttgart manufacturer, "could not exist for one month in Germany. The piano makers would not support it, and the editor would surely be thrashed after each one of his publications. I am surprised that the American piano makers support such a sheet.

"The existence of such a paper is a disgrace to the musical industries of America. I speak entirely independently, for Mr. Blumenberg was very careful to leave me very much alone in his attacks on the jury. He will find his match, however, in Mr. Thacher, who will see this whole business successfully through to the end."

And Professor Hlavac said, "As far as these attacks concern myself, I can afford to treat them with contempt. It is only a few weeks ago that this paper had not enough words of praise for me. I came to Chicago as an artist, for my art. I have done what I could to maintain the standard of music at the exhibition by my concerts and recitals. To be subjected to abuse simply because I became a member of the musical jury and so disappointed, without my knowledge, the editor of this paper, is contemptible. Such treatment is not likely to impress artists favorably with this country."

As for the *Courier's* editor, he went back to New York City to lick his wounds, and on October 25 he published the following lame comment:

"The W. W. Kimball Company started into the fair to get something and they have got it. A fine booth was erected, some elegantly incased pianos were displayed therein and Mr. Irving L. Holt was placed in charge of the display. There he has stuck and showed pianos and caught dealers—to be slangy. This booth has been well looked after, and the great number of dealers who have called have been ever well cared for. In addition to this work the Kimball pianos have been in a number of state buildings, as well as played in concert. Backing all this work, a splendid award was secured, which is being advertised all over the country.

"The W. W. Kimball Company went into the Fair to get something and they got it, as we said before. Their dealers all over the country will feel the effect of this good work. Enterprise, enthusiasm, guided by brains, have done everything for the Kimball piano. Nor must their organs be forgotten. It has been a great year for Kimball."

And *Freund's Musical Weekly,* which had played both sides of the fence, rang down the curtain on it all in an editorial on "The Only Kimball" in April, 1894, that ended with this curious and enigmatic comment:

"You may play trumps with Kimball until your hair is silvered and your molars tremble in their sockets, and then you will find the same old joker up his sleeve, and it takes your trick every time. Go to! As well look for the Lost Atlantis as to try to penetrate Kimball when he closes the crevices in his armor and throws out his torpedo nets. Read the Kimball awards, and then you will not be surprised at the Only Kimball's Machiavellian character."

20

"You will take a Kimball piano, a sandwich and one pint of old rye!"

Expansion was the Kimball keynote all through the final decade of the 19th century, and the company's steady progress was slowed only once—and then only temporarily. That was in the last half of 1893, when an extreme depression set in following the stock market crash of June 27. In that year there were 600 bank failures across the country. More than 15,000 commercial houses, including a number of piano and organ manufacturers, failed, and 74 railroads went into receivership.

For the Kimball company the excitement of the world's fair honors and the impetus they gave to sales helped to ease the whiplash sting of the panic. In that financially disastrous year of 1893, as *Freund's Musical Weekly* observed, "they were faced by the problem which many yearn for an opportunity of solving—what to do with all the idle money belonging in the firm's coffers?" Long experienced in the ups and downs of the economic tides, William Wallace Kimball was in a philosophic mood as he prepared to leave for a European tour in July, 1894.

"We must accustom ourselves," he said, "to a readjustment of valuation before we can come down to anything like a healthy condition of business. We have too much of everything. The supply is larger than the demand, and all this means a revaluation of prices on a lower basis. Of course, you will understand that this will cause a lower basis of wages for the working man. The tariff issue and everything connected with it points directly to this readjustment.

"We cannot hold ourselves aloof from the world. We must be a nation of progressive ideas and not retrogressive ideas. In order to meet European competition and build up our trade on a healthy basis and secure a good return upon the money invested, and a natural and not artificial condition of our workingmen, we must get at this readjustment of prices and values without loss of time. And until we get the wages and the prices adjusted . . . we cannot expect any boom in business."

Kimball estimated that the recovery from the depression would take "two or three or four years" at least. It actually took four.

Every effort of the company was directed in that year toward aggressively pushing sales. The Hallet & Davis representation was yielded to Lyon & Healy, in order to concentrate on the Kimball instruments, which now included a full concert grand.

The *Indicator* reported that Kimball's sales for the year were the greatest of any piano manufacturer in the world. And Marc Blumenberg's *Musical Courier* remarked in December that "it is not only the amount of business that is startling," but "it is also astonishing to realize what advances have been made by this house in the case work, the finish, and the artistic excellence of its instruments." This, Conway wryly remarked, was Blumenberg's lordly way of bestowing his own "World's Fair" award.

An improvement in the English trade also took place in 1894, following the transfer of the Kimball agency from Liverpool to Robert M. Marples, a dealer with extensive showrooms at No. 7, Cripplegate Buildings, in Wood Street, hard by London's ancient Cripplegate Church. The London music merchant had been a visitor to the World's Columbian Exposition the summer before and as a well-heeled cash buyer had convinced the company he could push its products abroad, particularly the portable pipe organ, which was a novelty in England. On September 3 he held an exhibition of his new American pianos and organs at the Victoria Hotel in Manchester. The results were good. There were three travelers on the road, he wrote to Conway, and he expected the Kimball pipe organs to catch on, particularly in Scotland, where the Presbyterians were beginning to give up their longtime prejudice against musical instruments in the worship.

After visiting in London a year later, Kimball expressed doubt there would be a large market there for his pianos: "You see, labor is cheaper there than with us, and the item of freight alone amounts to a good piano profit. I don't see how a manufacturer can produce his goods here, pay freight, and compete with the cheap labor there." His own factory employes had been granted a wage increase that May as the depression began to ease its grip.

Incidentally, *London Music* was pleased by Kimball's visit and noted that, unlike most American manufacturers it had seen, he did not deprecate the English piano. He merely observed that in England a craftsman followed an instrument all the way through its manufacture while in his own factories there were experts in each branch of the work.

Pre-Christmas sales in both the wholesale and retail departments in 1894 were the largest in Kimball history, surpassing the peak reached in the corresponding December two years before.

Credit for this excellent showing in time of depression was due largely to two influences—the debut of the full concert grand piano, introduced to Eastern audiences on a spring tour by the internationally famous Emil Liebling, and an aggressive use of testimonial advertising by Albert Cone.

Early in the year, when the first of the big, eight-foot-nine-inch, ebony-finish concert grands was ready, the Governor notified Liebling, always a reliable musical ally and a man whose artistic judgment had contributed immeasurably to the company's success.

After thoroughly testing it in his Kimball Hall studios, the veteran Liebling enthusiastically asked permission to use it for the rest of his current concert season.

His subsequent visit to the East, said the *Indicator*, "was in the nature of a triumphal march." Starting with a concert at New York City's Carnegie Music Hall on March 1, Liebling went on to play to flattering applause before audiences in Brooklyn, Washington, and Detroit. In April he swung south to Memphis and a similar success in the great Auditorium, and in July he played a special concert at Saratoga before the convention of the Music Teachers National Association. On every hand the new Kimball piano production was hailed as the equal of any made in the older Eastern factories.

Liebling was a showman as well as an artist. For a generation he occupied an exalted place in the Chicago musical colony. From 1884 until his death in 1914 he was intimately associated with the promotional end of the Kimball business. It was a case, the company explained, of "a legitimate unity of the artistic element and the productive merchant—each complements the other." With its pianos his inseparable companions, he traveled East, South and West, appearing before clubs, musical groups, schools, festivals, conventions, and concert audiences as a standard-bearer for the Kimball pianos.

Liebling's reputation as an artist and composer was brilliant. On the occasion of his Washington appearance that March 3, the Washington *Post* reported that the audience was liberally sprinkled with leading capital figures, including numerous senators, several Supreme Court justices, and the German ambassador and a party of ten. Brilliant flowers and foliage plants screened the footlights, flanked at either end by clumps of dark green palms. Easter lilies, set on massive marble pedestals, formed a centerpiece. Just before the frosty-haired Liebling walked dramatically onto the stage, the name "Kimball" flashed from a cluster of white incadescent lamps set against a green background, brilliantly illuminating the scene.

It was typical of the Liebling-Kimball performances, and Kimball agents and dealers were expected to follow up such affairs with flocks of orders. Which, more often than not, they did.

According to Morris A. Gutstein's "A Priceless Heritage," the story of Chicago's Jewish colony, Liebling came from a family of noted Jewish musicians. Born in Pless, Germany, in 1852, he studied piano at Wiemar under Franz Liszt and at Vienna with Julius Dachs. He began his career in America by teaching music at Georgetown, Kentucky, where he first settled in 1867.

As a promising young artist, he went to Chicago in 1872 and was befriended by Kimball, whose hospitable home was often the center of a circle of devoted music lovers. The relationship begun with the company in those early days endured until his death on January 20, 1914, in his Astor Street home on Chicago's Near North Side Gold Coast. It was fitting that the music of a Kimball pipe organ was played at the funeral services in St. Chrysostom's Church. Among the pallbearers were C. N. Kimball and Edgar C. Smith, longtime associates in the company. Liebling was mourned by a large personal following in and out of the music trades. It included not only those who had heard him play in concerts, but also a legion of pupils, the many who had played his widely known compositions, and those who were acquainted with his musical lectures and his large output of writing and criticism. For many years he had edited the *Musical Herald,* a handsome illustrated magazine launched in the 80s, published intermittently for free distribution as a Kimball promotional organ, and discontinued after his death. His younger brother, George Liebling, a Berlin pianist, toured America in the 1920s.

Treasurer Cone's big venture into the testimonial field, begun with the Adelina Patti endorsement of 1889, picked up pace during the world's fair and continued to roll merrily along until his death in 1900, when others took over.

One of his able allies in this endeavor was Edgar C. Smith, manager of the Chicago retail warerooms and in those days known far

173

and wide as the "Beau Brummel" of the piano business. He came to the company from Waterloo, Iowa, in 1880 with an introduction from L. S. Parsons, one of the early Kimball dealers in Iowa.

An impressive salesman with a winning personality, Smith had a way of making customers feel important. "He completely disarmed them," recalls James V. Sill. "People wound up by thanking him for selling them a piano."

Right-hand man as head salesman under him for many years was George Schleiffarth, who composed such hit songs of the 90s as "Doris" and "Ambolena Snow." Smith joined the company's board of directors in 1914 and served till 1930, when he retired after 50 years as a Kimball man.

Another man who aided Cone in gathering artist testimonials was F. Wight Neumann, a hustling, bearded impresario who had fourth floor offices in Kimball Hall from which he conducted two operations which he called the Star Lecture Course and the Society for the Cultivation of Music.

Both Smith and Neumann were well acquainted with the leading musical talents of the day. Both were qualified by temperament and training for the delicate task of approaching these artists tactfully and seeking their approval for the Kimball piano.

The shy, soft-spoken Cone preferred to remain in the background, directing operations. With virtually unlimited advertising funds at his disposal, he hired the hard-working Neumann to acquaint prospective artist friends with the Kimball pianos and to offer them contract arrangements in exchange for their testimony. Often this called for entertaining on a lavish scale, and the Neumann expense accounts were terrific. All the contract terms were finally arranged by Cone personally; and he rigorously insisted that every artist who endorsed a piano for Kimball must actually use one. It was a requisite that many another user of piano testimonials overlooked in those days.

Smith, in turn, would then take over and year after year would meet and greet the artists and wine and dine them when they came back to Chicago from all over the world. Thus their enthusiasm for the Kimball piano was kept alive and fresh.

174

Just as he had done with the Patti-Tamagno company in 1889, Cone managed in the spring of 1894 to capture the wholesale endorsements of the leading artists of the Abbey & Grau grand opera company on its visit to Chicago. The stars the company signed included Madame Emma Calve, Jean and Edouard de Rezke, Luigi Mancinelli, Lillian Nordica, Sophia Scalchi, Fernando de Lucia, Pol Plancon, and Francisco Vigas. In 1896 the leading artists of a third great company, the German troupe of the Damrosch Opera Company, was added to the lengthening list. Walter Damrosch himself, the great musical leader and director of the New York Symphony Orchestra, testified, "I have examined the Kimball Piano, and it gives me pleasure to state that it has a pure, refined and powerful tone. The action is light and responsive to a rare degree." Among the Damrosch artists who also endorsed the Kimball were Max Alvary, Katharina Lohse-Klafsky, Johanna Gadski, William Mertens, Paul Lange, Conrad Behrens, Louise Mulder, Marie Maurer, and Mina Schilling.

In each case, a special advertising booklet, illustrated with halftones of the artists, was used to carry the endorsements to customers and to the music trade in general.

Lest the list of Kimball friends should get too hoity-toity for the everyday trade, Cone also solicited the praise of such oddly assorted personages as the Belgian violinist Cesar Thomson; Dr. A. Conan Doyle, the author of the Sherlock Holmes stories; the popular bandmaster John Philip Sousa, and "the airy, fairy" Lillian Russell, the comic opera queen. When the Sultan of Johore decorated the soprano Minnie Hauk, Cone took occasion in an advertisement published in the Chicago *Tribune* to point out that she remained American in her preferences: She still played a Kimball piano.

Music Trades ran a wry comment about this time:

"I do believe if Kimball were to say:

" 'Neumann! You leave tonight for the North Pole. You will take a Kimball piano, a sandwich and one pint of old rye! You will play that piano at the Pole and come back with a signed testimonial!'

"Neumann would reply: 'Yes, Mr. Kimball! In what language would you prefer the testimonial?'

"And then Neumann would disappear and within two weeks would reappear, and the morning after all the Chicago dailies would have a flaming announcement: 'This Time THE KIMBALL PIANO Has Secured a BLANKET MORTGAGE on the TESTIMONIAL BUSINESS in the shape of an ENDORSEMENT FROM THE NORTH POLE!' "

Cone went right ahead getting testimonials and advertising them widely, while the piano sales soared. He liked an endorsement, no matter where it came from. In 1898 he had the pleasure of advertising the decision of Dr. Ziegfeld's Chicago Musical College, the country's largest, to switch from Steinways to Kimballs. This meant the sale of fifty pianos, among them fifteen parlor grands and a full concert grand.

After many years of service to the company, Wight Neumann left in 1897 to accept an appointment as U.S. Consul in Cologne, Germany. There were many who suspected the diplomatic honor was a company reward, arranged by the politically influential E. S. Conway, though Conway never admitted it.

One of the happiest moments of Cone's life came on a January afternoon in 1894 when an office surprise party, arranged by Neumann to celebrate the treasurer's 25th anniversary with the company, greeted him as he returned from lunch. On his desk, under silken draperies, sat a pair of magnificant pink-and-gold Sevres vases, hand-painted and standing four feet high. The staff had chipped in $700 to buy them. His voice trembled and his eyes misted as he thanked them all, listened to Conway's sentimental, brotherly reminiscences of their long years together, and then slipped quietly away to his Drexel Boulevard home to reflect upon the rich friendships he had gathered.

Accompanying the vases was a brief remembrance note signed by his beloved associates, including Kimball, Conway, Neumann, Liebling, Smith, W. W. Lufkin, E. B. Bartlett, G. J. Gouchois, J. B. Thiery, C. C. Dunbar, L. A. Dozois, A. L. Fierlein, E. R. Blanchard, J. R. Pollock, H. A. Wise, Miss Dartnell, Miss Dunkinson, Miss Patterson, H. B. Reynolds, R. E. Davis, S. J. McCormick, C.

W. Davis, Eugene Whelan, H. H. Hinton, C. F. Balch, A. Fuller, L. H. Davis, L. H. Barnitt, R. M. Brown, L. A. Crittenton, S. H. Mooney, Thomas Smythe, E. F. Greenwood, C. B. Woodruff, H. L. Goodrow, John Borwell, G. E. Alley, W. T. Bradbury, John Farley, Luke Yore, Frank Webb, Miss Hamilton, Mrs. Kelley, F. Klug, Dennis Donovan, John R. Green, and E. A. Cox.

In a day before advertising got its long pants, Cone was one of its greatest practitioners. Many said he was the equal of old Charles F. Tretbar, the bald genius of the Steinway organization. His resources were infinite, his imagination vivid, and his writing style versatile. He loved nothing better than to turn a hand to the kind of bucolic copy that sold pianos in the hinterlands. For example, in the 90s he prepared this item as a reading notice sent out to the Sedalia (Missouri) agent for insertion in the local papers:

PIANO TALK NO. 5

Some months after I had told Conway what I thought of that $85,000 check I was again in Chicago. Pretty soon Mr. Kimball saw me, and was quite cordial, evidently in a very good humor. "Ah!" says he, "our Missouri sharp, I believe?" "Yes, sir," says I. "Have you seen our 'new scale Kimball?'" says he. "No, sir," says I. "Come," says he: "there they are. Now examine them. Pull them all to pieces, and tell us how you like them." So when he came back again I had, sure enough, pulled the piano to pieces. And says I: "Mr. Kimball, some things about them I don't like." I noticed he scowled a little. "Well," says he, "what don't you like?" "I don't like the plate," says I. "What's the matter with the plate?" says he. "Too much gingerbread and flummididdle work," says I. "What do you mean?" says he. "I mean," says I, "that I don't like those carbuncles and things on the casting." "Why," says he, "other fine pianos—Steinways and others—have them." "Yes," says I, "Steinways have made their big name and can afford to act the fool if they're a mind to. You ain't Steinway yet, and will have to hustle like fun to get there; you're just starting, and that's different. Now I always have believed that the cleaner the plate the clearer the tone."

Mr. Conway was just passing, and Mr. Kimball called him, and had me to say it over again. "What do you think of that, Conway?" says he. "A Missouri puke telling us how to build pianos." He didn't get mad and Conway just nodded his head and smiled. But don't you

177

forget it, the next "new scale piano" I saw had no wrinkles on the plate, and ever since that time it has been a hummer and Steinway ain't in it. The Kimball plate has been just the smoothest and cleanest of any, and the tone is the clearest, best and purest of the whole list. Oh, yes, I'm glad I'm a Kimball man, only I sometimes wish I had some of the money that plate has made for the W. W. Kimball Company.

Yours truly,

W. SHARP

The catalogs of suggested advertisements which Cone prepared for the use of local agents were highly praised in their day, both by the men for whom they produced sales and by such advertising authorities as the *Inland Printer* and *Printer's Ink*.

Charles Austin Bates, the critical authority for the latter publication, repeatedly praised his catalogs for their appeal. He pronounced the 1896 edition, with its portraits of musical authorities, an advance over any he had ever seen. But he twitted Cone for some of his long, involved sentences. And he took a swipe at the prevailing trade practice of listing pianos at about $800 "when they know, and the dealer knows and the public knows, that they are never going to get more than $350 or $400 for that piano."

Bates' criticism was one of the strong influences that led Cone to press for and finally win a one-price system in the trade.

Cone's broadsides, profusely illustrated with portraits of the artists who endorsed the Kimball piano; his paid reading notices, which even today can mislead a reader into believing they were printed as legitimate news; his "Piano Primer," with which he instructed the children of his generation in the undying merits of the company—all these were the carefully thought out products of a well-ordered mind.

His advertising philosophy was simple: Judicious advertising in the daily papers pays. Half a century later the piano business still agrees.

"The company's success," he modestly said, "is due to the sagacity and broad business policy of its founder. Its advertising is but one of several secondary means which have been utilized to further its interests."

A frail man, never quite well, Cone nevertheless was happy and open-hearted, "a man whose ingenuousness was irresistible." He made annual vacation visits to Colorado Springs, beginning in 1886. He traveled widely around the country for his health—to Old Point Comfort, Maine, or to Pass Christian, Mississippi, where Conway liked to hang out, or to Florida with the Kimballs. Once he took a six-week trip to California for his health—and brought back orders for 150 pianos. A mere bagatelle where Cone was concerned, said the *Presto*. As a young man he sang with the Apollo Quartet. Suave, courteous, polished, he became in his years as treasurer and advertising manager one of the most forceful and widely admired men in the piano trade.

Death, from pneumonia, came to Albert Gardner Cone on Wednesday morning, March 28, 1900, in his fashionable Chicago home at 4148 Drexel Boulevard. He was buried on the following Friday with C. N. Kimball, Edgar C. Smith, E. E. Conway, Carle C. Conway, H. A. Wise, E. R. Blanchard, C. C. Dunbar, and L. A. Dozois as pallbearers. He would have been 48 that September.

His sister, Evalyne, and her husband, W. W. Kimball, were vacationing in Coronado Beach, California, when the telegram came announcing his death. To his widow, Ella, the sister of the real estate man W. A. Bond, he left $75,000 and household effects. His estate was estimated at $325,000 in personal property and $25,000 in real estate. Among his bequests were $50,000 to the Chicago Home for Incurables, $10,000 to the Chicago Homeopathic Hospital, and $5,000 each to several family members, including the Governor, Mrs. Kimball, and his brother Irving H.

A measure of how the stockholders felt about his 30 years of "splendid service and sterling integrity" was provided on the morning of Saturday, May 19, following his death. At a special meeting called by the Governor, they voted unanimously to pay a "complimentary contribution" of $45,000 to Ella Bond Cone—being $1,500 a year salary for a period of 30 years."

21

"They can build a better pipe organ for a given sum of money than any other builder."

I<small>N THE</small> Kimball company's first century there were three great manufacturing epochs—reed organs, pianos, and pipe organs. The second alone endures and carries on today. The glorious years of organ-building are long since past, and there remains only an incalculable host of memories—the light of recollection in an old timer's eyes, a thousand and one faded clippings tucked into family Bibles, or into the scrapbooks of the faithful; the rousing strains of innumerable far-off reed organs, playing "In the Sweet By and By"; a haunting interlude of Bach, floating in grandeur from the great golden throat of a Kimball pipe organ somewhere out there, perhaps on the other side of the world.

First came the lowly reed organ, which soared to swift popularity after it came of age and reigned for a time as the queen of the 19th-century parlor. Then its popularity dwindled after the first decade of the present century, until at last the company closed the books on a fabulous and opulent era—half its lifetime—in which it had dominated the field as the world's largest reed organ manufacturer. On September 30, 1922, it boxed up the last of the Kimball reed organs—the 403,390th—and shipped it on its lonely way. In the catalog it was a style 661, oak.

The second epoch, emerging soon after the reed organ period began, was piano manufacturing. It likewise brought to the company a position of world leadership. It is an epoch that has had no end, and it continues in great strength today as the adventure of a new Kimball century begins.

After the piano's first triumph, there came the third great epoch of manufacture with the advent of the stationary pipe organ. It opened in 1894 as a sequel to Frederic W. Hedgeland's development a short time before of the portable pipe organ.

With the cost-conscious W. W. Lufkin watching his every move, the inventive young Englishman built his pioneering stationary organ a year before the company erected its first pipe organ factory. Working in the cramped quarters where he turned out the smaller instruments, he utilized the portable's principles to design a larger organ with 625 pipes and eighteen registers. The tests were completed on June 22, 1894, and it was shipped out on the same day to Kewanee, Illinois, to be set up and installed under Hedgeland's supervision in the auditorium of the First Methodist Church.

For its first instrument of this type—"highly prized," the papers said, "for its clear and melodious tone"—the Kimball company received a modest $1,500. And Lufkin heaved a big sigh when the cost sheets showed that on it the factory had just about broken even.

This small beginning marked the opening of a memorable forty-eight-year period that came to an end on September 26, 1942, when the 7,326th Kimball pipe organ was shipped out to the Good Hope Lutheran Church of Bucyrus, Ohio.

After that, the manufacture of the big organs ceased, primarily because of the World War II restrictions on the metals and other critical materials that went into them. A secondary reason was the decline in profits that afflicted the organ department. It was never

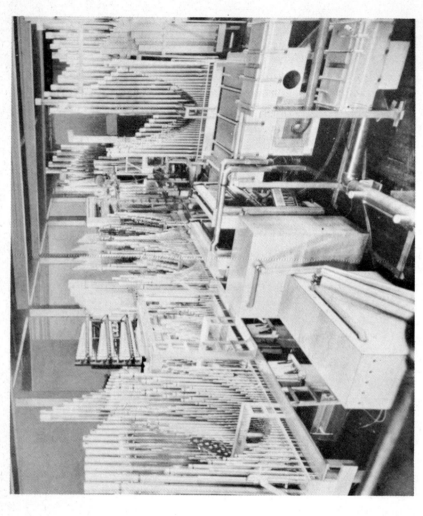

One of the most famous of the Kimball pipe organs was this one, built for the Public Auditorium in Pretoria, the Transvaal, Union of South Africa. It is shown here in the erecting room at organ factory.

a great money earner, the pro-piano men within the company tell you with a shrug of the shoulder. The record of one of the latter-day organs tends to support their view: In April, 1941, the company shipped out an instrument built for the wheat-farming parishioners of the Dutch Reformed Church in Moorreesburg, Cape of Good Hope Province, Union of South Africa. It was billed for $5,500 and cost the factory a cool $5,078.12. By the time it was installed, the cost sheets show, a total of $5,317.88 had been expended, leaving a paper profit of $182.12.

In the long years between Kewanee and Bucyrus, the company produced millions of dollars worth of great pipe organs for churches, temples, and cathedrals, fashionable residences, universities, theaters, auditoriums, ballrooms, and radio stations. The market extended into almost every quarter of the globe, and with it the prestige of the Kimball name.

Among the larger and more expensive of these instruments were the $65,000 pipe organ erected in 1935 in the Municipal Auditorium at Pretoria, capital of the Transvaal, Union of South Africa, and the great $135,000 installation in the auditorium of the Roxy Theater in New York City.

The many remodeling commissions that were handled through the years included a reconstruction in 1900 and 1901 of the giant Mormon Tabernacle organ in Salt Lake City. This famous instrument, the second largest in the country at the time, was built originally by the followers of Joseph Smith.

In the pipe organ department the company blended the inventive and scientific skills of factory-trained experts with the traditionally painstaking craftsmanship of old-school organ architects. On its staff were some of the greatest organ authorities in the world, devoted men whose aim was tonal perfection. In the course of their work they made a great number of significant contributions to the advance of the organ builder's ancient art.

The manufacture of this "king of the instruments" had its effect on piano making, also. For it gave the company an advantage that few of its rivals enjoyed: The piano and organ departments, akin in so many ways and operated in the same cluster of factory buildings, shared their knowledge and experience. From a pipe organ engineer, for example, came the suggestion for the exclusive "pipe organ" tone chamber that is a feature of the Consolette piano today.

Finally, as E. S. Conway foresaw, when Hedgeland first went to work for Kimball, the piano sales division made highly effective use of the company's worldwide reputation in organ making. A piano buyer, the potent sales argument ran, could in all safety base his selection of a Kimball piano wholly on the fame enjoyed by the company as an acknowledged leader in pipe organ design.

Progress and development came rapidly after the Kewanee installation in 1894. Within a year the company was—and blame the *Musical Times* for the pun—in "full blown" pipe organ manufacture. Walter T. Bradbury, a hustling salesman, was in charge of Chicago contacts, and he brought in some big orders in those early years, including one for an elaborate residential organ to be installed in the Dearborn Street home of the wealthy Dr. Nicholas Senn, the famous U.S. Army surgeon, and another in evangelist Dwight L. Moody's church at LaSalle Street and Chicago Avenue.

The Senn contract paid a dividend in 1897 when Mrs. Senn presented a $10,000, three-manual organ to St. Chrysostom's Church. It was necessary to take a part of the roof off that Clark Street structure in order to install it.

The affluent Mrs. A. L. Benjamin of Milwaukee was another customer for a residential organ, as was W. W. Kimball's friend George Pullman, who had the company build for his Prairie Avenue home a fancy mahogany instrument, finished in vermilion. It was used the first time at the wedding of his daughter Florence on Friday evening, April 29, 1896.

Down in South Bend, Indiana, the millionaire Studebaker brothers decided they should have some of Kimball's new pipe organs. They ordered two three-manual jobs in May, 1898, for their plush new Studebaker Building on Chicago's Michigan Avenue, and a two-manual installation, with automatic player attached, for the Studebaker Opera House in South Bend. Frederick S. Fish, the son-in-law of old John Mohler Studebaker, came up to Chicago and watched in fascination as the big organs were put together.

One of the fanciest of the early commissions was the two-manual organ erected in 1895 in the South Side home of the Chicago society leader Mrs. Horatio O. Stone, who had cut her biggest swath as a hostess to Oscar Wilde. It was encased in antique finish Spanish mahogany, and on the middle belt were eight Corinthian columns with massive carved caps, which in turn supported a large and exquisitely carved canopy.

The rapid growth of the new business forced the company to start work immediately in 1894 on the first pipe organ factory, which became known as building D. It was completed in May of the next year, and brought greater speed to the work. The First Methodist Episcopal Church of Tuscola, Illinois, placed an order on October 1 of that year for a two-manual organ, and five weeks later, on November 7, it was ready for use. In the following year, 1896, W. S. B. Matthews, the editor of *Music,* wrote: "They [the Kimball company] can build a better organ for a given sum of money than any other builder."

In its first factory the company was able to make all the metal and wooden pipes, all the actions, keys, and cases, and the famous tubular pneumatic action that Hedgeland had invented. The factory was another five-story structure, containing 96,000 square feet, its principal feature being a great two-floor erecting room, 80 by 80 feet in area and 30 feet high. Immediately off it were the stock rooms and the "voicing" room, where the final adjustments were made and the organ given its innumerable gradations of tone. This plant served the department as headquarters until 1907, when an even more adequate building, with a still larger erecting room, was occupied. This second facility, factory H, was five stories high, with a total floorage of 60,000 square feet. The plans were drawn by the Kimball architect William Strippelman, who had designed all the new buildings erected since the company started.

The need for this addition had been obvious with the increasing demands made upon the department. In 1905 a high point was reached when A. M. Shuey, manager of pipe organ sales for the Kimball branch store in Minneapolis, casually sent in a $21,000 order for an instrument to be erected in the Municipal Auditorium. This forty-ton mammoth was the fourth largest pipe organ in the United States at the time. It measured 20 x 20 x 40 feet and contained 4,000 pipes, including one that was thirty-three feet long and two feet in diameter. It took six railroad cars to haul the big organ to Minneapolis.

More than a quarter of a century later, in 1931, the second W. W. Kimball, son of C. N. Kimball and president of today's Kimball company, helped to design and build another huge pipe organ for the same auditorium. This time it was a $100,000 instrument, a large two-console, five-manual organ of vast tonal resources. One of the world's largest, it had 102 speaking stops and seven percussions. It was installed in specially built chambers on both sides of the great stage.

Some of the more famous installations over the years, all specially designed, built, and voiced for their own locations, include the following: Christ Episcopal Church, Nassau, Bahama Islands; St. Peter's Episcopal Church, Cambridge, Massachusetts; Municipal Auditorium, Worcester, Massachusetts; St. Margaret's Roman Catholic Church, Des Moines; St. John's Episcopal Cathedral, Denver; First Congregational Church, Oklahoma City; Messiah Lutheran Church, Minneapolis; St. Peter's Lutheran Church, the Bronx, New York City; radio stations WABC, New York City, and WGN, Chicago; Thorne Hall, Northwestern University, Chicago campus; the ballroom of the Atlantic City Auditorium; First Congregational Church, Columbus, Ohio; Heinz Auditorium, Pittsburgh; Cornell College, Mount Vernon, Iowa; Second Baptist Church, Germantown, Pennsylvania; Coliseum Theater, Juneau, Alaska; Vassar College, Poughkeepsie, New York; Municipal Auditorium, Memphis, Tennessee; the First Presbyterian and First

Baptist churches in Hollywood, California; and the First Churches of Christ, Scientist, in Cambridge, San Francisco, and Vancouver, British Columbia, Canada.

Andrew Carnegie, the steel magnate, was an early fancier of the Kimball pipe organs and donated several of them to churches and institutions. Among them was the famous organ in St. Paul's Cathedral, Pittsburgh, modernized by Kimball in 1923 with the latest electric action and a four-manual console. The oil tycoon John D. Rockefeller presented a Kimball organ to the auditorium chapel of the Union Medical College in Peking, China, opened in the fall of 1919.

Throughout the pipe organ period there was a steady demand for the residential organ, and the company made many notable installations, all specially designed, in the homes of wealthy customers throughout the country. In 1937, a large organ with an automatic playing mechanism was built for Mrs. M. F. Yount, widow of a famous Texas oilman, and installed at her Spindletop Farm, near Lexington, Kentucky. Other buyers of residential organs included George E. Devendorf of Great Neck, Long Island, New York; D. A. Schulte of Red Bank, New Jersey; L. C. Phipps of Denver, and Stephen A. Gerrard of Cincinnati.

The manufacturing policy of the pipe organ department as it developed after the turn of the century was a departure from the path followed by most organ builders. With increased use of modern machinery and facilities the tendency had been for organ factories to desert the intimate relationship that had existed between customer and organ builder for many centuries in the long history of the craft. The practice in earlier days was for the organ builder to bring his tools to the job, in the manner of the carpenter, and perform his work under the employer's watchful eye. Now, with the work concentrated in giant factories remote from the final installation, the employer's watchful eye was missing. The craft of organ building had begun to suffer as shoddy workmanship and shoddy materials crept in.

The second W. W. Kimball, from the time he started work in the organ factory in the 1920s, was disturbed by this kind of competition in the trade. For more than an ordinary lifetime, the Kimball company had built in the tradition of good craftsmanship, honoring the buyer's trust and delivering millions of dollars worth of fine instruments. But it was becoming more evident all the time that something vital was missing—the old ability of the buyer to keep watch—and that unscrupulous builders were making it difficult for honest manufacturers to carry on.

So far as this factory was concerned, young Kimball decided, the buyer must be given an unequivocal basis of trust. So it was that under his growing influence the company developed a revolutionary type of buyer-builder relationship for the pipe organ trade—embodying in its contract a section that listed in specific terms every item of material, every specification of design which it would guarantee to include if entrusted with an order for manufacture. It was a policy of absolute frankness, and it further impressed the Kimball record for fidelity in the public mind.

To it perhaps can be attributed such world-ranging operations as the installation of the great Pretoria organ in South Africa in 1934, after Wallace Kimball had become the general manager of the pipe organ department. Rarely had a Kimball contract been obtained from such an unexpected source. It came in February, 1934, several years after John Connell, a Pretoria musician and orchestral conductor, toured America, ostensibly to give a series of recitals. In the course of that tour he played a Kimball pipe organ, and when the South African city fathers wanted an organ and sought his suggestions, he recommended that they send the order to Kimball, half a world away.

This great organ, with its 6,616 pipes and 160 stops and couplers, weighed seventy tons when put aboard an Illinois Central train and sent off to New Orleans for shipment by steamship to Africa. In its depths were 325 miles of electric wires, more than 4,000 magnets, and nearly 15,000 electrical contacts. All the latter were of silver.

The silver contact points were for the electrical connections under the keys of the Pretoria console. They were typical products of the Kimball company's research.

All the parts of the Kimball organs were built in the factory, where a rigid control of quality in material and workmanship was exercised at every stage, from the beginning of work to the final factory erection and testing before they were knocked down for shipment.

In developing the contact wires beneath the keys the company engineers could have relied upon what the standard handbooks had to say about the relative conductivity of metals. But to make absolutely sure they were using the best metal for the job, they ran extensive tests under actual working conditions, mechanically reproducing the action of the keys while testing many designs and materials. These included three silver alloys and two of phosphor bronze, tungsten, platinum, German silver, and other metals. The tests extended over six months, and in the course of them, a total of 16,588,800 electrical key contacts were made. The silver contacts finally chosen offered a durable and reliable guarantee against any breakdown at that point in the organ's electrical system.

Other unusual specifications for Kimball pipe organs were the fine alum-tanned sheepskin hinges and gussets that enclosed the framework of the air reservoirs; the individual motors to operate the swellbox shutters; the sealing of woodwork with lacquer instead of varnish, a technique adapted from the experience of automobile makers; and the expensive system of air control on the reservoirs, by which the company utilized three graduated valves instead of the single valve used by most manufacturers.

This three-valve system was thoroughly described in the authoritative organ-building handbook, "The Contemporary American Organ," written by the organist Dr. William H. Barnes, for whom the Kimballs built—to his own design—a notable three-manual organ in the First Baptist Church of Evanston.

Dr. Barnes remarked, in passing, that one organ builder had jested that the graduated three-valve system of regulating the high-pressure Kimball air reservoir reminded him of a farmer whose cat had kittens, whereupon he cut a small hole in the side of the barn to let the kittens get through and a larger hole for the mother cat.

But the fact is that the extra valves made it possible to regulate and steady the air pressure of the Kimball organ in a manner accomplished by no other manufacturer.

Dr. Barnes also credited the company with having demonstrated in its organs how to materially increase the wind pressure on the stops and thereby achieve a smoother, prompter, and more musical tone, without creating a corresponding increase in the volume of sound.

As for the Kimball automatic players, first developed by Hedgeland and put into use in September, 1897, then later perfected, Dr. Barnes described them as works "of fine accomplishment and remarkable ingenuity."

This authority also used the term "ingenious" to describe the pipe scale drawn in the Kimball factory by Joseph J. Carruthers, an English pipe organ builder who was a student of the great Robert Hope-Jones.

Carruthers was internationally known as a Kimball organ architect. He used to discuss the questions of organ tone at great length with Maurice Hardy, another of the company's experts. The Englishman's idea of the only perfect organ was the one in St. George's Hall in Liverpool, England, built by "Father" Willis in 1855. Whenever he heard a particularly effective American organ, he would say it sounded almost as well—but never quite as well—as the one back in Liverpool.

Another of the great Kimball organ builders was George Michel, a voicer of unusual capabilities, according to Wallace Kimball. Barnes wrote of Michel: "He has developed some orchestral reed tone, particularly English horns, French horns and saxophones . . . of excellent quality. The chorus reeds and strings that he has produced are also very superior."

Barnes also discussed Michel's development of a complete diapason chorus employing pure tin in all pipes from the four-foot octave on up, a recent example of which is embodied in the great Kimball organ in the auditorium at Worcester, Massachusetts. Of this development, Barnes wrote, "This is probably the first modern instance of such a chorus. The results are noteworthy for the clarity and cohesion of tone produced by the use of pure tin for these registers."

The company recognized that "the educated hand and eye and the trained hearing of the voicer can never be displaced by machines or mechanical processes if the organ is to be a true work of art," and George Michel was its great insurance policy for pipe organ perfection. It was Michel, more than any other man, who gave the Kimball pipe organ of the 20th century its great reputation.

22

"Kimballville! All out for Kimballville!"

"FROM THE time I entered the music trade of Chicago," said W. W. Kimball in 1902, "my idea was not only to bring the piano and organ to the highest degree of perfection possible with the mechanical resources of the world, but finally to realize so definite an economy in the conduct of the business in its every phase as to effect a practical benefit to the American nation. I have aimed to advance the mechanical principles of construction and so to economize the business as to furnish the highest grade of instruments in a greatly reduced cost to the public."

How well he accomplished this aim was already abundantly evident by the middle 90s. An industry-wide census in December, 1894, showed 179 piano manufacturers in the United States, with New York leading the list with 71 and Boston and Chicago with 20 each. A year later there were nine more manufacturers in Chicago. But of all the world's manufacturers, both of pianos and reed organs, the Kimball company could boast the largest output and the largest sales.

Its total production of pianos since building the first factory was nearing the 50,000 mark. And a short time away, in 1903, the year before the founder's death, the company would turn out its peak year's production of Kimballs for its first century—22,000 instruments—a record that was matched only once afterward, in 1911.

Marc Blumenberg's *Musical Courier* candidly observed on September 26, 1895, "The W. W. Kimball Company is without question the largest producer of pianos, with facilities unsurpassed and constantly improving. The concern now makes its own iron frames, its own keys, and actions, its own cases and designs. . . . There is no doubt that when the company began the manufacture of pianos there was an intention of producing at the lowest cost, but subsequently, while the policy of economy in production was not abandoned, the grade of the instrument was raised, necessarily increasing the cost, but not in proportion to its increased merits. It cannot be denied that without these merits the testimonials from the hosts of musicians which have been given to the Kimball piano could never have been obtained. . . ."

In the next spring, the apparently repentant Blumenberg went even farther in an "endorsement" of the Chicago-made Kimballs he had fought so bitterly: "In the construction the greatest care is evinced, and from the outside finish into the very deepest and obscure inside portions the best technical skill is applied. The result is a splendid tone and most sympathetic touch, and I do like to spend time playing them—for, as you probably do not know, I play the piano with more than suspected skill."

It was a warm May day when W. W. Kimball picked up the *Courier* on his return from lunch, peeled off the coat of his light-colored summer suit, and sat down on one of the large and comfortable circular divans to rest for a few moments in the main floor showroom of the Kimball Building. As his eyes lit upon Blumenberg's "endorsement," a smile, half scorn and half amusement, spread slowly over his benign countenance.

Then he glanced up to watch the workmen who were putting the final touches of red paint on a brand-new and massive ornamental metallic awning—a *porte cochère* Edgar Smith had called it—over-hanging the pavement in front of the Kimball entrance on Wabash Avenue. There was a need for such a covering on rainy days, Smith had told him, so that the ladies and well-dressed customers would not ruin their handsome attire. On its three sides in conspicuous raised letters were the words: "ORGANS—KIMBALL—PIANOS." It was a final stroke of modern elegance for the half-million-dollar Kimball Hall property, acquired just the year before in a deal in which the Kimball directors voted on June 19 to take over the $100,000 bonded indebtedness of the Chicago Music Hall Company. Within a month the Kimball company had paid off the mortgage in cash and obtained full title to one of Chicago's most valuable properties.

Kimball took a lot of kidding about his fancy new awning. The building stood on the inside of the Elevated "Loop," and the *Music Times* waggishly suggested that the "L" officials had entered into a conspiracy with Kimball to develop a new station at that point and call it Kimballville.

The editor conjured up visions of gentlemanly agents passing among the riders in the crowded commuter trains and announcing: "The next stop will be Kimballville. Passengers desirous of pur-chasing the piano endorsed by Patti and all the great operatic stars of the earth will be given exchange checks good for any train. Mr. Smith and his small army of good-looking assistants will be glad to welcome each and all. Kimballville! All out for Kimballville!"

The great manufacturer could well afford to smile at such sallies. The capital stock invested in the company at the time was $2,750,-000, and there were 1,400 employes on the payroll. At least 3,000 more men were dealers and salesmen for the enterprise. The output for the year, as scheduled by W. W. Lufkin, was to be 8,000 pianos and 12,000 organs. Competition had been whipped to a frazzle both at home and abroad; and even in the midst of the economic doldrums that still persisted in the wake of the 1893 panic, Lufkin was shooting for the mark of 40 pianos a day, an output hitherto unheard of in the history of piano manufacturing.

Wabash Avenue's "Music Row" was abuzz with the news that Kimball had entered with his friend Marshall Field and others into a new Chicago syndicate of businessmen seeking to enter the Venezuelan trade. In other areas of Latin America the trade was expanding. Two years later, Kimball would ship to Otto & Arzoz, Mexico City dealers, two carloads of pianos and organs, the largest shipment of its kind ever made to the Mexican market.

In February, 1895, Kimball had formed a subsidiary, the Whitney Piano and Supply Manufacturing Company, capitalized at $25,000, with an initial intention of manufacturing piano actions on a large scale. Part of the plan, which was never carried out, was to sell actions to other piano makers in order to keep production large enough for the operation to be self-sustaining. The incorporaters were Alvin Whitney, a Bostonian, who was Lufkin's action expert at the factory; Frank H. Whitney, a Quincy (Illinois) dealer in Kimball pianos, and Arthur E. Whitney, a Ohioan who had been one of the expert representatives E. S. Conway developed to travel from city to city and direct special sales for the various Kimball agencies.

John H. Whitney of Elyria, Ohio, the son of the latter Whitney and himself a onetime Kimball agent and dealer, recalled in 1956 that each of the three Whitneys smugly assumed it was he in particular who was being honored when Kimball decided to use the name on a new piano to be manufactured for the medium-priced market. Arthur was particularly pleased because it gave the salesman and the dealer a well-made and fairly attractive full-size upright that could be sold with more satisfaction than was afforded by the small, medium sized, and less well-made Hinzes.

As John tells it, the name of this particular instrument reminded too many people of the better known name of H. J. Heinz, the pickle manufacturer, and competitive piano men ridiculed the Hinze far and wide as the "pickle piano." This indeed was one of the considerations that led the company to discontinue its manufacture some years ago. The Whitneys, a substantial and popular product over the years, continued to be manufactured intermittently until 1953, by which time the total production had reached 165,300.

Good times were again in evidence in 1897. Herman H. Kohlsaat's daily Chicago *Times-Herald* reported in July: "Organs are the last things farmers buy, and they usually must have money ahead before they decide to get a little music in the house. During the last three months, however, the piano and organ business among the farmers of the West has picked up wonderfully. . . . The farmers are not asking for long time. They are paying cash with the orders. The trade is so brisk that one Chicago firm is increasing its plant at a cost of $107,000."

The company, of course, was Kimball, which, Conway said, was behind on its organ orders by 500 instruments. It was preparing to occupy the new $107,000 plant that August. The Chicago retail store was really rolling: On the first Saturday in June Ed Smith and his men sold 27 pianos off the floor.

The new addition, the fifth to be erected on the sprawling eleven acres of riverside grounds, was factory E, five stories high, and it increased the total floor area by 66,000 square feet. The capacity of the whole plant and its fourteen acres of floor space was now 40 pianos and 75 organs a day. And to celebrate the expansion the Kimball baseball team invited John V. Steger's piano makers up from their South Side plant for a picnic and ball game. The normally tight-fisted W. W. Lufkin shelled out a $25 prize to inspire his factory team.

One Saturday night while this plant was in process of construction one of Chicago's sudden summer windstorms came galloping up out of the Southwest and hurled an empty eight-ton water tank off the superstructure atop the building and onto the roof. The huge tank, which had just been put in place and was to have been bricked firmly into position on Monday, crashed through and

"Put On Your Old Gray Bonnet. . . ." A tally-ho full of music teachers visits the Kimball factory in 1900. At extreme left is C. N. Kimball. Near the rear wheel with foot on step is W. W. Lufkin. Seated on step near front wheel is Pianist Emil Liebling. Beside him is Edgar C. Smith. (*Photograph reproduced through courtesy of the Piano Trade Magazine, where it appeared in May, 1942.*)

lodged on the fifth floor, breaking all the water pipes connecting the automatic sprinklers. The escaping water flooded the building, causing $4,000 damage to richly finished hardwood stocks already stored there.

Such a mishap was hardly noticed in the continuing Kimball expansion. Bill Strippelman was at his drawing board again early in 1898, and in August the firm of Landquist & Nelson began putting up another five-story brick building, Factory F, the first unit of which had floor dimensions of 80 x 250 feet. The cost was $50,-000, bringing the total expended on the plant so far to $560,000. Plant capacity was now up to 55 pianos a day, Lufkin said. In the following year factory F was extended again with the addition of another section, 80 x 150 feet, costing $35,000 and bringing the total floor space to almost eighteen acres. The two units were eventually referred to as warehouses 1 and 2. The final five-story section, which became warehouses 3 and 4, and brought the total space in factory F to 240,000 square feet, was not erected until 1903. In the meantime, the company had added another 60,000 square feet by putting up still another five-story factory and office structure, which was known as factory G.

Watching his factory expand that year, the aging W. W. Kimball remarked to his nephew: "Pretty soon, Mr. Lufkin, you're going to run through the alphabet. Then what'll we do?"

Had he lived that long Kimball would have loved building H, the pipe organ factory erected in 1907, and especially building I, the great foundry and japanning room, one story high and 10,400 square feet in area, that Strippelman began erecting in November, 1909. Completed the following spring, the foundry realized the company's longtime desire to control the manufacture of every single one of the literally hundreds of thousands of parts that went into its instruments. With a further increase sometime later of 2,000 square feet, it brought the total factory area at the end of the 20th century's first decade to 808,400 square feet.

Behind the burst of rapid expansion as the century drew to a close was a heavy increase in business, which was reflected in good black ink on the company's books. An example was the $269,-774.94 that was passed to the surplus account on January 11, 1898, when the directors met and voted to bring new family blood into the executive structure by amending the by-laws and making C. N. Kimball their first vice president. At this same meeting the founder's other up-and-coming nephew, W. W. Lufkin, was awarded the title of general superintendent, which Secretary Conway had held up to then. At the next meeting, in 1899, a strife-ridden year in Chicago piano manufacturing, the surplus was further fattened with a handsome $380,108.97.

In this same year of 1899 the Kimball company looked ahead also to an expansion on its downtown site. It was one of those shrewd moments that characterized the career of W. W. Kimball and led more than one of his contemporaries to credit him with a rare intuition. At his suggestion the directors bought the southwest corner of Wabash Avenue and Jackson Boulevard from the heirs of A. J. Averill, paying $325,000 in cash and government bonds. The company now held a frontage of 120 feet on Wabash and 109 feet on Jackson. Eighteen years later, in 1917, it would dedicate on this site a magnificent new Kimball Building, the skyscraper on whose main floor the downtown store still operates today.

The purchase of the property completed, the 71-year-old manufacturer went off with his wife to Beverly Farms, Massachusetts, to put his golf grounds in order and "limber up my joints." But not before he had instructed A. H. Fischer, who represented the company on a Committee on Stencils established by the National Piano Manufacturers' Association, to join with the other committee members in urging all piano manufacturers to end or regulate the "promiscuous" stenciling of pianos.

He would not return to Chicago until September. Albert and Ella Cone were in Europe and not due back until the end of September. Conway was at his summer home in Delavan Lake, Wisconsin, for most of the summer. With all three gone, the company's affairs were left pretty much in the hands of C. N. Kimball.

The new vice president was taking it all in stride. The only thing that bothered him was the labor difficulty some of the Chicago piano makers had been having. The Kimball company had been remarkably free of such strife. He hoped the agitation would not spread and involve him while he was holding down the hot spot on Wabash Avenue.

23

Conway. "A power in the business life of Chicago
and a Hercules in the Western music trade."

"Sam, why don't you act like a gentleman? Get your big feet
off my desk, take off your hat, and let's get this trouble over with,"
said Edwin S. Conway one day early in January, 1900, as he returned to his office after lunching with his strike-weary associates
of Music Row and found an old friend waiting.

The silk-hatted visitor to whom he gave this gentle reprimand
was Samuel Gompers, president of the American Federation of
Labor, who had come to Chicago to intervene in the longest and
biggest labor dispute ever to strike the piano and organ industry.
The agreement Conway and Gompers worked out that afternoon
served as the basis for ending a three-month lockout of 4,000 workmen by nine of the seventeen piano and organ factories then
operating in Chicago.

Labor difficulties had beset the Chicago factories all through the
prosperous year of 1899, when they had turned out 34,375 pianos
and 68,750 organs. With production up 25 per cent over the preceding year, the workers were demanding better pay and shorter

201

hours. Their leader was Charles Dold, a Socialist and onetime cigar maker who was business agent of the Piano, Organ and Musical Instrument Workers' International Union of America and who later became the president of the Chicago Federation of Labor. Following a successful strike that June at the Bush & Gerts Piano Company, where he had won a union contract, he sought to organize the other Chicago factories. This brought on a strike at the Story & Clark Organ Company plant.

All the other manufacturers knew their turn was coming.

As the *Music Trades* editor, John C. Freund, commented, "He [Dold] had a strong case. The men deserved more wages. The great majority of the manufacturers were willing to give them more. At that moment, when he had his battle won, when the general prosperity warranted a raise in wages, he injected into the issue conditions, including the absolute recognition of the union, to which no self-respecting business man could submit."

On November 4, the major factories shut their doors. Involved, besides the struck Story & Clark plant, were the Kimball company, Smith & Barnes, George P. Bent & Company, the Hamilton Organ Company, the M. Schulz Company, Julius Bauer & Company, Adam Schaaf, and Newman Brothers. Weeks before the shutdown they were agreed on meeting the workers' demands for a wage increase and a uniform nine-hour day, but they balked at the "full and complete" recognition Dold wanted.

Almost daily during that long, bleak winter the industry leaders met to discuss their troubles and map strategy. Among them were Otto Schulz of the Schulz company, E. H. Story of Story & Clark, W. H. Matchett of George P. Bent, C. A. Smith and H. P. Nelson of Smith & Barnes, William Bauer of Julius Bauer, Charles W. Newman of Newman Brothers, and E. S. Conway and W. W. Lufkin of Kimball. In November, W. W. Kimball sent his nephew C. N. Kimball to the meetings of the Illinois State Arbitration Board at the Great Northern Hotel, where the workers aired their grievances. But nothing came of this, and the dispute continued.

When Gompers moved in to seek peace in January, the Chicago

factories nominated Conway as their spokesman. The agreement they achieved was submitted to a secret meeting of the workmen on Saturday, January 6, and approved by them over the protest of Dold. It called for the union to end its Story & Clark strike, for the manufacturers to end their lockout, and for the initiation of a nine-hour day in the factories and the reinstatement of strikers without discrimination. The companies also agreed to hold meetings with the workers to adjust wages upward, but they did not accede to the union recognition demand.

Both Gompers and John B. Lennon, the A. F. of L. treasurer, announced that the strikers' aims had been "practically and substantially achieved." Dold at first refused to recognize the agreement, but later gave in. Finally the companies set Tuesday, February 6, as the date for their reopening, and the workmen began to return.

The *Indicator* said on May 6, "The Chicago piano manufacturers are once more in sight of filling orders." It added that "the strike was a good and valuable lesson to all concerned, and is well worth all that it cost as a guide for the future." The Chicago *Tribune* estimated the loss to the companies at $1,000,000. The workers' loss in wages was placed at $700,000.

To Edwin S. Conway's skill and diplomacy in handling the issues went the major credit for the settlement. The fairmindedness he showed in the conferences with his friend Gompers set the tone for the excellent labor relations the Kimball company has enjoyed almost uninterruptedly since that date. In time the piano workers' union won and honorably maintained the recognition its early leaders fought for.

While his settlement of this dispute and his role of peacemaker among the warring factions at the World's Columbian Exposition were notable achievements, they were only incidental in the more than four great decades of business leadership that Conway gave to the Kimball company.

His greatest contributions lay in the building up of a highly

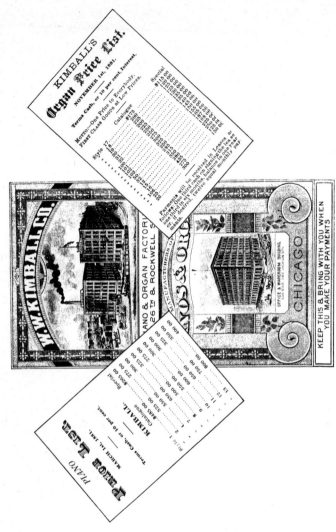

The company pioneered in installment selling, along with McCormick of reaper fame and Singer of sewing machine fame. At center is early payment book. Price lists for dealers show reductions from catalog.

effective sales organization and the development of a remarkably successful consignment sales system through which the company financed literally hundreds of dealerships it could not have otherwise had.

The consignment method grew out of the installment sales business in which W. W. Kimball pioneered in his piano and organ trade of the 1860s. It enabled the company to build up the first large-scale installment sales operations in the piano and organ industry. It provided the Kimball dealers with a substitute for capital in the days when bank credit was not readily available to them, and it was a principal factor in the financial success of the company in its first half century.

In essence it was a simple arrangement: The average dealer had little capital with which to purchase instruments. With its ample resources, the company would ship him pianos and organs on consignment. He signed an agreement under which title to the merchandise was retained by the company until it was paid for. The dealer would then collect installments from the purchaser, remitting to the company until the amount he owed was paid, at which time the title was turned back to him. Sometimes the company itself handled installment payments from the customer. In other cases the company mailed the regular monthly statements to the customer, who then would pay the dealer.

Many of the manufacturers of that period attempted to handle consignment sales, but all too often the effort proved disastrous when they became loaded up with worthless paper. The Kimball success was largely due to the method Conway developed of keeping an eye on the company's consignment interests. He made it the business of his salesmen to look after the "consignees," and they did so with such thoroughness that the company rarely suffered losses of consequence.

The Kimball travelers kept track of all dealers who held consignment goods, knew their personal and business habits, and were quick to spot phonies. If a dealer ran into difficulties in selling his wares, the Kimball man was there to help him, often with a heavily advertised special sale. As a result, the company rarely was caught by a dealer bankruptcy. The credit losses on consignment contracts rarely amounted to as much as $10,000 on millions of dollars worth of business annually, with the exception of the few depression years.

In "A Rich Heritage," a memoir of his father published in 1956, Carle Conway recalls a consignment episode in 1893 which made a lasting impression on him. He was fourteen in that depression year and had accompanied his father on a trip to Butte, Montana, to visit William C. Orton of Orton Brothers, a Kimball agency first established in the 1880s. The company had shipped three carloads of pianos to Butte, although the Ortons still owed money on previous purchases, and Conway had sent A. A. Fisher, one of his top special salesmen, to help the agency out of its difficulties.

"I remember our arrival in Butte," Carle wrote, and "the candid, almost tearful relief and gratitude with which Mr. Orton said, 'Mr. Conway, we think it's wonderful. We were broke, and you've sent out three carloads of pianos, and you've sent out a man to help us sell them, and you've provided us with a special sale, and now we're solvent again, and we're able to go ahead. . . . I think it's wonderful!'

"Father was touched, but he was also honest. I can remember his familiar gesture, turning his cigar over in his mouth, as he thought out his reply. Then he spoke with simple candor. 'Well, Will, *I* don't think it's wonderful. You know, when this depression struck, *we* were hit pretty hard, too. So we talked it over with the Governor and he said, "Well, if we don't do any business, I *know* we'll go broke. . . . So let's take the last chance. Let's take installment paper from these dealers. Let's go to the honest ones . . . and say we'll accept the installment paper that they get for the products, and we'll consign the pianos, and *we'll* do business *until* we go broke because there's no other choice. If we don't do business we're *bound* to go broke." '

". . . And that was really the start of the installment piano business as far as this company, the W. W. Kimball Company, was concerned. I think *that* experience, more than any other, is why they forged ahead so fast in the years that followed."

Actually, as has already been noted, the consignment business originated much earlier than Carle Conway supposes. But, as he added in his account, it was the Butte experience that prompted him in 1933—forty years afterward—to bail out the customers of his Continental Can Company by mailing out "six or eight million dollars in cash in thirty days after the banks closed" in another great depression. He credited the Kimball philosophy with having saved Continental Can in 1933, just as it did the Kimball company in 1893.

Edwin S. Conway in his prime was described by O. L. Fox as "a power in the business life of Chicago and a Hercules in the Western music trade." A stalwart man, six feet two, he was handsome, even debonair; a leader admired by his salesmen; a perfect mixer and a popular public speaker within and without the music trades. When a problem arose, George Hadley recalls, he would remove the inevitable cigar from his mouth and "grind his teeth like a horse while he paced back and forth in his office."

A man of great dignity, he could chuckle over his own awkward moments. John Harbison, a Kimball accountant who joined the company on November 1, 1900, and still is on the home office staff, recalls that one day Conway went out with a drayman to repossess a reed organ from a second-floor flat. As the two of them carried the organ down an outside stairway, the drayman in front and the Kimball executive following behind, the irate woman of the house kicked Conway in the rear every step of the way to the ground.

In his office, he more often than not sat with his feet on his desk. F. S. Shaw, then president of the Cable Company, said in 1904 that Conway told him he was best earning money for Kimball when he sat thus, apparently doing nothing. His big feet, incidentally, were a joke throughout the trade. One day, as Conway walked down the street in Dallas, Texas, a bootblack stepped up and asked, "Shine?" Conway looked down at his muddy shoes, and so did the boy, who stared in disbelief at the shoes and then back at his half a box of blacking. "Come off," he said, "I ain't doing business on a losing basis." And he started to run, until Conway lured him back with the promise of an extra dime.

Conway traveled widely to maintain the company's first-hand contacts with dealers and their problems. James V. Sill recalls: "It was not unusual for Conway to begin a trip to the Pacific Northwest by wiring the Kimball dealer in Milwaukee to board the train there and ride with him to Minneapolis. The Minneapolis dealer would ride with him to Fargo. Then the Bismarck dealer would board the train and accompany him to Butte. He could transact a whale of a lot of business in a short time in this way."

Devoted to his family, Conway on many occasions arranged his business trips so as to combine them with the family's vacations. Once they went to Alaska, and in 1898, while the boys Earle E. and Carle C. were away at college, the Conways took their daughter Sybil with them on a tour of Europe.

"He was one of the first men in the trade," one biographer reported, "to recognize the value of co-operative effort through association work. He was active in organizing local trade associations, and was one of the founders of the Chicago Piano Manufacturers' Association and at one time their president. He was also a charter member of the National Piano Manufacturers' Association and served one term as its president. His sane counsel was sought on every occasion when the manufacturers' association had any knotty problem to solve."

On October 5, 1896, Conway was honored by the home office staff and other Chicago friends who gave him a chest of table silver on the twenty-fifth anniversary of his first connection with the company. At the ceremonies, Albert Cone said of his long relationship with Conway, "I can conscientiously say that not one impatient word has ever passed between us."

The signers of the remembrance card that went with the gift were W. W. Kimball, A. G. Cone, Curtis N. Kimball, W. W. Lufkin, E. B. Bartlett, F. Wight Neumann, E. C. Smith, C. C. Dunbar,

Luke Yore, J. B. Thiery, John Farley, E. R. Blanchard, H. A. Wise, L. A. Dozois, J. R. Pollock, R. E. Davis, S. J. McCormick, E. A. Groff, R. C. Sweet, E. A. Cox, H. B. Rennolds, L. H. Barnitt, C. F. Balch, W. T. Bradbury, George E. Alley, C. C. Tuller, Nannie Dartnell, Emil Liebling, Frank P. Whitmore, H. N. Kanagy, J. O. Twichell, Frederic W. Hedgeland, John W. Northrop, William Bates Price, George Schleiffarth, L. A. Crittenton, H. Briggs, C. E. Conibear, H. L. Goodrow, Mary M. Kelly, E. S. Fink, Miss Regan, Miss Cloyd, W. H. Cotter, Miss Butts, Miss Rogers, and Miss Murphy.

As a personal friend of Presidents McKinley, Taft, and Theodore Roosevelt, Conway was a frequent White House visitor over many years. The Kimball company's rivals were astonished and chagrined in March, 1897, when the *Musical Times* quoted a Washington Sunday paper's report that President McKinley had selected a Kimball grand piano for the Blue Room of the White House. It was a personal triumph for Conway and his friendship with McKinley; and the *Indicator* rubbed it in by proclaiming: "The Kimball piano will be the piano of McKinley's administration.... The political field has not been until now cultivated, and the finest and richest plum of all—the endorsement of the administration—has just been gathered."

When the news reached Chicago, Conway was in Washington. But W. W. Kimball blandly told reporters:

"Mr. McKinley seems to be a man of rare judgment, and of course he ordered a Kimball piano. I wouldn't say anything about it if I were in your place, for it might look as though we were seeking an advertisement out of it—and we would dislike to be so misjudged.

"Mr. McKinley wanted the best piano money could buy and naturally he selected a Kimball. That's all there is to it."

In 1901, Secretary Conway saw his son Earle elected to the board of directors at the annual meeting of the Kimball company. It was in that year also that he acquired the title of Colonel, which would stay with him the rest of his life, by being appointed to the honorary post on the staff of Governor Yates of Illinois. And it was also in that year that Colonel Conway mistakenly predicted: "Reed organs will never die out."

When W. W. Kimball died in 1904, Colonel Conway was urged by the stockholders to assume command of the company. But he declined the presidency at the annual meeting on January 10, 1905, in favor of C. N. Kimball, and assumed Kimball's post as vice president, "feeling that the time had come when it was right that younger men and the larger stockholders in the company should fill the more active offices." Earle was made secretary in his father's place, and held the post until July 28, 1905, when he resigned as a director and as secretary to take over Hallet & Davis with his brother, Carle.

Colonel Conway remained in active command of the sales force until he began a semi-retirement in 1914.

Just before W. W. Kimball's death, Conway had summarized the company's activities for the preceding three years as follows: "In October, 1902, our company commenced to clean house because a resting spell was due. We cleaned house in 1903 and 1904, after the slump that began early in 1903. As early as September 1, this year, the slump began to show signs of abating. We are now planning four or five years of good trade ahead. Everybody may have to hustle harder for business, but there is plenty of it in sight if you are of a mind to go after it."

In the "resting spell" emphasis had been placed on collecting accounts, closing up lapsed contracts, and getting partial payment paper rather than in making long lists of sales.

That the housecleaning was indeed profitable is evident from the earnings reports of these years. In 1901 the earnings were 39 per cent on the capital stock, with $250,776.78 passed on to surplus; in 1902 the earnings were 40 per cent, with $315,081.42 placed in surplus; in 1903 the figures were 20 per cent and $577,568.85.

By January 8, 1907, Vice President Conway could report to the stockholders and put on the record the following summary:

"Accounts receivable, including branch stores and roadmen,

January 1, 1906, was $644,083. In that account was $47,000 pipe organs, which has been transferred since into lease account, which would leave accounts receivable, figured on the same basis as now, January 1, 1906, $597,083.

"Accounts receivable the first of January, 1907, including branch stores and roadmen, is $566,684, showing a decrease during the year of $30,399."

This he considered "a showing indeed not unsatisfactory, when we take into account that the highwater mark of commercial expansion was reached about July 1, 1906, since which date our energies were bent largely to drawing in our business and weeding out all questionable accounts, the result being that we enter the year 1908 with a minimum of outstanding accounts, and our general business very healthy, notwithstanding the condition of the country. All things considered, I look on the results obtained in 1907 as satisfactory. I hardly dare hope for as good a showing for the year 1908. In my judgment we will not see a noticeable change for the better before the middle of 1909. Prior to the slump of last October we had enjoyed ten years of phenomenal industrial prosperity, and when the pendulum swings it usually goes farther than we wish. However, I look on these dips as essential, and with our large capital, splendid organization and no indebtedness, we have a right to believe that we will get more than our share of the business of the country during a period of restricted general business. We are to be congratulated on the showing of the year 1907." After a 30 per cent dividend, there was $199,285.68 available to be placed in surplus.

The company's profit showing was improved in 1908 after a slow start in the first few months and was made without expanding the amount of accounts receivable. There was enough on hand to pay a $479,200 dividend (40 per cent) to the stockholders on January 12, 1909, and to put $225,090.12 in the surplus account.

At the 1911 meeting a $431,280 dividend (36 per cent) was voted and $205,342.70 was placed in surplus. The next profit figures announced were at the annual meeting of January 12, 1914, when a

27 per cent dividend of $323,806 was declared and $143,302.79 was added to the surplus.

It was at this meeting that Colonel Conway submitted a request dated September 3, 1913, which stated that after 42 years of continuous service with the Kimball organization he had decided to withdraw from active work at the end of 1913 and devote a part of his time to travel and recreation.

His wishes were accepted by the directors, who granted him a leave of absence, expressing the hope that he would be with them whenever possible and give them counsel and fellowship. On the Colonel's motion, the charter and by-laws were amended to create a second vice presidency, to which E. B. Bartlett was elected. Bartlett had been serving as a director and secretary of the company since Earle Conway's leavetaking in 1905. His place as secretary was filled by the election of George L. Hadley, the brother-in-law of President C. N. Kimball.

On February 22, following this action, Colonel and Mrs. Conway left for a three-month European tour with their good friend, J. C. Stubbs, vice president of the Southern Pacific Railroad in charge of legal matters.

For the next few years, Colonel Conway spent most of his efforts in the company's behalf traveling around to the various branch houses and among the dealers, assisting them with the new elements—the player piano and the talking machine—which were revolutionizing the business. High prices and the war in Europe were also having their effect. By 1917 the Kimball earnings were down to $108,000 and after payment of this nine per cent dividend in January, 1918, there was a piddling $12,861.77 left to add to surplus.

Colonel Conway, visiting W. B. Roberts Jr.'s Kansas City branch with W. H. Cotter in November, 1917, observed: "Like all other industries throughout the country, despite high prices the piano and talking machine businesses [he had ceased to even talk about the reed organ] are being forced to attempt to meet demands that only the war spirit of a nation could have brought about."

Raw materials, the machinery of industry, and most of the labor supply were given over to war needs.

"It is a patriotic move," Conway added, "and the man who grieves because he cannot meet the demands of his trade . . . the man who bemoans and whines over the loss of the big profits he would otherwise be able to take advantage of, is unpatriotic and of a selfishness almost greater than that of the bond slacker, and he should be repressed."

The next year, 1918, was somewhat better for the company, with earnings up to 12 per cent, or $144,000, and a surplus of $151,-480.93. And in 1919 the company boosted its earnings to 21 per cent, paying $252,000 in dividends and putting a whopping $457,-845.48 in the surplus account on January 13, 1920.

Colonel Conway died before this meeting, on Tuesday, November 4, 1919. He had been ill for six months in his two-story frame home at 226 Maple Avenue in Oak Park, just west of Chicago, where he had lived for forty years. The funeral was held at 2 o'clock on the following Friday afternoon.

The *Oak Parker* mourned him in an editorial, "When a Good Man Passes On," which said, in part, "Before and fundamental to all other community assets is the wealth and glory of good citizenship. Oak Park just now suffers the loss of one, in the person of E. S. Conway, who was for many years an active, vital, personal power for civic and social righteousness. . . . There is no community wealth measured by the standards of gold or silver that compares with the sterling qualities of the type of manhood and citizen lived in our community by Mr. Conway."

In addition to his years with Kimball, first as secretary then as vice president, he had served for years as president of the Cicero Water, Gas and Electric Company, and at one time as president of the Chicago, Fort Madison & Des Moines Railroad, later purchased by the Burlington. He was a member of the First Baptist Church of Oak Park and the Oak Park and Marquette clubs, the Delavan Country Club of Delavan Lake, Wisconsin, the Chicago Athletic Association, the Press Club of Chicago, and the Union

213

League Club of Chicago. A founder of the Cicero Lodge (later Edwin Stapleton Conway Lodge) of the Odd Fellows, he was a principal promoter of the Odd Fellows Home in Lincoln, Illinois.

The directors on January 13, 1920, named W. W. Lufkin to succeed Conway as first vice president. Lufkin retained his post as general superintendent for the company. E. R. Blanchard, who had served as auditor since Albert Cone's death in 1900, was named treasurer to succeed Lufkin, who had held the treasurer's title since 1911. (The treasurership was vacant from Cone's death until 1910, when Secretary Bartlett was elected to fill it. He resigned in Lufkin's favor a year later.)

24

"The great business built up by his sagacity is the best monument to the genius that distinguished his career."

DESPITE THEIR long years of intimate relationship in the music business, it was typical of W. W. Kimball to write to Edwin S. Conway on Saturday, September 8, 1900, from the Hotel Stephanie in Baden-Baden a letter that began with a formal salutation:

> My Dear Mr. Conway,
>
> Your letter was received and read with much pleasure. Was glad to hear from you.
>
> My face will be turned towards home. Leave for Paris Sunday night and sail on the steamer *Deutschland* on the 15th. Expect to be in Chicago on or before the first.
>
> I shall be glad to get back. To see you all. And with [regards] to yourself and family, I am
>
> Sincerely yours,
> W. W. KIMBALL.

In the summer of 1904, on the eve of another departure for Europe, Mr. Kimball was stricken with a dropsical condition and confined to the great French chateau at 1801 Prairie Avenue. In

215

the long months that followed, literally hundreds of old friends in and out of the company visited his bedside to cheer him along. Although he joked about his friend Jordan the undertaker, "waiting like a vulture" to grab him off, he knew the end was near.

On Friday afternoon, December 16, at 5 o'clock, William Wallace Kimball, the 76-year-old dean of the Chicago music trade, drew his last breath. An era of musical greatness was at an end.

The funeral services were held in the Kimball home at 2 o'clock on the following Sunday afternoon with the Reverend W. O. Waters of Grace Episcopal Church in charge. They were simple and unostentatious, "as it had been the great desire of W. W. Kimball," said the *Indicator,* "that his funeral should be in accord with the principles on which he had based his life." Telegrams of condolence poured in from all over the world. The floral offerings were abundant and costly.

Among Mr. Kimball's good friends attending the service were the following, all of whom went with the funeral cortege to Graceland Cemetery as honorary pallbearers: Marshall Field, E. S. Conway, H. H. Porter, Henry Dibblee, C. W. Butterfield, Lambert Tree, Robert Todd Lincoln, Robert Hall McCormick, Eugene S. Pike, J. J. Glessner, Watson Blair, Charles H. Deere, and Augustus H. Eddy. The active pallbearers were all business associates: Carle C. Conway, E. B. Bartlett, Edgar C. Smith, E. R. Blanchard, L. A. Dozois, C. C. Dunbar, H. A. Wise, and W. H. Cotter.

On the following Wednesday afternoon at 2 o'clock the Chicago Piano and Organ Association held a special memorial service at the Wellington Hotel. Resolutions in honor of Mr. Kimball were offered by a committee including F. S. Shaw, George P. Bent, J. P. Byrne, George B. Armstrong, and W. L. Bush. Shaw, Bush, Bent, Byrne, and Platt P. Gibbs spoke brief eulogies.

In their resolution the manufacturer's colleagues said, "He was one of the heroic types of Western development. . . . What Jonas Chickering meant to the manufacturing field, W. W. Kimball was in the field of commercialization—a pioneer. He first proved that pianos of excellent quality can be made rapidly and sold rapidly.

It was he who first placed the methods of the piano industry on a plane identical with that occupied by the great industries of the country."

They took note also that in 1904 the production of Kimball pianos, reed organs, and pipe organs would total 40,000 units and that the company's payroll numbered 1,500 employes.

Final tributes were also prepared by the several organizations in which Mr. Kimball had maintained a membership—the Chicago Club, the Calumet Club, the Washington Park Club, the Wheaton Club, the Illinois and national manufacturers' associations, and the Essex County Club of Massachusetts.

The will of W. W. Kimball was filed in Probate Court in Chicago in January, 1905. It named Curtis N. Kimball as his executor.

To Evalyne M. Kimball was bequeathed $1,800,000 in stocks and bonds (other than Kimball company stock), together with the Prairie Avenue mansion. A codicil provided an additional $100,-000 for the widow. The will also provided that if the stocks and bonds mentioned were not enough to make up at market value the $1,800,000 specified, the deficiency was to be made good out of Kimball's shares of stock in the company.

Special interest was attached to the distribution of the shares of Kimball stock. To his niece from Rumford, Maine, the former Eva Kimball, then Mrs. Warren M. Salisbury, the manufacturer left the largest single block of shares—3,234. To his nephews, C. N. Kimball, who followed him as president, and W. W. Lufkin he left equal allotments of 2,383 shares. Two hundred shares were left to Virgil W. Kimball of Chicago, a son of the manufacturer's nephew William J. Kimball of Rumford.

Two brothers and three sisters of Mr. Kimball received $20,000 each. The brothers were David W., still living on the Iowa farm, and Virgil D., the father of Mrs. Salisbury, still on the old place at Rumford. The sisters were Lucy Ann Lufkin and Columbia Kimball, both of Rumford, and Elizabeth Gleason of Mexico, Maine. The widow and children of Mrs. Gleason's son Harry were left $10,000.

217

The real estate owned by Mr. Kimball, the amount of which was not specified, was left in equal shares to his widow Evalyne, his niece Eva K. Salisbury, and the nephews C. N. Kimball and W. W. Lufkin.

There was no indication in the will of the total value of the estate, although the *Indicator* said in its issue of January 2, 1909, that it was estimated at $9,000,000.

At a special meeting of the Kimball directors on December 19, 1904, a resolution of condolence was adopted. It read:

"William Wallace Kimball was a man of rare nature. He was the embodiment of gentleness, and one of the most considerate of men. This trait in his disposition endeared him to all that were in his employ, or that were connected with him in the discharge of daily tasks. Yet with all his genuine sympathy, his interest for his fellows, his unvarying courtesy and desire to minister to the comfort of those about him, he was ever the exemplar for the young in all the characteristics of the aggressive, progressive, honorable and ambitious merchant and manufacturer. No one was his superior in any of the distinctive marks by which the man of genius in trade is known, few his equal. He was the soul of honor. The great business built up by his sagacity, his earnestness of purpose, his unquenchable ambition, and his inflexible integrity is the best monument to the genius that distinguished his career.

"In this tangible manner we wish to testify to the love and esteem and admiration in which the memory of our late associate and the president of the company is held.

"Therefore be it resolved that this memorial be formally entered upon the records of the corporation and a copy, properly engrossed, be sent to the bereaved widow."

The signers were Curtis N. Kimball, Edwin S. Conway, Wallace W. Lufkin, and Earle E. Conway.

At the January 10, 1905, stockholders meeting, at which Vice President C. N. Kimball was in the chair, Mrs. Eva Salisbury was elected a director to take the place of W. W. Kimball. C. N., Colonel Conway, Lufkin, and Earle E. Conway were re-elected. In the following year, Warren M. Salisbury replaced his wife on the board. He remained in the post until his death in 1917, and Virgil W. Kimball was elected in 1918 to replace him.

Mrs. Salisbury's son, Kimball, joined the directorate in 1921, to fill the vacancy that had existed since Colonel Conway's death in 1919. He remained active until he resigned in 1948.

Mrs. W. W. Kimball continued to make news in Chicago and in Europe long after her husband's death. She spent much of her time in art galleries in London and Paris, searching out the paintings that the Art Institute later inherited and the priceless jade figurines she fancied.

When she returned to her Prairie Avenue home from Europe in 1913 with her famous acquisition of Rembrandt's likeness of his father, she hung it in the reception room near the entrance. The Chicago *Tribune* commented on the "ingenious electric system" which "augments the night watchman in protecting the half million dollars' worth of paintings which comprise the Kimball collection."

Apparently she used more care in protecting the paintings than she did in guarding her expensive jewels. Several times in her latter years her losses of gems became, as the Chicago *Evening Journal* put it, "a topic of discussion in Chicago's society circles." Once, while returning from a dinner at the Marshall Fields, she somehow became separated from a $1,500 brooch. This was in 1908, at about the same time that she was reported to have lost diamonds valued at $10,000. Later she reported that the brooch had been returned. On the evening of December 6, 1911, she lost a $1,500 diamond-studded pendant while leaving the Auditorium Theater after a grand opera performance. The loss did not seem to concern her, said the *Journal*. She had not notified the police.

"I put an ad in the paper," she said. "I haven't received any answers yet, but I may get returns later."

There is no indication in the record that anyone ever claimed the reward she offered.

Art collectors of her day credited her with extraordinary shrewdness in raiding the European galleries. When she obtained Millet's "The Shepherdess" for $75,000 it was said to be worth twice as much. The $150,000 she paid for Turner's "Dutch Fishing Boats" was reported to be much less than it was actually worth.

In October, 1919, when she was 79, her brother Irving H. Cone of Los Angeles filed a petition before Judge Henry Horner in Probate Court, asserting that she was incapable of managing her affairs and asking that a conservator be named for the estate, "which amounts to not more than $1,000,000." A companion, Miss Alice Voight, had lived with her at the Prairie Avenue mansion since Mr. Kimball's death. The Northern Trust Company and John H. Coulter, an attorney, were named conservators, and Mrs. Kimball went away with her companion for a rest.

In April, 1920, while Mrs. Kimball was out of the city, Coulter informed the Art Institute that it could take the famous Kimball art collection and put it on display for the public.

"After her death the collection will go to the Kimball heirs, of whom there are about a dozen," he announced. "If Mrs. Kimball made a will years ago, giving the collection to the institute, then of course, it will remain there. The jades and gems are in the vault of the Northern Trust Company and, as far as I know, will remain there."

An inventory of the home showed the estate to be valued at $2,800,000, or $1,800,000 more than Irving Cone had estimated in his petition. Mrs. Kimball had $2,318,673 in cash, stocks and bonds. Par value of the stock was placed at $1,546,700. The mansion was estimated at $42,500. Its contents were placed at $389,626, and the jewelry at the bank was estimated at $43,642. The paintings were valued at $333,240, although William V. O'Brien of the O'Brien Art Gallery immediately protested that they would bring $1,000,-000 at auction.

In October, 1920, Mrs. Kimball returned to her beloved home and became sunk in inconsolable grief upon finding her prized paintings missing. She looked at the great empty walls, where her priceless art works had hung, and wept. They were not only the masterpieces in whose quest she had spent years of effort. They were a part of her memorable years with W. W. Kimball, a link with the days of her youth, with happy hours in Italy, France and Spain—days of splendor and rich excitement in which the whole world of art and beauty had been her happy hunting ground. Her sorrow, it seemed, was more than her 80 years could bear.

When Judge Horner, who had permitted the transfer of paintings to the institute, heard of her black despair, he sent for her; and in what was said at the time to be one of the most unusual court actions ever recorded in Cook County, he reversed his decision and ordered the Art Institute to return Mrs. Kimball's paintings to the old home on Prairie Avenue. There they remained for the rest of her life.

Evalyne M. Kimball died on June 13, 1921, following an attack of pneumonia. At her funeral the pallbearers included twenty-three prominent Chicagoans: Charles L. Hutchinson, John A. Spoor, Martin A. Ryerson, Watson Blair, Edward Blair, Clarence Young, Orson Smith, Solomon A. Smith, Dr. A. R. Reynolds, John J. Mitchell, Samuel Insull, W. J. Chalmers, John S. Runnels, Henry H. Porter, Eugene R. Pike, Charles C. Pike, Dr. Frank Billings, Cyrus H. McCormick, Frank O. Lowden, A. C. Bartlett, Stanley Field, Harold A. Howard, and A. A. Sprague.

The Art Institute was quick to speak up. "We hope eventually to acquire the Kimball collection," said Clarence A. Hough, its comptroller. For some years he had been sending the institute's hanger regularly to the Kimball home, as its owner experimented with various vantage points from which to view her prizes. Mrs. Salisbury merely said, "Mrs. Kimball did not speak at any time regarding the disposal of her paintings. I do not know if she has bequeathed them to the Art Institute."

A few days later, on June 21, the will was filed in Probate Court. It left the paintings to the institute; and though a codicil stated that they were to be left with Mrs. Salisbury through her lifetime, the niece immediately announced she would relinquish that right.

The estate was valued finally at $2,640,000, of which $2,600,000 was in personal property and $40,000 in real estate. Perpetual trust funds were set up for three charities—the Newsboys' and Boot-blacks' Association, $100,000; Children's Memorial Hospital, $50,000; and the Visiting Nurse Association, $50,000. Eighteen persons among the beneficiaries had died since the will was first written in 1912. Among them were Stephen McGrath, the mail carrier on Prairie Avenue for many years. A maid and a butler who were left $5,000 apiece had forfeited their bequests by falling in love and becoming Mr. and Mrs. John Farley.

The principal beneficiary was Mrs. Salisbury, who not only received the residuary estate but the $100,000 bequeathed to her husband, Warren M., who had died in 1917. Their son, Kimball, received $100,000, as did Mrs. Josephine Noble of Chicago, a niece of Mrs. Kimball. The brother Irving received only a trust estate, from which he would receive the annual income of $200,000.

A court contest, charging undue influence, was shortly begun by several of the heirs, including Irving Cone and Mrs. Noble, but it lost out and was finally abandoned in 1922.

A curious footnote to Mrs. Kimball's will was recorded in 1955 with the publication of Arthur Meeker Jr.'s "Chicago, With Love." Mrs. Kimball made a $5,000 bequest to the senior Arthur Meekers, who were Prairie Avenue friends and neighbors. Their son, who has long lived in Europe, wrote: "Old Mrs. W. W. Kimball . . . sticks in my mind because she once showed us children the collection of 'Old Masters' she kept in her Renaissance castle—one, of course, of each master. Her collection of nieces was locally just as celebrated; towards the end of her life she imported a series of them in turn from the East to serve as companions, sending them back to be credited—as though they'd been parcels from Field's—when they proved unsatisfactory. Finally one stuck and became her heir."

Mrs. Salisbury's inheritance brought about a realignment in the interests of the major stockholders of the Kimball company. As of December 27, 1922, following an increase in the capital stock from

$1,200,000 to $2,500,000, the three principal holders were President C. N. Kimball, with 6,317 shares; W. W. Lufkin, 6,469, and Mrs. Salisbury, 5,160. The capital stock was again increased in 1924 to $4,000,000.

Following the death of Mrs. Salisbury on October 31, 1945, her personal secretary and financial adviser, Miss Helen C. Dillon, was named trustee under her will. Miss Dillon was elected to the directorate in 1947 and withdrew the interests of the Eva K. Salisbury estate in the following year, at the time Kimball Salisbury withdrew. The holdings of these interests at that time were: the estate of Eva K. Salisbury, 3,459 shares, and Kimball Salisbury, 3,635. No member of the Salisbury group ever assumed active participation in the operations of the company, aside from their activities as members of the board.

For many years Mrs. Salisbury divided her time between her home at 1100 Lake Shore Drive in Chicago and her magnificent summer residence, Tor Court, in the Berkshires on the east shore of Onota Lake, at Pittsfield, Massachusetts. One of its features was a Kimball pipe organ.

Kimball Salisbury was one of the many Kimballites to see active service in World War II. He entered the naval service as an ensign, became a lieutenant commander and in 1943 was placed in command of the naval aircraft training base at St. Augustine, Florida. Now retired, he lives in the Chicago suburb of Lake Forest.

25

"It was amazing! People would rush into the store and say, 'This is mine! This is mine!'"

Dᴇꜱᴄʀɪʙɪɴɢ Colonel Edwin S. Conway's "great selling organization," Arthur Loesser noted in "Men, Women and Pianos" that a Kimball salesman, writing in 1880, "said that he had sold their instruments for fourteen years all over the 'West' and that the name of Kimball was as familiar there as that of Grant."

Among the great salesmen of the company's peak years none was more widely known than A. A. Fisher, the expert on "special sales" and the father of Bud Fisher, the cartoonist, whose real name was Bud Conway (after the Colonel) Fisher.

Fisher joined the Kimball company in 1876 and under Conway developed into a sales and advertising genius who struck terror into the hearts of his competitors with his technique for special sales. His greatest period of activity was in the 90s, when he traveled about the country staging these events to clean out the stocks of stagnant stores.

A typical exploit was the sale he conducted in December, 1895, for Arthur E. Whitney, who operated Whitney's Music Store at 97 East Third street, St. Paul, Minnesota, from 1882 until hard times forced him to shut his doors in March, 1894. Whitney had stored about one hundred pianos and operated for more than a year as a wholesale agent for Kimball in Minnesota. But in December, 1895, he still had the one hundred pianos on his hands in St. Paul, and Conway assigned Fisher to the task of helping him unload.

Renting the old C. O. Rice & Company store at 140-142 East Sixth Street, opposite the Ryan Hotel, Fisher installed the Whitney stock and put up his special signs. Then he inserted a column-long reading notice in a Sunday edition of the St. Paul *Pioneer*, heading it: "ANOTHER TERRIBLE FALL. Five Hundred Go to the Bottom with a Crash. In their Maker's hands—One Hundred of Them to Be Executed in St. Paul, and the Slaughter Begins Monday—The Most Remarkable Undertaking Ever Attempted by One Man."

The advertisement proclaimed that as a general wholesale agent of the Kimball company he had been authorized to sell 500 new upright pianos "at the exact manufacturer's wholesale cost" and that St. Paul had been chosen to receive 100 of them. He added that "at the end of six days they will either go to Chicago in my pocket or in a box."

John H. Whitney, the son of Arthur E., was only fifteen at the time, but he watched the phenomenal operation, and he recalled in 1956 that the store was sold out "to the bare walls" before the week was over.

"It was amazing," he said. "People would rush into the store and put their hands on a piano possessively and say, 'This is mine! This is mine!'

"My dad had a lot of sheet music on hand. Other dealers came in and bought it up by the foot. Dad would stack the music on the counter, grab a ruler and measure it off. Sometimes a dealer would stick his hand over and press down to be sure he got full measure."

Following the St. Paul sale, Arthur Whitney rested for a while and, as times got better, began an adaptation of the Fisher methods by moving from town to town, opening a store, running it until he had exploited all its immediate possibilities, and then shutting it down to open another store in some other town. Among the towns in which he operated, John recalls, were Duluth, Minnesota; Superior, Wisconsin, and Ironwood, Ishpeming, Bessemer, and Marquette, Michigan—in a line across the iron and copper mining country at the south end of Lake Superior from Duluth to Sault Ste. Marie, Michigan. New merchandise was offered in these special sales, which lasted from four to seven weeks in each town. The process was to open a regularly licensed piano store to avoid local restrictions against transient business. Newspapers and handbills advertised the wares, and installment contracts were offered, although they were carefully screened against potential losses.

John Whitney later tried the special sale technique himself in Ishpeming, opening a store in December, 1916, and expecting to close out in six months. He stayed eight years and in the meantime had opened a second store. R. M. Brown and William E. Day, both Kimball special salesmen, closed these stores out for him in 1924. After that he moved to Minneapolis and for about four years operated one or two special sales a year in Ishpeming and Negaunee, Michigan, until he retired in 1928.

The A. A. Fisher technique aroused the industry all through the middle 90s. In Fort Wayne, Indiana, where he staged a sale in March and April, 1894, a group of local music dealers publicly attacked him in a libelous newspaper announcement which said, "The Fort Wayne public has been amazingly gulled during the past week by a piano sale which is being conducted at the Arcade after the fashion of a fake clothing sale which strikes the city every once in a while." Then, after a column of abuse of the Kimball piano, the dealers said:

"Where will the buyer find Mr. Fisher, in thirty days after a sale is made, when the piano is warped, the glue cracks off [indicating that they were varnished with glue], the action falls to pieces, the case splits down the back, or the strings snap into a jumble with every change of weather? . . . The Fort Wayne piano dealers are responsible when they say that the public is being mercilessly skinned. . . ."

Fisher struck back and demanded a retraction. He got it from both the Kyle Music Company and Jacobs & Conklin, two of the more prominent dealers involved, as well as from the Fort Wayne *Morning Journal,* which had published the defamatory material.

Freund's Musical Weekly later commented that "in the many vigorous personal attacks upon Fisher he not only held his own ably but compelled his traducers to openly apologize for their interference. The weaker dealers he did not consider as at all worthy of his steel, and before they knew just how they stood they found themselves on quicksands, from which they scurried in mortal fear. The whole incident goes to show that interference with a man who knows what he is about, and has courage enough to carry out his plans, is utterly foolish and reacts upon its progenitors."

Musical Times described the Fisher methods as "contemptible." And Marc A. Blumenberg's *Musical Courier,* now leaning to the side of Kimball, after years of bitter attacks, deplored the Fisher methods and called him "an element that produces strife" but at the same time said: "They had no business, no moral right to attack him; he did not attack them. In every case that the future will bring forth, Fisher will win if he is attacked!" It exhorted local dealers to meet the Fisher sales methods with "high-toned, intellectual doses of scientific advertising and competition."

Presumably the mildness of the Blumenberg attack was occasioned by the fact that at this time he was, as *Music Trades* said in 1898, practicing his "organized blackmail" against W. W. Kimball.

Incidentally, it was not until 1902 that justice finally caught up with the notorious *Courier* editor. It came when the great Victor Herbert sued him for libel after a vitriolic attack in the issue of July 17, 1901, had accused the composer of plagiarizing comic operas. The case went to trial in October, 1902, and the jury awarded Herbert a $15,000 verdict, reduced to $5,158.40 on appeal.

"Everyone was happy because he had won and everyone admired his courage in bringing suit," wrote Edward N. Waters in "Victor Herbert: A Life in Music," published in 1955. "The ill repute of the *Musical Courier* was extraordinary, but no one had dared to attack it or correct it."

Waters describes the victory banquet that followed. On that occasion, Walter Damrosch said that Herbert's suit had "done more to break the miserable power of the *Musical Courier* than anything that has ever happened." Upon the same occasion, William Dalliba Dutton, president of the National Piano Manufacturers' Association, "described how the paper unethically gouged money from the group he represented."

Waters further cited John C. Freund's article in *Musical America* of October 29, 1898, in which the *Music Trades* editor discussed "organized blackmail" as practiced by "a certain notorious musical paper." "How?" asked Waters. "Very simple to describe. The unnamed journal would send a representative to an artist newly arrived in New York. The artist would be asked for a sum of money: if paid, favorable criticism would result; if unpaid, the artist could expect the opposite. . . .

"Freund described another method. The unnamed journal would induce a professional artist to insert an advertising card in its columns for three months. The cost would be $100 or $200, but the promised benefits seldom appeared. At the end of another term another bill would be sent, although no order had been given to continue the card. This would go on until the poor victim was billed for several hundred dollars. When he refused to pay, the journal would threaten the prevention of engagement, and bad reviews or no reviews at all. Its agent—generally a woman—would persuade the victim to settle for $200 in cash and a note for the balance. The artist, frequently with a family to provide for, usually capitulated."

Blumenberg died in Paris on March 27, 1913. The Kimball company, with the advent of C. N. Kimball to the presidency, finally withdrew all its advertising from the *Courier*. Some years after the Herbert trial, George Hadley recalls, C. N. and Mrs. Kimball "were strolling in a Baden-Baden park one morning when they espied a dejected old man sitting on a bench and realized there was something familiar about his countenance. Stepping back to make sure, lo and behold, there was the penniless Marc Blumenberg." And C. N., forgetting all that had passed before, reached into his pocket and befriended the old Kimball enemy.

Another of Kimball's special salesmen whose activity was as productive as Fisher's, although less widely publicized, was the late William H. Cotter, who worked for the company for more than fifty years. He was a distant relative of Conway. Born in Springfield, Ohio, in 1858, a year after W. W. Kimball began his business, Cotter at twenty-two took his first Kimball job as a reed organ salesman in Missouri. In 1885 he opened a branch store in Moberly, Missouri, where he remained for six years. Then Conway called him to Chicago to become a general sales traveler, which was the position he held until he retired in September, 1930.

George Hadley recalls that it was Cotter who in the late 90s developed an extensive mail order operation for the company out of his knowledge of the rural piano and organ market in the Middle West. It was about this time that the major catalog houses, Sears, Roebuck & Company, and Montgomery Ward & Company, began to offer pianos by mail. Cotter was quick to see that the Kimball company, with hundreds of local dealers throughout the country, could offer repair and tuning services the big mail order concerns were unable to provide. On the strength of this, he ran extensive mail order advertising in newspapers and farm magazines and did a thriving coupon order business until it was abandoned after the turn of the century.

Cotter's big talent, however, lay in the special sales. His advertising copy pulled out all the stops. A scrapbook of his reading notices discloses the following headlines: "PIANOS GO DOWN." "THEY ARE GOING!" "MUST BE SOLD. $5,000 WORTH OF PIANOS AND ORGANS." "WHEN WE DISCOUNT IT COUNTS." "TO QUIT BUSINESS!" "IT HURTS COMPETITORS." "IT IS POSSIBLE!" "THANKSGIVING DAY." "TERRIBLE FALL! The Burchfield Stock WILL NOT LAST LONG." "THE END HAS COME." " 'TWAS A TERRIBLE FALL." "THEY ARRIVED TOO LATE." "IT'S MUSIC FOR THE MULTITUDE."

Cotter was a loyal Kimballite to the end. His scrapbook in the archives has tucked inside it a piece of his homegrown verse on "The House of Kimball" which contains the stanza:

> Great men have lived in every age—
> Their lives are a living symbol.
> No greater merchant prince e'er lived
> Than William Wallace Kimball.

He was no Keats, this Bill Cotter, but he could sell pianos.

Another of the oldtime Kimball salesmen was Ben King, the poet-humorist of St. Joseph, Michigan, who was also an accomplished musician. John McGovern, a literary friend, wrote of one of his pieces of mimicry:

"He frowzled his hair and became Paderewski, who forthwith fell upon the piano tooth and nail, tore up the track, derailed the symphony, went downstairs and shook the furnace, fainted at the pedals and was carried out rigid by supers—the greatest pianist of any age."

The Chicago *Daily Press* said on February 17, 1892, that "Ben has probably sold more Kimball pianos than any other one man in America."

Besides traveling on the road, he spent long periods selling for Edgar C. Smith at Kimball's Chicago warerooms. His stories about his piano-selling experiences were a regular feature of the gatherings of his literary friends at the city's Whitechapel Club.

Once when he was traveling from town to town in Nebraska he was overtaken by a band of Sioux. He had a Kimball piano in his wagon, and the Indians insisted that he unload it and play for them. It was bad enough, he reported, when his playing of "Johnny, Get Your Gun" excited the red-skinned squaws to pulling his hair and embracing him with delight. But when the Sioux then carried off his piano without even signing an installment contract, it broke his heart.

Another time, after selling a Chicago woman a Kimball on the installment plan, he was surprised to find her in the store the next day in a state of mild excitement.

"I want those installments," she said, "that go with my piano."

"Your installments, madam?" asked Ben. "Why, what do you mean?"

"I bought that piano on installments, didn't I?"

"Certainly, madam!"

"Well, when your men set it up they didn't put on the installments, and that is what I have come for. Everybody knows that when the casters are set in those little glass installments, the tone is much better than if it sits on the carpet."

So Ben quickly gave her the little glass cups in which the casters were supposed to rest. And an "installment" sale was saved.

Ben had another favorite story—about the piano he sold one day to a man who was erecting a house on School Street in Chicago. It was Saturday afternoon when it was delivered, and the draymen were unable to get it through the hallway. A derrick being used in the construction was employed to lift it, with the intention of putting it into the house through a second-floor window. But the derrick stuck midway in the operation and left the piano dangling in midair all through the night and into the next day, when a big rain came down. On Monday the operation was completed, and with some trepidation the owner tried the piano for the first time.

"Great was his joy," said Ben, "to find the rain had improved its tone rather than injured it. Which just goes to show that you can't hurt a Kimball piano."

Ben King died at 37 in Bowling Green, Kentucky, one April night in 1894, after making a platform appearance with his good Chicago friend, the humorist Opie Read. At the time of his death a single volume contained all of his works, but his famous lament that there was "nothing to do but work, nothing to eat but food" has provoked chuckles wherever English is read.

King's tale of the rain-soaked Kimball has something in common with the "tornado pianos" of the 90s. In April, 1899, the Kimball company made much in a pamphlet entitled "And There Arose a Mighty Wind" of a Kimball upright that survived an April tornado in Kirksville, Missouri, with only one pedal broken. The Bush & Gerts people followed that up with a report about one of their pianos that had survived a Nebraska tornado. Later that year the *Indicator* took note of still another "cyclone piano" that had cropped up and said, "Just how many thousand feet this instrument was blown is not stated, but, like all the rest of the many cyclone pianos, it came out of the great disturbance as good as new."

Still another of the great Kimball salesmen was Gilbert Smith, a Southerner who headquartered in Atlanta, Georgia. A long, skinny, be-mustached gentleman with mutton-chop sideburns, he wore a silk hat, a high celluloid collar and narrow-cuffed trousers "that made his legs look like condensed Gothic exclamation points or a frozen-throated soprano's high C's."

Born on a Tennessee farm, Smith began selling pianos and organs in 1874 and retired in March, 1909. In the 80s and 90s, "when piano salesmen wore top hats and frock coats, carried silk umbrellas and had a sweetheart in every town," he went to Georgia to sell to the farmers. One of the favorite musical centers of the salesmen of that day was the town of Jug Tavern, now Winder, in the heart of Georgia's peanut belt.

Smith was in Washington with Conway in 1897 to attend the installation of President McKinley's Kimball grand. So excited was he by that event that he had a leather worker make him up a valise that was an exact copy in miniature of the President's piano. When rival salesmen twitted him about it, he shyly disclaimed any advertising motive and merely said he had it made in that shape because he could put his socks in it without folding them.

Maurice W. Buckley of Chicago, who retired in the summer of 1956 at 81, was one of the oldtime Kimball salesmen. From July, 1900, when he entered the company's employ, until he retired, he sold more than 25,000 pianos and organs. One of his customers paid for his piano with a bushel basket full of dollar bills. Another was a member of the Al Capone gang, although Buckley did not know until later who the buyer was.

One of the salesmen whose name is mercifully lost in the files came into the Chicago office one day shortly before W. W. Kimball's death with an order that soon had the whole Kimball Building shaking.

Nobody dared to fill it without getting the approval of the ailing company leader, and nobody dared approach him at that time for fear of upsetting him.

The story was recalled recently by Charles Washburn, author of "Come Into My Parlor," the biography of the notorious Everleigh sisters of Chicago red light fame. Here it is, just as Washburn related it to the writer:

"The gold-plated player piano in the Everleigh Club from 1905 until its closing in 1911 was made by the Stuyvesant Piano Company of New York. I owned the piano until recently.

"The Kimball company were first consulted on making them a gold player—the cost was no object—and spurned a $5,000 payment when the company learned the player was to go into a bordello and not in a home. The sisters and I have often laughed about this and both have told me how they tried to mislead Kimball officials by saying the piano was to go into a 'private conservatory of music.' Incidentally, the club did have a library, so why not a conservatory?"

26

"Anyone without musical knowledge can play the instrument."

Soon after the success of its first stationary pipe organs, the Kimball company was caught up, as was every other piano and organ manufacturer around the turn of the century, in the new rage for self-playing organs and player pianos.

Though nobody at the time could have foreseen it, these were revolutionary developments, especially as they affected the future of the piano making industry. By 1919 the players constituted more than half of the output of American piano factories, and the decline of the straight piano was well under way. But an even more important influence was at work and destined to have far-reaching consequences. Within themselves the new mechanical inventions were unwittingly feeding the flames of another revolution, which would shortly come with the tremendous upsurge in popularity of Thomas A. Edison's phonograph. The players and their offspring, the more expensive completely automatic electric reproducing pianos, were creating within the public consciousness—or subconsciousness, perhaps—a habit of passive listening to an instrument that fed the monstrous whirlwind of the phonograph revolution. And when this development was followed quickly by the perfection of the home radio and, after that, the television set, the habit so firmly seized upon by the phonograph was further solidified.

All these were crucial, if slowly unfolding, phases in the history of the W. W. Kimball Company, but with its background of decades of trial and triumph, it had learned to weather the passing storms, to study and analyze the trends of the times, to make the necessary adjustments all along the line, and to continue with steadfast purpose toward the principal goal of making a quality musical instrument at reasonable cost.

Mechanically activated or automatic musical instruments had their origins in remote antiquity. There were barrel organs, for instance, as early as the fifteenth century. Centuries of experimentation therefore lay behind the pneumatic playing mechanisms for organs and pianos developed in the late 19th century. American inventors were intrigued in 1876 when a French player-piano invention known as the "Pianista," designed by a man named Fourneaux, was exhibited at the Philadelphia Centennial Exposition. Spurred by this imperfect gadget, they were soon at work on their own designs.

As early as 1880 the idea of a paper-roll playing mechanism was applied to the old parlor reed organ, and by the 90s any number of cabinet type "push-up" mechanisms had been developed for attachment to the straight piano.

The first hint of the Kimball company's interest in these machines came in 1896 when *Music Trades* ran a brief Chicago dispatch, dated August 27, which reported that Frederic W. Hedgeland, the Kimball organ expert, had just completed the company's first electric piano. "The instrument is a marvel and will astonish the trade when it gets on the market," the paper added. The report, however, was a bit premature; the Kimball piano player was five years away.

It was in the Kimball organ that the Hedgeland patents on player mechanisms were first employed commercially. These patents dated from March 8, 1892, and were embodied in a self-playing organ placed on the market in 1897.

"The latest improvement," the company said, "consists of a most ingenious pneumatic device which may be placed on either pipe or reed organs, rendering them self-playing without interfering with the regular use of the instrument by the organist. Anyone without musical knowledge can play the instrument and control its expression, variety and power by the use of paper music rolls, the notes in which are perforated or cut by direct electrical connection with the keyboard of an instrument while being played by a skilled performer, thus reproducing in the perforated roll the interpretation of an artist."

The first of these instruments was installed in Kimball Hall for public demonstration.

For a time in 1897, the Aeolian Organ Company of New York City, which was busy on its own developing similar player mechanisms and preparing to market a piano player, threatened a law suit against Hedgeland and Kimball, alleging patent infringement. But after W. B. Tremaine, Harry Tremaine, and S. A. Krause of the Aeolian company traveled to Chicago and inspected the Hedgeland devices freely at Kimball's invitation, the threat was abandoned.

The Aeolian company put its first cabinet type pedal-operated piano-playing mechanism, an invention of E. S. Votey, on the market in 1900. It called it the "Pianola," and the name caught hold and soon became a generic term for all piano players.

Kimball's entry into the field followed in September, 1901, when the "Artist-Mechanism" was introduced. It was a cabinet instrument, similar in outline to the general shape of a piano, and attachable to any piano.

It was the principal topic of conversation on August 31 as the Kimball employes held their annual picnic-excursion at Santa Fe Park. Vice President C. N. Kimball reported July and August business the largest in history. Company enthusiasm was stronger than ever after the labor difficulty of two years before; and the factory picnic committee headed by J. Heffernan whooped it up for Hedgeland's new device. Helping him were M. Nelson, A. L. Coakes, H. Prueter, J. Stoicke, S. Lamp, C. Rose, C. Lorenz, C. Ireman, A. Lunaburg, G. Thomas, K. Johnson, H. H. Lennisch, G. Whitelaw, P. Reckow, Herr Weiser, J. Sturenfeldt, D. Beatley, C. Lenartson, R. B. Murray and H. Krebs.

In a handsome booklet the company proudly described its new piano player's "sensitive and tireless fingers":

"These fingers work exactly like those of a professional manipulator, and in the matter of technique are found to have a freedom from error, a deftness and reliability of touch superior to any human hand."

Emil Liebling wrote glowingly of the Kimball's "magic fingers—fingers that actually strike the piano string as the human hand does through the key" while the "music roll guides these fingers through the delicacies and difficulties that could be conquered only by years of arduous work."

Within two years the Kimball player was becoming a staple of the trade. But there was an increasing demand for a self-contained player piano, and in the spring of 1904 the company put its first instruments of this type on the market. By 1906 the sales of the detachable cabinet players dropped off, and by the end of the decade they were fast becoming extinct.

In the depression year of 1907, piano production for the nation as a whole dropped from the 1906 peak of 251,500 to 176,000. But the vogue for player pianos continued, and 50 more manufacturers began to make them, to bring the total of makes on the market to 165.

It was in this year that the phonograph began to make its first great inroads into the piano field, with the Victor Talking Machine Company advertising in trade papers to urge piano dealers to take on its product. A typical appeal ran: "HOW MANY PEOPLE IN YOUR TOWN are able to buy a piano? How many people can buy one?

237

How many more are able to buy and to play a Victor Talking Machine? Selling pianos is all right as far as it goes, but you ought to have the Victor business too."

In 1909 the Kimball company introduced its first 88-note player piano. It was in this year also that the company shipped its 200,-000th piano, the decal for which, says George L. Hadley, "I personally designed." The company in this year also manufactured its 320,000th reed organ and its 5,000th pipe organ.

After declaring a 36 per cent dividend, $431,280, and placing $205,342.70 in the surplus account, at its annual meeting on January 10, 1911, the company, along with the 433 other U.S. piano manufacturers, began to show signs of suffering from the talking machine invasion. This was the year the first hornless phonograph appeared. At the end of the year the Kimball company rather obscurely said that the "profit on the amount of business done was up to the average in proportion to volume."

The next year, however, things were better and, although it published no figures, the company said it had enjoyed a record-breaking business. It reported a heavy growth in demand for its player pianos and its better styles of uprights. The player piano business, it said, had increased by 800 per cent in four years.

By 1915, players were still gaining, but the piano business in general was in a slump. The talking machine was really rolling, with the Aeolian company having entered the field to compete with Victor, Edison, and Columbia. P. J. Healy, the Chicago merchant, said that in his store the talking machine had already replaced the lower-priced piano, although it had increased the sales of players and top-grade pianos. The Kimball company decided it had better join the phonograph bandwagon or get lost in the shuffle.

By 1919, the tremendous vogue for players had completely swamped the straight piano field. There were 176,888 of them manufactured nationally as against 156,158 straight pianos. The peak was reached in 1923, when the total of players reached 192,-713, as against 150,337 straights.

The Kimball Story

From about 1913 to 1925 the electrically operated, completely automatic reproducing piano was a popular feature in the higher priced market, and the Kimball company produced a popular version in a grand in which the music roll was placed in a convenient drawer beneath the key-bed. It had a three-fold utility, the company said: "For use with the DeLuxe library of music rolls which automatically provide the interpretations of the masters; for playing manually—and the piano is in no way affected for this purpose by the installation of the Welte-Mignon reproducing action; and for use with straight 88-note rolls with which one makes his own expression or interpretation."

In 1932, just before the player piano went into a quick eclipse, the company bought the Welte-Tripp Organ Corporation of Sound Beach, Connecticut, along with its music roll libraries, recording devices, patents, good will, machinery, and right to manufacture. The deal was handled by William Wallace Kimball, then the head of the pipe organ department, and now the president of the company. But it soon had a white elephant on its hands, for the coming of the depression had already combined with the phonograph to deal both the player piano and the player organ a death blow. Not a single player was manufactured in the black year of 1932.

This year was, indeed, the low point for piano manufacturing in the United States, with fewer than 30,00 instruments turned out by all the factories. The decline began in the middle 1920s after a 1923 peak of 343,050 instruments—the best production record since the all-time high year of 1909, when there were 364,545 instruments manufactured. In 1927, the figure was down to 212,166 and the steady decline continued. By 1929 the total was 120,754; by 1930, it was 67,716; and in 1931 production dipped for the first time under the 50,000 mark.

The Kimball company had seen the trouble coming for the piano business when the dance craze that began around 1913 started Mr. Edison's talking machine on its dizzy climb to popularity. After six new companies in 1914 had invaded the field held tightly by Victor, Columbia, and Edison, the Kimball staff was set to work on a phonograph. The basic patents held on the Edison invention by these original members of the patent pool were expiring one by one, and the Aeolian and Sonora companies were among the first to hop in as competitors.

When C. N. Kimball gave the go-ahead on phonographs, the man to whom W. W. Lufkin turned was Albert A. Huseby, an inventive Norwegian who joined the company in 1894 after coming to Chicago to lead a band at the world's fair. His first job at the factory had been that of setting up a key-making department, of which he became the superintendent.

Old timers recall that Huseby once designed a new type of piano keyboard in which the balance rail pin was fitted into the key instead of on the rail. When Lufkin turned it down as impractical, he sold it to John Steger, who tried it without success. When Huseby came back to the factory to ask for his old job back, Lufkin put him to work in the foundry he was building. "You can be superintendent," he told Huseby, "at $35.00 a week."

The Norwegian knew nothing about a foundry and the casting of iron piano plates, but he read up on the subject and mastered the job. In time he invented many labor-saving machines that Lufkin used to advantage. Once he developed a device that would mechanically apply the seven coats of Zanzibar polish usually put on a piano by hand. In the patent papers, he named a revolving screw that he had included as one of its "unusual features." The Patent Office promptly wrote back that it was sorry about his not being able to patent this device, but Archimedes invented the screw.

Huseby's keen, quick ability to master new fields prompted Lufkin to give him the important assignment to develop a Kimball phonograph. The first thing he did was to write to Thomas A. Edison and ask him why the vibration of a needle on a diaphragm would reproduce the human voice. Edison replied cagily that he wished he knew.

The first of Huseby's phonograph patents was filed on December 17, 1915—No. 1,198,636; and although the first perfected instrument was not shipped out until June 26, 1917, the company showed a pilot model publicly in September, 1916.

Back of that long delay was another Huseby invention—"the swinging tone arm"—which failed. As the early model was first described by the company, "The motor board is slotted where the tone arm goes into the cabinet, allowing the arm to swing freely. After placing a record on the turntable, the operator simply swings the tone arm toward the center pin to a point where the needle is directly over the last groove in the record. The automatic stop knob on the front is then turned until it stops, the tone arm is swung back to the outer edge of the record, and the machine is ready to play."

Huseby was proud of this device, and when he first demonstrated it he called in George B. Lufkin, Edwin S. Conway, C. N. Kimball, Edgar Smith, W. W. Lufkin, E. B. Bartlett, Frank P. Whitmore, Eugene Whelan, and others of the big brass to watch.

All were enthusiastic except Conway, who said: "No, the damned thing won't work."

Despite this warning, the new Kimball phonograph, style 135, complete with "swinging tone arm," was introduced and sent to dealers all over the country. Just as Conway had predicted, "the damned thing" was a failure: the tone arm was so sensitive it skipped grooves all over the record. All the instruments had to be called back in while Huseby went looking for a ready-made substitute.

In time the perfected Kimball phonograph took its place in the market as an outstanding instrument, equal in workmanship, tone, beauty, and ease of operation to any of its rivals. The *Indicator* made special mention of its "very exceptional case work," which was in oak, mahogany and walnut.

In a variation on Victor's "His Master's Voice" illustration of a dog listening to a talking machine horn, the Kimball ad men dreamed up a picture that was called "Baby's First Opera." It showed a little girl standing with her ear close to the tone chamber of a Kimball phonograph. On her innocent face was a look of wonderment, which was supposed to impress viewers with the naturalness of tone she heard. Below the picture was the caption: "I want to see the lady come out."

Ben F. Duvall, a former vice president who spent 31 years with the Kimball company before resigning in 1955, recalls that in the phonograph's heyday the company shipped whole carloads at a time. Production was often up to 350 a week. Turntables were purchased in $40,000 quantities at a time as the sales soared.

"And it was all high-profit merchandise," adds Duvall.

The last Kimball phonographs left the factory on October 24, 1925. In the eight-year period of their manufacture the company sold 56,999 instruments, along with millions of records, which were a big item of business in the Kimball branch stores.

After the phonograph splurge was over, the remaining cabinet stock was converted to the manufacture of a Kimball radio, discontinued in the 30s. The company was not equipped to manufacture radio parts, and its radio operations consisted of installing chassis which it obtained from the Federal Radio Corporation of Buffalo, New York.

27

The Old Guard. "It was one of C. N. Kimball's great sources of strength."

C. N. KIMBALL's 31-year span as the second president of the W. W. Kimball Company was the transitional period between the old order and the new, between the vast 19th-century manufacturing and selling organization that just grew, like Topsy, in the great age of the commercial piano and the modernized version of today.

From the beginning, the men who went to work for W. W. Kimball were in the majority of cases men who looked upon their jobs as lifetime associations. As we have noted elsewhere, the loyalty of Kimball men was widely remarked in the music trade. This was especially true of the men in the executive ranks. One of C. N. Kimball's great sources of strength was his knowledge that in his busy, often troubled years as the company's leader, he was strongly surrounded and supported by what he liked to call the "Old Guard."

The Kimball Old Guard was, loosely speaking, the executive group and the home office staff C. N. Kimball inherited at his uncle's death. With them he carried on in the long-established patterns of the business as he had learned them. The executive changes over the more than three decades of his presidency, from 1905 to 1936, were remarkably few, even for a tightly knit family-owned corporation. Some there were, indeed, who thought the changes, when they came, in Kimball's latter years, were later than they should have been.

When C. N. assumed office in 1905, his executive associates were the veteran Colonel Edwin S. Conway, vice president; Earle E. Conway, his son, secretary; W. W. Lufkin, general superintendent; and E. R. Blanchard, auditor. Later that year, when Earle Conway resigned, E. B. Bartlett was elected to fill his post, and three years later was also made treasurer. In 1911, Lufkin took over the treasurer's duties while retaining his job as general superintendent.

In 1914, when it was decided to establish a second vice presidency, to which Bartlett was elected, C. N. brought in his brother-in-law George L. Hadley as secretary. And when Hadley resigned in 1917, Vice President Bartlett again assumed the secretary's job.

Still more family blood was brought into the executive end of the business in 1918 when Lufkin called in his brother, George, to become factory superintendent.

W. W. Lufkin was elected a vice president in 1920 following the death of Conway and retained his title as general superintendent. Auditor Blanchard, at the same time, was elected to fill the treasurer's post previously held by Lufkin.

In 1921, another Old Guard face appeared with the veteran Frank P. Whitmore's election as secretary to relieve Vice President Bartlett of that task.

With the exception of Earle E. Conway, all these members of the aging ranks remained for the greater part of C. N.'s administration the men in whose hands he reposed the varied details of company operations. The first break in the pattern came in 1925 when James V. Sill became assistant secretary. Ten years later he was elected to a vice presidency. More new faces came with the 1930s,

Part of the "Old Guard" of the Kimball company. Left to right, top: Edgar C. Smith, E. S. Conway, E. B. Bartlett, L. A. Dozois. Center: Eugene Whelan, C. N. Kimball, W. W. Lufkin, Louis A. Crittenton. Bottom: W. H. Cotter, George L. Hadley, E. R. Blanchard, C. C. Dunbar.

when C. N.'s two sons, David W. and William Wallace Kimball, entered the executive rank. David was made assistant to Treasurer Blanchard in 1932 and in 1934 became treasurer upon his resignation. Wallace was elected a vice president in 1933, when Bartlett retired. It was the destiny of Sill and the two younger Kimballs to become the links between the Kimball company as its founder had left it and the organization of today.

Earle E. Conway's brief executive term followed a successful period as a general agent for the company in Iowa and Nebraska, dating from his graduation in 1896 from Beloit College at Beloit, Wisconsin. His brother Carle C., a Yale University graduate of 1899, went to work for Kimball in September of that year at age 22. For about a year he sold instruments in the Minneapolis branch store, and after that he traveled with William H. Cotter, taking that special salesman's sensational piano ads to the newspapers and wangling preferred space with the aid of convivial schooners of beer and his own persuasive personality. After this experience he went into special selling on his own in Aurora, Joliet, Elgin, and other towns near Chicago. In time Carle led the list of retail salesmen, both in total volume and percentage of cash.

On July 7, 1905, having built up considerable holdings in Kimball stock, the Conway boys decided to move. Earle addressed a letter to the company in which he offered to sell his and Carle's shares "and take our pay in pianos and organs," to be delivered to them in Boston. They had joined the year before with E. N. Kimball Jr., in a plan to rebuild the long-established Hallet & Davis organization. They were highly successful in this work until the piano decline set in, and Hallet & Davis was finally taken over by Winter & Company.

Incidentally, Colonel Conway's decision to name his sons with double initials—E. E. and C. C.—stemmed from his belief that the double initials W. W. had brought good fortune to his beloved Governor Kimball. Conway's daughter bore the name Sybil Sylvia.

Edward R. Blanchard's service began in 1887, when he entered the "lease," or installment contract, department. This was a year after he came to Chicago as a 22-year-old book salesman.

Sill recalls that Blanchard once told him he had read 3,000 books. Thin, straight, intellectual, he would sit at lunchtime and tell his associates about the latest book he had read. "It was a waste of time for you to read it afterward," says Sill. "He would tell you everything of value in it." One of his other hobbies was invention. The *Indicator* reported on May 16, 1908, that he had patented several automobile appliances.

After selling his stock to the company and retiring as treasurer, Blanchard moved from his suburban Oak Park home to Pasadena, California, where he died in 1945.

Among his Old Guard intimates, there was none more beloved by C. N. Kimball than Earle Brewster Bartlett, who served the company for more than half a century, primarily as a salesman and executive, and in a contributing capacity as a technical expert.

A onetime farm boy, born in 1858 near Frankfort, Wisconsin, Bartlett came to Chicago at 22 and went to work as a retail salesman. He was a mathematical wizard, even without a pencil, old timers say. His first room-mate was C. N., who had arrived from Iowa a year before him. After a short time Bartlett was transferred to the company's branch store at Rockford, Illinois, but he was recalled by E. S. Conway in 1883 to enter the wholesale department, from which he advanced to secretary and vice president.

A great student of piano construction and an excellent technician, Bartlett took an active part in industry conferences. Typical was his comment on November 27, 1917, when the Kimball sales manager, Eugene Whelan, attending a meeting of music trade salesmen and technicians in Chicago, asked, "Why are there holes in the plate of a grand?" Somebody answered that it was to let the tone come out. The practical-minded Bartlett spoke up: "The plate of any piano is designed to sustain largely the tension of the strings. Of the metal, you need enough to do the work. The reason why there are holes is because the iron is not needed at the places where the holes are, and for no other reason." Somebody said, "It is a matter of economy, then?" "Yes," said Bartlett, "saving of freight also."

Bartlett was credited by the company with being one of the few men in the music industry who could completely design pipe organ and piano scales. He served a term as president of the National Piano Manufacturers' Association and another as president of the Chicago Piano and Organ Association.

Golf was Bartlett's main hobby, although he once built a sailboat on the rear porch of his Chicago home. He was a member of the Bob O'Link Golf Club, of which C. N. was a founding member and first treasurer, and of the Union League Club.

In 1930, he cashed in his stock holdings with the company and was given an extra $5,000 in recognition of his half a century of service since 1880. Three years later he resigned and went to Houston, Texas, to live. After that, until his death in 1944 at 85, he made at least two trips a year to Chicago, where he would return to his old desk, which the company kept reserved for him, and there while away many a pleasant hour reliving the old days with the company. In 1940 he was host at the Union League Club at a dinner for his old associates.

Bartlett once said that he learned two principles of good business when he first went to work for Kimball. "They were these: Never to write a short letter, and never to let a customer go away angry."

George Louis Hadley, C. N.'s brother-in-law, was 21 when he joined the Kimball company in the fall of 1897. He had attended the Chicopee Falls (Massachusetts) public schools and the Burdett Business College in Boston and at 19 had been treasurer of a sail cloth company on the Boston wharf. For a time in 1895 he managed a Boston bicycle factory, capitalizing on his bicycle racing background.

When C. N. got Hadley his first job with Kimball, he thought he ought to give the newcomer some good advice. On the first pay day afterward, he took him over to the First National Bank and introduced him to David Forgan, the president, suggesting on the way that George should save his money. Kimball's eyes fairly popped when the young fellow from Boston pulled a bank draft for $3,200 out of his pocket and deposited it. It represented his savings on his Boston jobs.

Hadley early in 1898 began selling reed organs and pianos around Hampton, Iowa, and thereafter put in sixteen years on the road during which he handled various branch store operations. In 1907 he opened a four-story Kimball agency at Farmer and Bates streets in Detroit, and started running contest advertisements in the newspapers.

A year later he reported that he had sold 650 Kimball instruments there, including several church organs. W. W. Radcliffe, the Cincinnati branch man, then took over, and Hadley moved into other fields. By the time he became secretary in 1914, he was managing 22 branch stores for the company.

One of his most successful sales operations occurred in 1912 at Nashville, Tennessee, when he sold 52 pianos at one time to Belmont (now Ward-Belmont) College, a noted Southern finishing school, over which the Reverend Ira D. Landith presided as regent. The sale was engineered with the help of Edouard Hesselberg, a distinguished Russian concert pianist who was musical director at Belmont from 1905 to 1912. Hesselberg was under contract as a Kimball artist and arranged to give a concert to demonstrate the Kimball's virtues. Hadley recalls that in order to lend dignity to the concert he scurried around all over town looking for rental tuxedos for the various members of the company's Nashville agency who attended.

With the sale, the agency acquired all the old pianos at Belmont, and Hadley set out to sell them. A resourceful man, he located an abandoned hospital in the heart of town, took an option on it, and moved in the traded-in stock. A wire to W. W. Lufkin brought down an expert refinisher and a repair man from the Chicago factory. Hadley chalked in the grains on the piano cases, some of which were of green oak, and the refinisher, an expert on stains and varnishes, went to work. Soon they had a dazzling array of refurbished pianos ready for the wareroom, and Hadley took a full-page ad in the Nashville *Banner* to proclaim, "Beautiful Pianos from Belmont." Such was the school's reputation, he says, that for three or four years afterward Nashvillians kept coming into the store to ask for "one of those pianos from Belmont."

Hesselberg assisted Hadley in a number of other sales efforts. He was the father of Melvyn Edouard Hesselberg, known to the screen and stage today as Melvyn Douglas. In 1956, when Douglas appeared in Chicago in the play "Inherit the Wind," he recalled that as a young man in Chicago he worked for the Kimball company briefly. The Hesselbergs often visited C. N.'s Highland Park home after leaving Nashville to live in Chicago.

When the phonograph rage was at its height, Hadley resigned to start his own Chicago business manufacturing the Valuphone. He sold out in 1921 to the Wizard Phonograph Company and in 1926 rejoined Kimball as an East Coast representative with headquarters at the branch store in Washington, D. C.

The Kimball business was dead in Washington at the time, and Hadley decided to resort to Albert G. Cone's artist testimonials to see if they would still sell pianos. He had Emma Manning, then secretary to C. N., dig up all the old photographic plates of artists and with them made up full-page advertisements for the Washington papers.

He also prepared a larger folder in similar style and blanketed the city of Washington with them. The distribution was made by boys who rode through the streets and left a handbill at every other house on the east side of the street. Just why this choice was made, Hadley can't recall, but it sold pianos and put the store back in business.

In 1943, Hadley sold the Washington dealership to Earl Campbell of New York City, a former official of the Hammond Organ Company. Since that time the handsome, white-haired veteran has been retired, living in Miami and Boston. Sill recalls him as "a gracious, resourceful, hard-working executive; highly respected and much beloved; a good merchandiser, a perfectionist, and a man who understood people better than almost any man I ever knew."

George B. Lufkin, W. W.'s younger brother, served as factory superintendent from the time of his election in 1918 until he was made a vice president on February 18, 1946. As such, he supervised many of the important changes and additions in buildings and equipment.

George was born on September 13, 1874, attended preparatory school at Kent's Hill, Maine, and was graduated from Wesleyan University, Middletown, Connecticut, in 1902. For two years he taught chemistry and coached baseball and football at Wyoming Seminary, Wilkes-Barre, Pennsylvania. In 1903 he married Sara Elizabeth Eaton, his boyhood sweetheart, and in 1904, the year W. W. Kimball died, he moved to Chicago and began work in the factory as a yard laborer.

As a youth, he was known as one of the best baseball pitchers in New England and played on semi-professional and professional clubs in the area. At 60 he won the Chicago city horseshoe pitching championship.

In Oak Park, where he lived at 205 South Elmwood Avenue, he sang in the choir of the Washington Boulevard Methodist Church. He was a member of the Chicago Historical Society and the Art Institute of Chicago.

George B. Lufkin died at 75 on Saturday, April 22, 1950. His wife, two sons, and two daughters now survive him. One of the sons, Eaton, is employed by the company. The other, George B. Jr., is a Chicago insurance broker. The daughters are Mrs. Alice Gonzales of Champaign, Illinois, and Mrs. Marjorie Brunkow of River Forest.

Slender, six-foot-two-inch Frank P. Whitmore was blushing furiously as he stood at E. R. Blanchard's desk in the lease ledger department on January 25, 1895, and watched the Kimball bookkeeper smile at the clipping in his hand.

Blanchard was amused at the job-seeking want ad that Chester

Whitmore, a young Chicago law school night student from Burlington, Iowa, had put in the paper in behalf of his younger brother. It said: "GREEN COUNTRY BOY. NOT AFRAID OF WORK."

Frank got the job, and on January 29 he went to work for Blanchard at $10 a week.

Eight years later, with $2,000 saved, he went out to Fairbury, Nebraska, to join his brother-in-law George White as partner in the White Piano Company, a Kimball agency. It was in this period that Whitmore discovered what he calls "the easiest plan for selling pianos I ever had."

Because he knew the Mormons in the Western country were a music-loving people, he decided to ship some pianos to a sister of White's, who owned a ranch near Thermopolis, Wyoming. Then he took a train to Cody, where the ranch woman met him and proceeded to drive him by wagon and mule team all through the Mormon farm and ranch district on a piano-selling tour. He picked up 30 orders for pianos in as many days.

The easy selling came, says Whitmore, when he discovered that if he sold one wife of a Mormon settler a piano or an organ, all the other wives would be jealous and insist on having one for their homes also. It was a chain-selling proposition that worked.

Whitmore later ran the Kimball retail store and branch wholesale outlet in Topeka, Kansas, where he founded the city's first Rotary Club. Still later he managed the Kansas City branch. He returned to the home office to take over as secretary in 1920 and lived at 644 Abbotsford Road, in the North Shore suburb of Kenilworth, until his retirement in 1941.

During his years as secretary he was in charge of the company's Western wholesale accounts from Chicago to the Pacific Coast. He was president of the Chicago Piano and Organ Association in 1926 and 1927.

When he retired, the *Piano Trade Magazine* described him as "a sound business thinker, modest and affable" and a man "held in deep affection by hundreds in the music business." He now lives with his wife Elizabeth in Orlando, Florida, where, at 83, he is still one of the livelier members of the beautiful Orlando Country Club.

A longtime associate, Ben F. Duvall, succeeded him as secretary. Of Whitmore, Duvall says, "Mr. Whitmore was a shrewd, friendly, patient man—a man who seemed automatically to know the answers to business problems."

Eugene Whelan, one of the oldest in point of service among the Old Guard members, died on April 5, 1956, at 84. He was manager of the Chicago retail store from the time of Edgar C. Smith's retirement in 1930 until 1941.

A native of Maine, Whelan joined the Kimball company late in the 1880s as a house-to-house piano salesman and eventually became assistant manager under Smith. A devout Catholic, he brought to the company a considerable Catholic trade. On one Saturday afternoon, George Hadley counted twenty-six nuns in the Kimball warerooms, inspecting the piano and organ stock with Whelan. In 1898 Whelan married Josephine Kipley, daughter of Chief of Police Joseph Kipley of Chicago.

There were others, not in the official family, whom C. N. considered Old Guard members. Among them were Smith, C. C. Dunbar, L. A. Dozois, and L. A. Crittenton.

Charles C. Dunbar was for 34 years a member of the home office staff. He died in 1926 at age 54.

Edgar C. Smith died at 71 in 1932, two years after retiring. When he withdrew his stock interest in 1929 and 1930, he was given additional company checks totaling $20,150 in recognition of his long and devoted service.

Laurence A. "Larry" Dozois, the home office cashier for many years, started under W. W. Kimball. When the company erected its new skyscraper building at Wabash Avenue and Jackson Boulevard in 1916, he became the Kimball rental manager, succeeding the late Harry A. Wise, who handled such matters for many years. Dozois withdrew his 50 shares of stock and retired in 1921. He was given an additional $2,500 as "final recognition of his long and faithful service."

The dapper, earnest, deeply religious Louis Allen Crittenton was a man on whom Conway, Bartlett, and Hadley depended for disposing of enormous quantities of correspondence. Hadley recalls him as a "perfectly wonderful man."

At noontime, instead of going out for lunch, Crittenton would sit in his office, eating a lunch he had brought from home. Newsboys from the street would come in to see him at his leisure, bringing him their troubles.

"He would talk with them as they sat down by his desk," says Hadley. "Then he would say, 'Let's pray,' and all the little newsboys would kneel down by his desk and pray with him."

Crittenton died in May, 1953, in the Baptist Home and Hospital in Maywood, just west of Oak Park. He was 83.

28

Curtis N. Kimball. "He leaves us all richer in
spirit and experience for having known him."

Wʜᴇɴ Curtis Nathaniel Kimball died in 1936, the *Piano Trade
Magazine* summarized his career by describing him as one of the
"most conspicuously successful figures" in the piano and organ
industry, a man "known to thousands of piano dealers, and re-
vered and respected in the trade, [but] in no sense a mixer." *Music
Trades* took note of the "unusual ability and distinction" that
marked his thirty-one years as the Kimball company's leader. Both
magazines observed that, although he kept a tight rein, he had left
most of the details of its operations to his associates. The *Diapason,*
official journal of the American Guild of Organists, and the piano
trade paper *Presto-Times* commented on his conservative nature.
The former added that his conservatism had sometimes caused
him to be "misunderstood."

Diapason took its cue from the Kimball directors themselves,
who drafted a resolution which read: "Curtis N. Kimball was a
man of rare accomplishment. He succeeded in office as president
of this company a man who was truly a genius; yet he was fully
equal to the responsibility which became his.

"He was a man of sound judgment, often so far-seeing as to be misunderstood, yet never lacking the courage of his convictions. And time after time his judgments and prophecies were indicated by subsequent events.

"He possessed remarkable strength of character, was straightforward in thought and action but was possessed of a modest and simple nature with a wise tolerance for the views of others. He was a profound student, a man of great dignity, yet always approachable, with a commanding personality which never failed to impress all who knew him. His integrity was never questioned, his administration one of fairness, kindness and justice, and he leaves us all richer in spirit and experience for having known him."

When all these comments are added together, they become an accurate, even penetrating assessment of C. N. Kimball's career. For the leadership he gave to the company was of a generally high order. It was traditional and conservative. But what it may have lacked in daring was counterbalanced by the loyalty and harmony he maintained in the executive rank and by his preservation of the family control entrusted to him by his uncle.

There were those within and without the company who believed his extremely cautious administration and his reluctance to take an active part in music trade affairs held the company back and prevented the full development of its potential. And there is indeed some evidence that the company dragged its heels in the prosperous early 1920s at a time when it might well have been pioneering new ideas, new designs, and new sales methods in the face of a declining piano market. Long accustomed to easy prosperity and reluctant to try anything new, C. N. and the Old Guard were slow to respond to the changing demands of the times. The company lost valuable ground to competitors for a time as newer, more modern piano styles outbid it in the marketplace.

But to his credit it must be said that at long last C. N. saw, just before the bone-crushing 1929 financial crash and the depression that followed, that if the company were to move ahead in the industry it so long had led, it must throw off its inertia. Once he saw the necessity, he moved with resolution, albeit with characteristic fairness, to persuade his old friends to step aside and let fresh, aggressive, younger men tackle the new problems which confronted the company.

The various comments of the trade magazines and the directors at his death suggested, if they did not clearly isolate, some of the elusive threads of what seems at this distance to have been an essentially tragic weave that ran through the fabric of C. N.'s career as leader.

His avoidance of the limelight was part of a reticence which sprang from a mild-mannered New England heritage and could not be changed; it was an integral part of a personality and character that was, as the *Presto-Times* said, "of peculiar strength and influence." And although those who knew Kimball best were aware of his essential warmth and friendliness, this brooding, sensitive man was acutely aware of—and hated the fact of—his being misunderstood.

This was one of the tragic threads. Another was the fateful and difficult series of changes with which his administration was faced.

As one of the three principal heirs of W. W. Kimball, C. N. began his leadership in 1905 under propitious circumstances, only to have the piano and organ business as he knew it undergo a continuing succession of upheavals, climaxed by the coming of the depression, whose shattering blows drove the Kimball enterprise to the very edge of disaster. When he assumed control the company was a smoothly-knit organization, the greatest of its kind in the world and at the pinnacle of success. In the years to come he would witness the death of the once-popular reed organ, the rise of the phonograph and the radio as rivals of the piano, the sudden death of the player market, and the final slide of the whole piano industry into the 1932 abyss of all-time low production.

In the face of all these difficulties, his achievement in bringing the company through its most critical years must be accorded a high place in the industry's records. One measure of his overall success as a leader was contained in the obituary the Highland

Landmarks in the music industry are these Kimball Buildings of the past. Top: State and Jackson streets, 1887; center: Wabash and Jackson, 1891; bottom: the skyscraper erected at the latter site in 1916.

The Kimball Story

Park *Press* ran on August 6, 1936: "A man of keen business acumen, Mr. Kimball was inclined to be conservative, careful, and sure in his methods; as witness, a few years ago in the midst of the depression there appeared in the financial section of one of Chicago's dailies a statement that the Kimball Building on the corner of Jackson and Wabash [built under his administration in 1916 and 1917], was the only building in the Loop which had never been encumbered with a mortgage."

The $2,000,000 sixteen-story Kimball Building was indeed a monument to C. N.'s careful planning, and it served for four decades as the headquarters for the Kimball general offices and retail and wholesale operations. It was vacated by the company in the spring of 1956, along with the sprawling Kimball factory at 2611 South California Avenue (the latter-day address of the old Twenty-sixth and Rockwell layout), when all operations were combined in a brand new $2,000,000 plant in suburban Melrose Park.

Although Harry A. Wise, the Kimball real estate agent, had been negotiating for purchase of the Wabash and Jackson lease-holds for some years before, it was not until May 6, 1914, that it became generally known that C. N. was planning to erect a more modern building, "in consideration of probable future needs," on the site where the old building stood. On that date the directors voted to buy the property occupied under a lease from Hulburd Dunlevy since 1890. It was the last of several leaseholds to be purchased before construction could start.

The decision to build was announced in the Chicago *Daily News* of January 29, 1915. As architects, C. N. had chosen the celebrated Chicago firm of Graham, Burnham & Company, assigning to them the difficult task of designing a building to be erected in three sections while the old Kimball Building was progressively demolished. The *Wall Street Journal* marveled at the time over this construction project, which was completed with a minimum of disruption to the old building's tenants.

"The new building was built and financed by C. N. on individual construction contracts for each type of work, and in some instances new corporate groups were formed to better serve economical requirements," George Hadley recalls.

The company moved a part of its operations into the fourth and eighth floors in April, 1916, although the handsome brick, steel, and granite structure was not finished until the following year. Eventually it occupied most of the first, fourth, sixth, and seventh floors, while other tenants, largely in the musical profession, rented the rest of the space. The total floorage was 241,000 square feet. There were three basements, ten elevators, and an attic.

On the second floor was the beautifully appointed 500-seat Kimball Hall, for more than a third of a century a popular resort of music lovers. In acoustical design, heating, lighting, and ventilation, no expense was spared to justify the company's claim that it was "Chicago's most versatile concert hall." Some of the world's leading concert artists, recitalists, and musical organizations appeared there. And this, said *Music News,* gave the lie to "the fallacy of assuming that in Chicago inferior artists play at Kimball Hall and the better ones at Orchestra Hall." *Down Beat* a few years ago thought it "an ideal spot for a jazz concert." The Budapest String Quartet, the Fine Arts Quartet, the Tudor Madrigal Singers, Eva Le Gallienne, Anna Russell, Liberace, the Bali Java Dancers, Sigmund Rothschild, and the Salzburg Marionette Theatre were among the diversified performers to appear there. The hall's former manager, James Fisher, who is now assistant to Rolla A. Burke, retail sales manager, recalls that the first Chicago radio broadcasts came from its stage.

When the competition of television and other influences caused Kimball Hall finally to shut its doors in March, 1955, John Justin Smith, in a nostalgic article in the Chicago *Daily News,* mourned the once famous concert hall as "a house of hope and heartbreaks." He recalled the ghosts of hundreds of young musicians who found glory and despair within its four walls: Among them was an Iowa girl who studied voice for five years, plunged her last $500 into a fancy Kimball Hall debut, walked out on its stage—and faced an audience of three persons.

The Kimball Building itself was sold in July, 1955, to the Chicago Title and Trust Company, which acted as a trustee for an undisclosed interest. That October it was announced that the building had been given to De Paul University by the Frank J. Lewis Foundation. The Kimball company retains its downtown piano warerooms on the first, second, and fourth floors under a rental arrangement.

A need for basic changes in the company's ways began to assert itself forcefully to C. N. Kimball in the middle 20s. It was then that he began his long-range program to revitalize the executive rank with an infusion of new blood. James V. Sill—"Vic" to his intimates—came in as assistant secretary at the 1925 annual meeting, when the by-laws were amended to include that post. In the following year C. N. and the other directors authorized the president's son David, who had been working on collections, to sign payroll checks at the factory "without any title at the present time." And in 1929, the other son, Wallace, moved onto the board of directors, replacing E. R. Blanchard.

In the meantime, C. N., on January 3, 1927, had addressed a significant letter to Treasurer Blanchard: "Whereas during the past ten to twelve years about one million and one half dollars have been put into permanent capital in our office building, and also a further requirement of more than one-half million dollars has been met in taking up the Kimball shares of the Conway estate, and for the further reason that at the present time and for several years past nearly double the amount of capital is required to accomplish the same operations as heretofore, it is now the sense of the board and officers that a dividend of 8 per cent, payable in three-year notes of the W. W. Kimball Company, bearing interest at the rate of 5 per cent and payable quarterly, should be issued at once. . . ."

The company skipped an annual meeting in 1929 for the first time in years, and in the following January, after declaring 1927 and 1928 dividends, it recorded a 1928 figure of $78,384.73 in ominous red ink in the record of the surplus account. Then on April 1 an adjourned special meeting of the stockholders voted to amend the articles of incorporation to broaden the company's scope beyond its original purpose of 1882, which was merely "the manufacture and sale of musical instruments."

As revised, the article read: "The object for which it is formed is to manufacture, buy, or otherwise acquire, own, mortgage, pledge, lease, sell and transfer or otherwise dispose of, to trade and deal in, furniture, pianos, organs, phonographs, talking machines, radios, musical instruments, appliances, parts, accessories and supplies of all kinds and other goods, wares, merchandise and personal property of every kind and description."

Behind this move, which C. N. made broad enough to include almost anything the company might have to manufacture to survive—"even chamberpots," cracked one of the directors—was the manufacture in the piano and organ factory of a line of laboratory and vocational furniture. This work had begun under George B. Lufkin's general supervision in the fall of 1928, when the bottom fell out of the player piano market. The company's expert on laboratory equipment was Arthur E. Kaltenbrun, who later became sales manager for the division.

It was largely this development which saved the Kimball company in the depression and enabled it to keep its factory busy while many another less versatile piano manufacturer went under.

The first sale of vocational furniture was made to the Kiefer Hospital of Detroit, Michigan. It was a $17,738.45 order and was the closing entry in the company books for 1928. This manufacturing phase continued through the next decade and into the World War II period. The last sale was made on May 12, 1943, to the Armour Research Foundation in Chicago.

In January, 1931, there was only a small ray of hope in C. N.'s annual comment to the stockholders. He reported: "The public mind has been very much absorbed with the radio and also the diversions offered by the automobile and in addition to these is the fact that today the installment selling has expanded to a point where there is practically nothing which is not offered to the public on this plan. It therefore becomes apparent that in the matter of easy credits, the piano trade has nothing exceptional to offer as compared to other trades and with the public so much absorbed in other things, the same attention as heretofore cannot be given to the piano either as piece of furniture or an educational medium. However, it seems to be the general impression with our own trade as well as the trade in general that with the diminishing number of factories engaged in piano production, we are getting quite close to the time when the pressure of overproduction will be very much relieved."

The annual losses from 1928 through 1933 were staggering, rising from the $78,384.73 of 1928 to a peak of $745,370.16 in 1931, and then dropping to $389,021.60 in 1933, after which the red ink disappeared from the ledger.

When the depression was at its worst, there was considerable talk among the directors, in the winter and spring of 1933, of calling it quits for good. While the stockholders were still too stunned to take any action in January, on March 2 a special meeting of the directors was called "to decide whether we would keep the factory closed and curtail operations to a liquidating basis or start work on some more stock of styles now nearly exhausted."

After hearing reports from Secretary Whitmore and his assistant, "Vic" Sill, the board "decided to go ahead on a conservative basis for the remainder of the year and if conditions have not improved by that time we could again consider the advisability of a liquidating program."

Two months later the present W. W. Kimball moved up to replace E. B. Bartlett as vice president. It was not an auspicious occasion for his promotion, for at this same meeting a loss of $659,-869.81 for 1932 was written into the books in the now familiar red ink.

It was about this time that C. N. indulged in one of his rare out-bursts of temper. A lifelong Republican, he had no use for Frank-lin Roosevelt's New Deal. One day one of the accountants handed him an income tax blank covering the Missouri branch operation and asked him to sign it. C. N. looked at it, tore it up on the spot, and told the astonished underling, "Send 'em last year's almanac and tell 'em to go to hell!"

At the annual meeting of 1935, the last one to which he made a formal report, President Kimball thought that in spite of Roose-velt, things looked considerably better: "As a brief outline of the present outlook, namely—about 10 years ago those who read the signs with some degree of accuracy began to exercise quite definite restrictions on their former operations, especially as to credits. Within the last five years general liquidation has been fairly well accomplished, thus preparing the foundation for building up anew. This is bound to work some benefit and with sane handling in all economic and political affairs would have by this time made general conditions for everyone fairly comfortable. Some of our departments are further advanced on the road to recovery than others, so that while 1934 in some particulars is an improvement on 1933, there is, however, much to be done all along the line, es-pecially in our retail, organ and furniture departments."

The next January things were just a little better, with $18,967 left over to add to the surplus after a dividend of $104,087.50 had been declared on earnings for 1935. Still the gain was too modest to give much comfort to Curtis Nathaniel Kimball, who would not see the summer through.

Two years after his election to the presidency, C. N. and Fannie Hadley Kimball moved with their children from 5441 East End Avenue, on Chicago's South Side, into Ridgewood, a great three-story brick mansion on a wooded forty-acre estate in the fashion-able North Shore suburb of Highland Park. When he picked out the site, at 320 South Green Bay Road, the year before, Kimball had his workmen haul in a stack of two-by-fours and erect a staging 25 feet high from which he could look westward over the wooded Skokie River Valley. He wanted to determine how best to locate his new home to take advantage of the view.

Marian A. White, writing of the Valley of the Skokie in "Upland, Vale and Grove," published in 1911, described the setting of the Kimball home as follows:

" 'Ridgewood!' Another appropriate designation. For the home itself is on a ridge or crest of a group of the fairest-crowned uplands that command an extensive view of the peaceful vale slumbering in a consciousness of reposeful comeliness and grace. A pergola-like archway and a hedge of sweet peas and other free, flowering varieties separate, yet unite, this main upland from a gentle slope that is under cultivation, providing fruits and vegetables in season for the home table. Beyond, far, far beyond, in a southwesterly direction, first up, then down, and again down and up, billow the grove-crested uplands toward the horizon. It is another view of the valley.

"Again to the west, and from a vantage point of the home itself, where most of the undergrowth has been cleared, and the trees given opportunity to reach and spread through the most enchanting vistas, the valley again comes to view. A few of the old-time farm buildings are holding a distant slope, while the Skokie glimmers as a thread of silver ingeniously wrought into a bit of tapestry, whereby the varied hues are held in one harmonious whole.

"To the northwest and from the same point of view, tier after tier of upland and grove, in which many stately landmarks of the original forest appear, greet one with an infinitude of pleasurable surprises, for it never appears exactly the same, although always beautiful, ever inspiring, this Valley of the Skokie."

A striking feature of Ridgewood was the pipe organ that Kimball installed as a memorial to W. W. Kimball. "The home was designed for the organ and the organ for the home," he told a party of newsmen on Monday evening, June 1, 1908, when he entertained at an informal recital. Kimball sat at the organ keyboard and Emil Liebling at the mahogany grand, which occupied a position at one end of the large library and living room. The organ was mounted on the first landing of the broad staircase that led up to the reception hall. Its console was in a first-floor niche at the side of the stairs. The organ woodwork was finished in white enamel, the pipes in plain gold.

It was in this home that the four Kimball children—William Wallace, David Wheeler, Mary Hadley, and Elizabeth Moore—were to grow to maturity. "Those of us who knew them [the Kimball family] during those years," said the Highland Park *Press*, "will always remember the beautiful home life which they exemplified, their activities in church and school, and above all, the enduring and constant example of the American home at its best, with its staunch American tradition surviving, steady and true, in a changing world."

Here, too, C. N.'s sister, Isabel Moore Kimball of Brooklyn, New York, would on October 26, 1929, unveil her stone sculpture "Creation," an interpretation through 19 beautifully carved figures of Addison's hymn. The famed sculptor Lorado Taft was principal speaker at the unveiling.

The Kimball boys were born on Chicago's South Side when the family lived in an apartment building at Cornell Avenue and 54th Street. Wallace was the first, born March 3, 1901, and David followed on May 14, 1902. In Highland Park, where their father was president of School District 108, both boys started to school at the Lincoln grade school, subsequently replaced by a modern building. They went on to the Deerfield-Shields township (now Highland Park) high school. David set a world's interscholastic record for the 220-yard low hurdle while in high school. It stood for 20 years.

After high school, Wallace attended Dartmouth College, where he was active in football and track. At the end of two years he left in 1921 to enter the business as a bookkeeper. The following year he married his high school sweetheart, Dorothy Purdy, and with some financial help from his father built a small home just north of

Ridgewood. He drew the plans himself, and had the home erected by the Zion Industries, while he and Dorothy checked its progress day by day.

After working in the collection department and then for a time in the retail store, he was transferred to the factory in 1925 to work as a $13-a-week draftsman, learning pipe organ layout. R. P. Elliott was then in charge of the pipe organ department. The long distance and poor transportation from Highland Park to the factory brought a move into a Chicago apartment and, two years later, another to the southwestern suburb of Hinsdale, where the young couple built a new home.

When Wallace entered the organ department, O. J. Hagstrom was chief of the manufacturing division, and George Michel and Joseph J. Carruthers were the top technicians. From these men he learned the details of construction, the principles of design, the tonal requirements, the identities of thousands of organ parts, and the intricacies of their assembly. After that he worked with organ installation crews until 1932, when he was placed in charge of the manufacturing division. Two years later, when Elliott left, he became head of the entire pipe organ department, including sales, service, and manufacturing. It was this post that he held when his father died.

David Kimball's association with the company began when he went into the collection department in 1922 after having attended the University of Illinois and Cornell University. A year after he joined the home office, he married Mary Knox Winton of Duluth, Minnesota, and they settled in Evanston, just north of Chicago.

The 57-year association of Curtis Nathaniel Kimball with his uncle's business came to an end at 9:20 A.M. Thursday, July 30, 1936, in the Presbyterian Hospital of Chicago, where he died following an operation.

News of his passing shocked the delegates to the summer conventions of the music trades, then in session in Chicago. Many of them stayed over for the funeral service, which was held at Ridgewood on Saturday afternoon, August 1. Burial was in the Garden of Memories Cemetery in North Chicago.

Besides his wife and sons, he left the two daughters, Elizabeth and Mary, who by now was Mrs. Harold F. Van Steenderen. Kimball was a member of the Highland Park Presbyterian Church, and a life member of the Art Institute of Chicago and the Chicago Historical Society. His other memberships included the Chicago Club and the Highland Park and Bob O'Link country clubs.

By the time of his death, he had already distributed a substantial part of his wealth to his family. On June 4, 1937, an inheritance tax return filed at Waukegan, Illinois, by his executor, H. H. Benjamin, showed C. N.'s estate to be $529,561. After a tax payment of $5,973, the remainder was left to Fannie Hadley Kimball and her four children. Mrs. Kimball lived on until 1942, when she died at 73, and was buried beside her husband.

29

"The House of Kimball is now at war."

Wallace W. Lufkin, succeeding to the presidency of the W. W. Kimball Company after the death of C. N. Kimball in 1936, spent the last nine years of his remarkable career as top executive of the manufacturing enterprise to which he gave so many decades of devoted service. They were years marked by enormous difficulties arising from World War II.

While C. N. had prepared the way for the younger men upon whom he expected the responsibility for leadership to fall, tradition and sentiment dictated another course. On August 4, 1936, at a special meeting of the board of directors, the 77-year-old Lufkin, a principal heir to the founder and by then the largest individual stockholder, was elected unanimously to become the company's third president.

"None of the Kimball concern . . . considered anything else," said the *Piano Trade Magazine*. "Mr. Lufkin had long been like a godfather to all of them and he is loved and honored by all his co-officials."

The other executive posts remained unchanged: Wallace Kimball and James V. Sill were vice presidents, David W. Kimball was treasurer, and Frank P. Whitmore was secretary. While Lufkin was an able, experienced leader and a man whose opinions and counsels were in many respects valuable, his election inevitably meant a continuation of the Old Guard influence of conservatism. It was soon apparent to Sill and the two Kimballs, the younger members of the official family, that theirs was to be a responsibility of overcoming inertia. It became a critical responsibility with the coming of World War II and brought a showdown between the old and the new forces in the company's affairs.

Out of this showdown came major contributions to the American war effort and with them the perfection of new manufacturing processes and new achievements in piano making that have set the pace for Kimball's second century.

Earnings for 1936 topped a comfortable $300,000, with $122,-038.95 carried to surplus after a dividend payment of $182,154. But by January, 1938, Wallace Kimball and his associates were deeply concerned over the fact that the company had lost ground in 1937 while its competitors were forging ahead. Piano sales in general were reported at their best point in fifteen years in midsummer of that year, when the National Piano Manufacturers' Association met in its thirty-sixth annual convention in New York City. But on January 24, 1938, the Kimball directors, after declaring a dividend of $104,115, were able to place only $71,827.23 in the surplus account.

Wallace Kimball thought he had spotted two definite reasons for the poor showing—inefficiency at the factory, where production costs were up, and a failure to keep up with the trends in piano taste, which was cutting sales. In both instances, the company's Old Guard inheritance seemed to be at the root of the trouble.

For some time, Kimball had paid increasing attention to the piano interests at the factory, where the mild and easy going George B. Lufkin, the president's aging brother, remained in overall command. The real boss of the piano department was still another oldster, the inventive Albert A. Huseby of foundry, key-making, and phonograph fame, who by now had spent 43 years in factory service. (Huseby remained with the company until 1943, when he died on April 20 in his Oak Park home at the age of 76.) An absolute dictator in the factory, as W. W. Lufkin had been before him, Huseby used to storm at his foremen, "You're not paid to think!" Once when W. W. Lufkin asked a draftsman what he was doing, the man looked up from his detailed sketches and replied, "Mr. Lufkin, I haven't the faintest idea. Mr. Huseby told me to make it."

Huseby's one-man rule extended even to arbitrary changes in factory schedules, revisions in design, and alterations in mechanical features without any authorization other than his own. These actions in turn were increasing labor costs and were responsible for the wholly undependable cost accounting figures which had been a cause of increasing worry.

When Kimball began to inquire into the second area of concern—the sharp drop in 1937 sales—he got a ready answer from salesmen and dealers. The fault lay in the company's failure to supply enough small console pianos, 36 inches and less, for the market. Although a 45-inch Consolette was introduced in 1936, President Lufkin had shown a marked lack of enthusiasm over the still smaller uprights, whose popularity was sweeping the country.

On February 7, at Kimball's urging, both these critical problems were thoroughly aired at a special meeting of the directors. George Lufkin and Huseby were directed to permit no further factory changes affecting costs without authorization. Kimball then cited a December survey of the music trade that had shown that 48 per cent of pianos sold that month were small models, and won an argument to step up the manufacture of 36-inch instruments.

Two other important steps were taken in the following year to strengthen the company's position. At Sill's suggestion, the directors voted to tighten up the accounts of dealers being financed by the company by placing them on a carrying charge basis. And Ben F. Duvall, one of the company's top wholesale salesmen, was named assistant secretary to aid his old friend and superior, Frank P. Whitmore. Two years later he succeeded Whitmore as secretary when the latter retired.

Although 1938 had yielded only $23,205.18 for the surplus after payment of a $104,090 dividend, business started picking up in 1939 and 1940 when, after a stepped up dividend payment of $156,120, there were still substantial added earnings—$106,189.21 and $185,372.97, respectively—to be recorded.

The brighter outlook was extra cause for celebration on September 11, 1939, when W. W. Lufkin was honored by the officers and directors at an 80th birthday luncheon in his honor at the Union League Club. Acknowledging his error in underestimating the console piano, the president jokingly reminded his associates that when the first "gas buggies" had appeared on the streets of Chicago he had predicted the automobile would not ever amount to much.

That the new role being played in the company's affairs by Wallace Kimball and his associates was producing results seemed apparent by 1941, when the company had the best merchandise turnover since the prosperous year of 1925. Vice President Sill reported at the annual meeting of January 26, 1942, that 1941 had shown the smallest percentage of repossessions in a quarter of a century and the largest percentage of cash sales.

The progress that had been made was cut short, however, on December 7, 1941, when Japanese bombers attacked Pearl Harbor, Hawaii, without warning and the United States suddenly found itself in the middle of World War II. At the annual meeting in January, Wallace Kimball read a government order curbing the use of tin, effective March 31, which meant the end of pipe organ manufacture, except for the using up of supplies already on hand or ordered.

All through 1941 the laboratory and vocational furniture division had been busy on defense work. More than fifty of its contracts, ranging from $500 to $30,000 each, had been either with governmental agencies or with customers engaged in government work. Among these were the Kankakee Ordnance Works, Elwood, Illinois; numerous Army camps throughout the country; the defense programs of several colleges, including the University of Texas; and such large industrial customers as E. I. du Pont de Nemours & Company.

With this record, Wallace Kimball felt the company already was in a good position to switch to more intensive war-oriented operations. He led a discussion of the probable war situation as it might affect the operations.

President Lufkin was of the opinion that the company was almost certain to have to shut down for the duration; but Kimball persuaded the directors to investigate what could be done in the production of war materials and he put through an official declaration that the company was "both willing and anxious to cooperate, in the manner that best befits it, with the country's victory program."

All through that spring of 1942 there were unofficial reports of an impending War Production Board order which would completely shut down all piano production. It came eventually, and made the shutdown effective July 31. In the meantime, as pipe organ and piano work dwindled to a standstill, the laboratory equipment and vocational furniture business carried on almost alone.

While President Lufkin was still gloomily talking about a complete suspension of operations, it seemed clear to Sill and Kimball that if the company did shut down, it would face an almost insuperable task in resuming work after the war was over. Both were convinced that there were military needs the company should and could meet with its facilities, if it only went after the contracts. Together determining early in April to put an end to temporizing, they delivered an ultimatum to the 83-year-old company leader to call a special board meeting at which a decision could be reached. The meeting was convened on April 8 and, with Lufkin's resistance now only passive, the board approved Kimball's proposal to bend every effort toward moving the factory into full-time production of war items.

"Our country's needs come first," said a company announcement. "For the 'duration' the high standards of quality, manufacturing, accurate design, and capacity to produce of the W. W. Kimball Company will be devoted almost exclusively to the manufacture of wartime equipment.

"We have a deep sense of responsibility to our many Kimball dealers and customers who, by their business and cooperation have placed us in a position to serve our country's needs so well—and it is indeed a pleasure and a privilege, in this our 85th anniversary year to say to you all at this time—thanks."

In August a great red, white, and blue sign—"Buy War Bonds"—went up on the south wall of the Kimball Building.

The first move toward obtaining war contracts was the issuance of an illustrated four-page bulletin which called the attention of prime contractors and sub-contractors to the fact that Kimball's "world's largest piano and organ factory offers its facilities for victory." The bulletin stressed the factory's 720,000 square feet of floor area, the abundance of skilled and semi-skilled employes, the woodworking and foundry facilities. It emphasized also the factory's versatile automatic hot glue press with which wood veneers could be turned out with utmost efficiency.

A costly Plycor hot glue press was purchased late in 1939 and installed in 1940 as Huseby experimented with the newly developed resin (he called them "raisin") glues for use in bonding wood. The immediate aim was the development of a laminated or plywood piano sounding board. It was a principle whose advantages had long been known; but a laminated board had never worked before because the animal glues of the past were not wholly waterproof. Kimball's first laminated sounding boards were tried out in 1939. Promising test results were already being achieved through the continuing experiments when the war intervened, and the press and the new glue processes were turned over to manufacturing plywood war products which had to meet the most severe tests.

The factory, now almost wholly run by Vice President Kimball, turned gradually to the manufacture of a wide variety of war items, both in the laboratory equipment and furniture field and in special applications of its woodworking and plywood facilities.

In 1943, the company advertised: "The House of Kimball is now at War. The huge Kimball factory is completely converted to the production of war work! So that the skilled hands that once provided musical America with the instruments of discriminating choice now supply a fighting America with products for victory!"

A whole new vocabulary was being learned by Kimball factory workers as they turned to new phases of manufacturing science, to new materials and new processes. Among the new words—strange ones, indeed, in a piano factory—were such as *nacelle, x-ray test, catalysts, differential density, glyceroe, anhydride, polarity, heat treating, phthalate, diathermic, tangential, longerons, polymerization, phenolic resin, anodic oxidation, dihedral,* and *compound curve.*

But the Kimball workers took it all in stride. The tasks they met were so new and different that they were a challenge to the factory forces. Among the most important of them was the production of 21 different aircraft parts or structures for three large plane manufacturers—the Boeing Airplane Company, the Lockheed Aircraft Corporation, and the Douglas Aircraft Company—as well as other military supplies. These included aircraft landing gear doors; a multiple seat assembly for paratroopers, with devices that automatically opened parachutes; bomb bay doors; a gunner's seat for the Army's half tractor truck; a protector for flare bombs; and an eight-foot (or more) high bulkhead, or partition, for warplane fuselages. The last was of honeycombed construction, with the short wood pieces that made up the honeycomb so accurately machined that they were assembled without glue, the plywood "skin" or exterior which was glued over the framework

275

Left: James V. Sill, retired general manager. His industry promotion has stimulated piano sales. Right: David W. and W. W. Kimball (pointing) inspect Douglas C-47 parts made by company in World War II.

holding the pieces in place. The honeycomb construction process, pioneered by Kimball and other manufacturers, was later converted to peacetime use in the manufacture of doors for private residences and industry.

The Signal Corps presented the company with a particularly difficult problem of plywood manufacture, which called for waterproof plywood, two-and-one-half-inches thick, made up of 27 plies. Kimball provided it.

The workmanship that went into these war products "was so meticulous," said *Piano Trade Magazine* in a 1947 review, "that the company was given preferred rating by the Army Air Forces, which included a notice to the aircraft companies that any part received with the Kimball inspection stamp could be installed without further inspection, except for obvious damage that might have occurred in shipment."

In 1945, after the dropping of the first atomic bomb on Hiroshima, it was disclosed in a company announcement that for three years the laboratory furniture division had been at work on the "top secret" atomic bomb program. Equipment it made was used in all three of the Manhattan Engineering District research centers— at the University of Chicago, at Oak Ridge, Tennessee, and at Hanford, Washington.

At the war's end the company could proudly boast that it had had not a single rejection of the tens of thousands of parts it had produced for the war effort. It was an "almost incredible record," said the *Piano Trade Magazine*.

Following Huseby's death in 1943, the principal work of developing the laminated sounding board was carried on by George W. Stanley Jr., who came to the company to succeed Huseby as chief engineer and to direct the aircraft work. During this period the company became one of the first manufacturers to make use of high frequency electronic gluing units. The postwar experiments included the testing of various woods, including mahogany and magnolia, for the laminated sounding board, but spruce was found, in the end, to give the most satisfactory results. One of the devices used in the experiments was a specially built "torture room" where steam-saturated air was fed in until the moisture content was at a maximum. The pianos being tested were subjected to alternate periods of extreme heat and humidity and extreme dryness until the glue bond and the ability of the sounding board to hold its resonating "crown," or special shell-like surface curvature, had been tested to the utmost.

Among the experiments carried on was the use of a secret, war-developed glue to bond wood-laminations front and rear to a center core of metal. This particular board was not adopted, but the experiment showed the lengths to which the Kimball engineers went to perfect the laminated sounding board.

Finally, on May, 1950, the *Piano Trade Magazine* announced the adoption by the Kimball company of its newly perfected Life-Crowned Toneboards in all Kimball upright pianos. The new sounding boards had been shipped out to dealers, unbeknownst to them, months before for testing in the field. The company retained a record of all such pianos shipped and after months had passed asked its dealers to have these particular pianos checked by servicemen. One dealer wrote back, "Our tuner came back with an extravagant story about how much better this piano was, and that it had a tremendously better tone."

The company described the Life-Crowned Toneboards as "probably the most important single improvement in piano construction during the last hundred years." Laminated sounding boards are now being used by several other leading manufacturers.

The special features of the Kimball board were patented on January 20, 1953, when registration No. 569,408 was approved by the Patent Office. Of three-layer construction, it takes advantage of the tendency of sound vibration to travel primarily with the grain of a wood. The grain of its hard-core middle layer runs in a direction opposite to the two outer tone-reflecting layers. In addition to claiming for it a superior tone quality, the company guarantees the Life-Crowned Toneboard will never split or crack.

In the summer of 1955, Wallace Kimball offered to overhaul the

Steinway grand in the Michigan Avenue clubroom of the Cliff Dwellers Club, of which he is a member. At the factory he ordered the instrument completely dismantled and rebuilt from the casters on up and, in addition, had a Life-Crowned Toneboard installed. The Cliff Dwellers is an organization of writers, artists, architects, musicians, and others interested in the arts, and among its members are a number of outstanding pianists. Kimball did not tell the musical members of the club about the change he had made until they had had an opportunity to play the instrument again and approve of the reconstruction that had been done. He chuckles as he recalls that two of the pianists, who are well-known Steinway artists, told him before they learned about the sounding board that the treble was better than ever before. At the annual Harvest Home party that fall, one of the club wags designed a special nameplate for the Steinway-Kimball grand, labeling it a "Steinball."

Despite the notable wartime achievements, there was little to cheer about in the annual meetings when the company's directors and stockholders faced the very real financial headaches the war was imposing. Annual losses were incurred for 1942, 1943, and 1944. Heavy factory expenditures were made in 1944 to prepare the company for a resumption of piano manufacturing following the two-year shutdown ordered by the War Production Board, and this accounted for an exceptionally heavy loss shown in the annual report on January 25, 1945. At this meeting the directors discussed the loss during the war of many of the company's highly trained piano technicians and agreed to initiate a program to train new employes for the postwar period, using its pre-war regulators and foremen. George Gottschalk, a 20-year veteran and a regulating foreman, was one of the leaders in this training plan. In 1946 and 1947 regular schools were conducted in the factory, and the company later said it had trained more piano technicians than any other company in the industry.

One of the reasons for the generally unsatisfactory financial showing during the war was the severe competition the company faced. Woodworking facilities were greatly in excess of demand throughout the country, and this was the only type of work the company could hope to handle with its machinery. The stockholders took comfort, however, at their 1944 meeting in the fact that "one of the indirect benefits we had received during the year's [1943] operations was a substantial improvement in our factory equipment and experience, which should be of value to us in the years to come."

The company decided in December, 1945, to dissolve its laboratory equipment and furniture division and devote its efforts exclusively to piano manufacture.

On December 6, 1945, President Lufkin died at 86. Wallace W. Lufkin was widely known in the music trades as the man "who had personally supervised the manufacture of more pianos and more reed organs than any other man in the history of the industry." A great factory manager in his prime, he fell heir in his declining years to executive responsibilities for which he was fitted neither by temperament nor experience. Yet among all the Old Guard members who worked with and survived W. W. Kimball, the founder, there was none perhaps who was more universally beloved and respected.

He lives on today in the memories of his associates at the factory and home office as a lovable and kind character, strong in courage and will, shrewd in his appraisals of men and events, and frugal in habits, despite his great wealth. Typical of the attitude of those who knew him well is a remark of Julia Boutet, who has served as private secretary to a line of company officials, including Frank P. Whitmore, Ben F. Duvall, and the present assistant secretary, Curtis P. Kimball, son of President Kimball: "Mr. Lufkin seemed like an old man the first time I ever saw him. He was lovable—one of the kindest, gentlest old men I ever knew."

Miss Boutet remembers his comings and goings vividly: One

day he came down casually to work and then, suddenly discovering that his toupee was on backward, lumbered hurriedly and red-facedly into his private office.

Another day, near the end, he fell as he walked with a cane through the main office. Refusing help, he got up and made his way into his own office, slammed the door, and in bitter embarrassment, banged his cane heavily across the top of his massive desk. Following this incident, Wallace Kimball noted a possibly hazardous situation for the elderly president at a point in the office where two steps led up to the entrance to one of the restrooms. He ordered a hand-rail installed on the wall. When Lufkin saw it, he was furious, recognizing instantly that it had been installed with him in mind, and he let Wallace know in no uncertain terms that he did not intend to use it.

His frugality was legendary. Miss Boutet used to spot him regularly as he lunched at a Thompson's restaurant on Wabash Avenue. Once, when he stopped to chat with an employe, he dropped a dime on the floor where it rolled out of sight, and he got down on his hands and knees to look for it before he took his leave.

Duvall recalls that one year, after having announced that he was planning to leave for Florida on the 10th or 12th of the month, Lufkin was still coming to the office as late as the 20th. When Duvall asked him why, he replied, "I've still got 20 rides left on my monthly commutation ticket." One of his curious habits, a relic of another age, was the wearing of celluloid collars, even after he became president of the company. In the hottest weather he would walk down Michigan Avenue with the collar off and only a neckband showing. Resenting the stares of passersby, he growled to Duvall, "I've a notion to stop these people and tell them I can write them a check for a million dollars."

Always sensitive about his increasing age, he came in one morning and confided that a woman had offered him her seat on the streetcar on his way over from the North Western Railway station. It so wounded him that he got off at the next stop and trudged the rest of the way to the office.

Sill recalls that one slippery day as they walked to the Union League Club for lunch he took Lufkin's arm at a rough spot in the sidewalk. When the manufacturer jerked away, Sill snapped back, "All right. You're going to break your damn neck at that crossing one of these days." Gruff as a bear himself at times, Lufkin admired a man who would talk back to him. At State Street he took Sill's arm as they crossed and from then on he accepted his aid whenever they walked together.

Sill also recalls that at 79 Lufkin had not made a will. He announced that fact one day and asked if Sill thought he should do so. Told that "the politicians will make money if you don't," he frowned and turned back to his business. Two weeks later a lawyer was in his office drawing up a will.

The Kimball company's third president in 88 years of history died on December 6, 1945, in his home at 273 Central Avenue, in Highland Park. He left an estate of $3,017,089, according to an inheritance tax return filed the following October by the Northern Trust Company, his executor. Federal taxes amounted to $1,025,089, and the state inheritance tax took $131,883. His daughter, Mrs. Juliette L. Tennant, received an estimated $831,748. Three granddaughters, Mrs. Jean Tennant, Mrs. Isabelle Morris, and Mrs. Barbara Reidy, received $334,129 each.

Although at his death he was known as the largest individual stockholder of the company, with approximately one-third of the capital stock, there were few who knew that from 1920 until his death, W. W. Lufkin refused to accept a cent of pay for his services as a Kimball executive.

30

"The greatest challenge the company has ever had."

A NEW and progressive spirit entered the Kimball company's operations with William Wallace Kimball's election to the presidency to succeed W. W. Lufkin. Here at last—for the first time since W. W. Kimball's death in 1904—was the chance so long awaited by the younger men as they chafed under Old Guard inertia. Here was the opportunity to reshape policies in vital areas of company operations, to move forward with fresh ideas and new viewpoints while still retaining the best features of what so many decades of tradition had built.

The second W. W. Kimball, a grand-nephew of the founder, became the fourth president of the W. W. Kimball Company on December 13, 1945, at a special meeting of the directors over which Vice President James V. Sill presided. Sill himself was re-elected and given the additional title of general manager. The elderly George B. Lufkin was installed as a vice president, relinquishing his post as factory superintendent, which was filled a few months later with the appointment of Ward E. Guest. David W. Kimball was re-elected treasurer. Ben F. Duvall, returning to the executive staff after wartime duties as a Navy officer, was re-elected to his old post as secretary, which Sill had filled in 1942.

Kimball's inaugural speech to his associates was brief and to the point. The company was faced with many problems and opportunities. They constituted, he said, "the greatest challenge the company has ever had." He pledged his determination to solve the problems and to realize the opportunities; and he called for the loyal support of the officers and directors.

Vast and far-reaching developments lay immediately ahead. For before the first postwar decade was ended, the company was destined to undertake an extensive modernization program, involving factory equipment and methods as well as operational procedures in the business end. In addition it would undergo a series of internal changes affecting both the makeup of the executive rank and the ownership of stock. Finally, as it neared the end of its first hundred years, it would leave the aging Kimball Building on Wabash Avenue and the sprawling Chicago factory, both of which had outlived their usefulness to the company, and strike out in new directions, in a modern plant and under a completely reorganized program which was geared to the needs of the second Kimball century.

The new spirit was evident from the start of W. W.'s administration. On the day he was elected, the directors abandoned the furniture operation because "it is foreign to the company's principal experience." In February, 1946, at the annual meeting, the president reported on the findings he had made in an extensive study of the factory operations. He thought the directors should pay attention to a whole series of needs—a better personnel policy, more modern machinery, an improved factory heating program, better dry kiln and lumber yard facilities, a wage incentive plan, better toilet facilities for the workers, a factory smoking room, a factory food service for employes. In March the directors decided unanimously after passing a first quarter dividend of 50 cents a share that no further dividends for 1945 should be anticipated unless earned. They also decided that an outside audit was needed,

Executive group photo, taken in January, 1947, shows, l. to r., D. W. Kimball, George B. Lufkin, W. W. Kimball, James V. Sill and B. F. Duvall. On wall is painting by Arthur Ferraris of founder.

along with changes in company accounting. As for the replacement of factory machinery, they agreed that individual machines ought to be replaced when a new machine would pay for itself within a short time and at the same time pay a profit in increased production. In April they decided to hold regular meetings of the directors once a month.

Among the things either started or accomplished in 1946, in addition to the audit and improvements in accounting procedures, were the inauguration of a group insurance plan for the employes; the building of a new $50,000 dry kiln and lumber yard system; the extensive modernization of factory equipment, and the installation of new heating equipment.

For the first time in company history, the directors early in 1947 were given a complete record of operating figures for the twelve months of the preceding year. In the fall the directors made another record with a decision to set up an annual budget each year, to be tied in with a monthly analysis of cash receipts and disbursements, with the figures carried forward month by month.

As the businesslike methods continued to be introduced, the profit figures began to show a steady improvement, despite the expenditure of considerable sums for capital improvements. The items committed for 1947 totaled $215,000.

With sales humming along under Sill, things were looking up in 1947 when President Kimball was confronted with a new dilemma. The Salisbury stock interests, holding a total of more than 7,000 shares, and the heirs of W. W. Lufkin, with a total of more than 8,000, expressed a desire to retire their stock from the corporation. The company lacked sufficient cash reserves to accomplish this. After considering various means of obtaining the necessary funds for the stock purchase, it was decided to place a first mortgage on the Kimball Building. W. W. then arranged with the First National Bank of Chicago for a mortgage loan of $1,000,000.

The stock transfer, involving 15,789 shares, was made on February 16, 1948. The major withdrawals were made by the Northern

Trust Company, for the Lufkin estate, 5,225 shares; Miss Helen C. Dillon, trustee under the estate of Evaline K. Salisbury, 3,459 shares, and Kimball Salisbury, 3,635 shares. The others withdrawing were Juliette L. Tennant; Robert A. and Isabelle Tennant Morris; Robert A. Morris as guardian for Kim L., a minor; T. Hamil and Barbara Tennant Reidy; Jean T. Tennant and Thomas N. Tennant.

It was during the protracted negotiations for these stock transfers that W. W. and David W. Kimball had the first of several brotherly disagreements over the conduct of company affairs. For some time, the younger brother had been telling W. W. he wanted a larger voice in company affairs than his post as director and treasurer gave him. And although W. W. considered turning over the president's chair to David, he feared the effect such a change might have in the trade. Finally, the problem was resolved in March, 1948, by the creation of the new office of chairman of the board, which David assumed, along with his title of treasurer.

When the company celebrated in June the completion of the 500,000th Kimball piano and invited 200 dealers from all over the United States to join in the ceremonies, it was David W. Kimball, chairman of the board, who addressed the gathering.

"Without such a great dealer organization," he told them, "we could never have made 500,000 Kimball pianos, and while this production record stands unmatched in the history of the piano industry, it is our determination that it shall be only a prologue to a future of better value and service as we start on our second half million pianos."

Seven piano retailers received "distinguished service plaques" at the ceremonies in recognition of having sold Kimball pianos for more than 50 years. They were the A. Hospe Company, Omaha, Nebraska, which had represented the company continuously for 70 years; the Hollenberg family of Memphis, three generations; Orton Brothers, Butte, Montana, 62 years; Seals Piano Company, Birmingham, Alabama, 65 years; Williams Piano Company, Sioux Falls, South Dakota, 61 years; San Antonio Music Company, San

At the new factory. Top: Joining veneer for Kimball "Life-Crowned Toneboard." Bottom: View of work area. Huge plant has 175,000 square feet of floor space.

Top: Setting hammers in pianos. Many Kimball craftsmen are lifetime employes.
Bottom: Regulating and inspection. Exacting standards are rigidly maintained.

Antonio, Texas, 57 years, and Walter D. Moses & Company, Richmond, Virginia, 69 years.

As a part of the celebration the company invited eight of its veteran craftsmen to gather around the 500,000th instrument and sing "You Are My Sunshine." Each had spent an average of 55 years in the Kimball factory, for a total of 439 years. Otto Ramm, then 80 and a 65-year veteran, played the piano while the singers were John Rezba, Gustave Havemann, John Fagerstrom, Vaclaw Strohmayer, John Sturenfeldt, George Michel, and Frank Boike.

David Wheeler Kimball remained as board chairman until February, 1953, when his older brother relinquished the presidency to him and stepped down to become vice president and general manager. This office had been left vacant by Sill, who resigned in 1952 to follow a more relaxed way of living, including some traveling he and Mrs. Sill had long deferred. The board chairmanship was abolished.

The long-sought term as president lasted only a little more than three months and was cut short on June 8, when David W. Kimball died at 50. For nearly three decades he and his wife had been among the leading social figures of the North Shore suburb of Winnetka, where they lived at 133 De Windt Road. He left an estate estimated at $355,000. His widow, Mary; a son, David W. Jr.; and a daughter, Mrs. Elizabeth K. Wanders, survived him.

Following his brother's death, W. W. Kimball again was elected to the presidency.

Perhaps the ablest of the Kimball executives upon whom W. W. relied in his program to modernize the company was the popular James V. Sill, who resigned as vice president and general manager in June, 1952, after forty-two years of service. He has since become president of the First Federal Savings and Loan Association in his Chicago North Shore suburban home town of Wilmette. More than any other man in the organization, Sill was equipped by experience and temperament to serve in an intermediary role between the older rank of Kimball executives and the leadership of today. Young in spirit, progressive, and energetic in sales and promotion throughout his long period with the company, he was never regarded as one of the Old Guard.

"Vic" Sill was born on a farm near Bloomington, Illinois, on July 21, 1895, and went to Chicago with his parents at the age of nine. Following the death of his father, he dropped out of school to go to work for George P. Bent & Company at fourteen. A year later, in 1910, he was hired by E. R. Blanchard as an office boy for Kimball at $6.00 a week. His first job was in the shipping department, and after that he became a stenographer for Secretary George L. Hadley. When Hadley left the company, Sill became an assistant shipping clerk, filling orders for parts and learning about the manufacturing end of the business. From this job he moved into wholesale as assistant manager. In 1925 he was elected assistant secretary of the company. Ten years later he became vice president in charge of sales. Finally, in 1946, he was chosen vice president and general manager.

One of the battles—a losing one—that Sill fought throughout most of his executive career with the company was an effort to get C. N. Kimball and W. W. Lufkin as presidents to take an active part in music trade affairs. Because the reticence of the two presidents led them to neglect this aspect of public relations, Sill found these duties falling increasingly upon his shoulders. Fortunately, he was suited to the role by his ability and his extrovert nature. Like E. S. Conway, who had been a dominating industry figure in the days of Founder Kimball's leadership, Sill eventually became the principal representative and spokesman for the company at annual meetings of the various industry groups. One of his first recognitions in the trade came in 1929, when he was elected president of the Chicago Piano and Organ Association.

Aside from his services to the company, Sill's most significant contribution to the music industry undoubtedly was the stimulus he gave to piano selling as chairman of the special promotion committee set up by the National Piano Manufacturers' Association in March, 1954.

Long concerned over the fact that the piano business was declining when everything else was booming, Sill got his first real opportunity to speak his mind on the subject to a national audience on June 5, 1951, a year before he left the Kimball company, when he was elected president of the association. The piano production situation was critical at the time because of the Korean war, but Sill realized that this was merely a temporary condition. He wasted no time in expounding upon what he felt was the real handicap of the industry—a failure to *sell* the piano as an instrument that would benefit the customer.

Outlining his philosophy for the *Piano Trade Magazine* of December, 1951, the Kimball general manager said:

"The future of the piano industry depends upon the enterprise of those in it, subject, of course, to temporary control periods like the present. For all practical purposes, the piano market has no serious limit or saturation point. Piano study is a part of the normal and proper education of children and, therefore, the volume of piano sales at any given time is closely related to the number of children going to school. For the next few years school attendance will reach an all-time high, and if we do our part, a growing market for pianos will be created. . . . No substitute for the piano has ever been found and it is unlikely that one ever will be found. Of course, no one can predict what inventive genius may accomplish in the future, but right now we, in our industry, still control one of the greatest sources of education and entertainment ever known. That the piano is the basic musical instrument is more than just a phrase. . . .

"There is a large so-called dormant market which needs but vigorous retail sales promotion to tap."

In almost every public statement he made during his presidency of the association Sill continued to stress the need for energetic sales approaches. The seeds he sowed fell on fertile ground. In March, 1954, the NPMA executive committee, of which W. W. Kimball was a member, asked Sill to head its special promotion committee. The chief assignment was to make a survey of the industry to determine why the piano business was making such a poor showing compared with other lines of business.

The findings that followed proved to be an eye-opener and caused Sill to "throw the book" at the piano industry in his first detailed report, made in the fall of 1954. He examined more than 2,000 piano advertisements in newspapers from coast to coast, visited hundreds of dealers, poked his inquisitive nose into every angle of the trade. He was astonished to discover that in fewer than five per cent of the piano advertisements was there any selling copy that pointed out how the use of a piano would benefit the purchaser. Most of the advertising of dealers and manufacturers was in terms of price or brand name.

Arguing for a complete change in advertising approach, Sill pointed out to the industry the necessity of using "selling phrases" in advertising an expensive item such as the piano, whose use is deferrable and whose advantages are not obvious at first glance.

"Go ahead and tell them about family ownership, about artists, about how old your company is, how strong you are," he wrote, "but also mention prominently—if you please—how piano study benefits people. Nobody could possibly have any other reason for wanting a piano, no matter how cheap, or even how good it might be."

To back this effort, Sill's committee prepared special "drop-in" newspaper mats of selling advertising that dealers might use, supplied multi-colored window cards that told the advantages of piano study, and hammered at manufacturers and dealers alike to sell piano benefits. Typical window messages read: "For every HOUR spent learning to play the *piano,* your child is assured a THOUSAND HOURS of pleasure in later life." "MUSIC develops your children's personality. When they learn to play the piano, they're having FUN WITH A FUTURE!" In two years the promotion committee put 4,000 window display and store cards into use; distributed 120,000 advertising mats to dealers, plus 400,000 pieces of direct mail material; sent piano selling messages to all dealers; and won a generally enthusiastic response from manufacturers in improving their own advertising by injecting stronger sales appeals.

In all these activities, Sill had the full co-operation and support of W. W. Kimball, just as he had in his years as an executive of the Kimball company.

At the association's 1956 meeting, the manufacturers were ready to credit Sill's committee with phenomenal results, although he modestly pointed out that there were other factors contributing to the increase in piano shipments. Nevertheless, the figures were pretty plain. There was a 16.17 per cent gain for 1955 over 1954. For the first four months in 1956 there had been a 39.73 per cent gain over the corresponding period of 1954, the first year in which the new promotional gospel was used. A checkup of retail advertising showed, Sill reported, that a revolution had taken place, with a heavy increase in the amount of "good selling copy."

"It is clear," he summed up, "that we are on our way upward and we are now sure that with the enthusiastic support of both retail merchants and manufacturers we can finally say that we have a future unlimited."

Having pointed the way to a practical program to increase sales, Sill resigned the promotion post to devote his time to his other interests as head of the Wilmette Savings and Loan Association and as a general business consultant. He was succeeded in September, 1956, by Frank L. Reed, president of the American Music Conference and public relations director for C. G. Conn, Limited, band instrument manufacturers.

Another of the Kimball executives who served as a contemporary of Sill and helped to bridge the gap between the Old Guard reign and the company of today was Benjamin F. Duvall, who resigned as vice president and secretary in August, 1955, to devote himself to other business interests.

Duvall, now living in semi-retirement at his suburban home in Glencoe, Illinois, on the North Shore, was one of the top piano salesmen of his day and is widely known throughout the music industry. His activities with the company included the development in the 1930s of a wholesale prospect list; the creation of extensive literature and sales manuals for retail dealers; and the direction of the Kimball "new era" program announced in March, 1954, in anticipation of the Kimball 100th Anniversary Year of 1957. This comprehensive program encompassed product refinements, the development of new piano styles, and extensive sales promotion activities.

Duvall is a native of Aledo, Illinois, born August 9, 1902. He began with the company in 1922 as a summertime stenographer for Secretary Whitmore, whose son Philip was a fraternity brother at the University of Illinois. Upon his graduation with a law degree in 1924, he again went to work for the company, first as a stenographer and later as a salesman. By 1930 he was so successful at selling that he was made assistant manager of the wholesale division. At the same time he was assisting Miss Emma Manning, then advertising manager, in advertising and promotion efforts.

It was in November, 1937, while serving as sales and promotion manager, that Duvall stage-managed one of the piano industry's most notable exhibitions of dealer-factory loyalty. The occasion was the memorable 80th anniversary banquet of the company, held at the Palmer House on November 15, with Duvall as master of ceremonies. Two hundred and ten men, including factory old timers, field men, and dealers from twenty-seven states, were guests of the company.

Five dealers who had handled Kimball pianos and/or organs for fifty years or more were given silver loving cups.

Among the recipients was the A. Hospe Company of Omaha, oldest dealer on the Kimball books today. The Hospe company was established in 1874 and has been doing business with Kimball since April 5, 1878. A. M. Sommar, vice president of Hospe, attended the 80th anniversary dinner, along with William Zitzmann, to accept the honor.

"During this period of almost 60 years," said Sommar, "our company has continuously sold Kimball pianos and always we have found the Kimball folk eager to extend the heartiest cooperation—

and in such manner as to eclipse the distinct commercial aspect of manufacturer-dealer relationships."

Another house represented was the Seals Piano Company of Birmingham, Alabama's oldest music house, established in 1882, the year Kimball was incorporated. Robert H. Seals, who went to Chicago with Albert Seals to accept the honor, described the company as "our friend for 54 years." The others who were honored were the Williams Piano Company of Sioux Falls, South Dakota, represented by A. E. Godfrey; Walter D. Moses & Company of Richmond, Virginia, a Kimball dealer since 1879; and the Orton Brothers of Butte, Montana, a 51-year veteran.

A remarkable demonstration of dealer loyalty was the presentation of a plaque signed by more than 50 Kimball dealers as a birthday remembrance. The signatures were gathered by Forrest J. Wilking of the Marion Music Company, Indianapolis, who presented the idea to Duvall.

In 1939, Duvall was named assistant secretary of the company, and in 1941, with the resignation of Frank P. Whitmore, he became secretary.

One of Duvall's outstanding promotional efforts was a tie-up in 1941 with the motion picture "Angels With Broken Wings," starring Binnie Barnes and Gilbert Roland, in which much of the action was in a music store heavily stocked with Kimball pianos.

Duvall's business career was interrupted by World War II, in which he served forty months in Naval service—sixteen of them on carrier duty in the Pacific as an air combat intelligence officer. He won six battle stars and held the rank of lieutenant commander at the war's end. Resuming his post as secretary in September, 1945, he served as sales manager and was elevated in 1952 to a vice presidency.

The *Piano Trade Magazine* said of him at the time: "The respect the music dealers of the United States have for Mr. Duvall's character and ability is reflected in the fact that he served as treasurer of the National Association of Music Merchants last year and this year was elected secretary."

Ben Duvall's popularity among the dealers was but a reflection of his sincere efforts to further their interests. He regards the company's attitude toward its dealers over the last hundred years as chiefly responsible for its successes. Although retired, he still talks like a "Kimball man." He told the writer recently:

"Our policy was to help our dealers in every way we could and to make outstanding merchants of them. We often set them up in business, financed them, told them what was right, what was wrong. We made some of the greatest dealers in the business today. And that built loyalty for the Kimball company. I would say the company's strong dealer organization is its greatest claim to fame."

31

"The largest and costliest factory built in the piano industry since the decline of the player."

Iт нas been a long journey from the little Lake Street establishment of 1857 to the magnificent new headquarters of the W. W. Kimball Company of 1957.

Like the first W. W. Kimball of one hundred years ago, his modern namesake and the other able, experienced men who direct the various divisions of the revitalized Kimball organization of today are looking enthusiastically forward, not backward.

The great traditions of a century of piano and organ craftsmanship, and of service to the musical needs of the nation and the world, have been united with modern efficiency in the beautifully designed new factory and home office building. Throughout the great plant a pride of accomplishment and a supreme confidence in the future of the music industry dominate every phase of operations, from policy creation and planning to production. As in its earliest years of manufacturing, the company's chief goal remains the achievement of that degree of progress and maximum efficiency that will guarantee the greatest possible value to Kimball customers.

Behind the "new look" there lies a triumphant story of revolutionary change that is already a classic in the annals of industrial progress.

It is the story of how, in less than two years and without a single interruption in the forward pace of the business, the Kimball company turned its back completely on outmoded buildings and operations and moved lock, stock, and barrel into a bright new future on the very eve of its second century.

Involved in this vast program of modernization was a crucial series of decisions that included the sale of the skyscraper Kimball Building in downtown Chicago, the sale and abandonment of the huge factory complex at Twenty-sixth Street and California Avenue, and the erection and complete equipment of the $2,150,000 factory and home office at Cornell and Armitage avenues in Melrose Park, Illinois, just northwest of Chicago.

The first of these momentous decisions, which drew front-page headlines in the daily newspapers and wrote a daring new chapter in music trade history, came on a February day in 1955. It was a day that W. W. Kimball, the man who charted every dramatic step of the new program, will not soon forget. For within less than eight hours the whole pattern for the company's advance into its second one hundred years was laid out in a series of swift and closely integrated decisions. In a single day the long-contemplated moves which had been pending for months were translated into action. They included three distinct transactions, all of which had to be meshed together in order to accomplish the necessary result, and all involving a head-spinning multiplicity of detail.

But at the day's end, when the weary W. W. Kimball sat down with his wife for a pre-dinner chat in the living room of their suburban Hinsdale home, he felt, with good reason, that the occasion called for champagne. The three steps taken that day had broken a new pathway to the company's future: The stock of David W. Kimball and of the youngest Kimball sister, Elizabeth, had been retired, further consolidating W. W.'s control. The old factory buildings and the site were sold to the International Harvester Company for $445,000 in a cash transaction. And a contract was signed with J. Emil Anderson & Son, a prominent Chicago builder, for the erection of the company's new home.

Only the sale of the 39-year-old Kimball Building at Wabash Avenue and Jackson Boulevard remained to be accomplished, and the negotiations for that purpose were already under way. This sale was finally consummated on July 28, with Oliver S. Turner and Clifford A. Zoll of Oliver S. Turner & Company, real estate brokers, and Levinson, Becker & Peebles, the Kimball law firm, handling the details.

On Saturday, June 14, six weeks before the closing of the Kimball Building sale, three generations of Kimballs participated in groundbreaking ceremonies for the new plant. It was a memorable moment for the family tradition as President Kimball yielded the shovel and stood back, tall and beaming, his graying hair blowing in the wind, to watch his sons, W. W. Kimball Jr., vice president, and Curtis P. Kimball, assistant secretary, and his three-year-old grandson Billy take their turns at turning over the turf.

N. C. Dezendorf, who sold pianos as a youth and is now a vice president of General Motors Corporation and general manager of the Electro-Motive Division at La Grange, Illinois, was principal speaker at the ceremonies.

His remarks evoked—instinctively and appropriately—that special blending of idealistic and commercial impulses that has always characterized the industry in which the Kimball company has played so dominant a part.

"Juvenile delinquents," said Dezendorf, "do not come from musical homes. There are more than two and a half million youngsters studying the piano in this country. Music is something that any family can enjoy together. A musical home is a loving home. Juvenile delinquents don't come from homes where there is love. That is why the erection of this great new piano factory is more than just another magnificent industrial advance but is also a significant contribution to our social and cultural development."

All through 1955, following the turning-point decisions of Feb-

The second W. W. Kimball (top), grand nephew of the founder, is president of the company today. Lower photo: President Kimball, his sons Curtis P. (left) and W. W. Jr. and grandson Billy at 1955 groundbreaking for new factory building.

At groundbreaking for Melrose Park plant in 1955. L. to r., B. F. Duvall, vice president of Kimball; Rep. Arthur W. Sprague; Don M. Peebles, Levinson, Becker & Peebles; R. W. Jones, Illinois Manufacturers Association; Rep. Joseph J. Lelivelt; Louis E. Nelson, First National Bank, Maywood, Illinois; W. W. Kimball, president of the Kimball company; H. T. Reishus, International Harvester; N. C. Dezendorf, Electro-Motive Division, General Motors; Paul W. Brandel and A. Harold Anderson, J. Emil Anderson & Son; Bentley G. McCloud Jr., First National Bank, Chicago; Sen. Arthur J. Bidwill; and Mayor Andy Frenzel of Melrose Park.

ruary, President Kimball moved vigorously to re-examine every aspect of company affairs and to strengthen his organization to meet the challenges that lay ahead.

For several years Vice President Duvall had been pressing him to recognize the industry and talents already amply demonstrated by the fourth generation of Kimballs to be associated with the firm since its founding in 1857. The other directors were similarly inclined. Accordingly, in April they elected the Kimball sons, William Wallace Jr., then thirty, and Curtis P., twenty-eight, to be vice president and assistant secretary, respectively. Each had from childhood shown an inclination to follow in the family tradition of piano making and during vacations from Dartmouth College had begun to learn the business from the ground up by working in a variety of factory jobs. In addition, they had spent a great deal of evening time in study of the business end of the company's affairs under the tutorship of Duvall and Sill.

W. W. Jr. entered Dartmouth College in June, 1943, following his graduation from high school, but World War II interrupted his college training. After service as a bombardier lieutenant in the Army Air Force, he returned to Dartmouth and was graduated in 1949. At that time he joined the firm officially as a factory worker. Working his way through the ranks, he became general factory foreman in 1952 and was placed in charge of production control in 1954. In addition to serving as vice president, he is presently the factory manager, in charge of all manufacturing functions. He assumed this post in January, 1956, succeeding Garfield Chalmers, one of several interim managers who followed George B. Lufkin.

Young Curtis Kimball, an honorably discharged Navy veteran of World War II, joined the company formally in 1950 after his graduation from Dartmouth and spent his first two years as a salesman in the Chicago retail operations. From there he entered the wholesale division, where he later became an assistant manager. His present duties include those of wholesale sales manager, embracing the direction of the home office assistants and nine district

Executive group at home office conference, 1957: from left to right, Otto J. Skoda, Service Manager; Charles Cullinane, Production Manager; Merton E. Rowan, Controller; Robert A. Laube, Personnel Manager; W. W. Kimball Jr., Vice President and Factory Manager; W. W. Kimball Sr., President and Treasurer; Curtis P. Kimball, Assistant Secretary and Sales Manager; William D. Parsons, Assistant Sales Manager; Rolla A. Burke, Retail Sales Manager; Theodore H. Krumwiede, Assistant Sales Manager and Advertising.

sales managers. Among the major innovations which he is implementing in the Kimball Centennial Year is a new form of dealer incentive which is intended to play a substantial part in continuing the expansion of sales.

Following the historical pattern of the past, the company is developing its young men for the important jobs of tomorrow. Typical of the younger Kimball men are Theodore H. "Ted" Krumwiede, the energetic assistant wholesale manager in charge of advertising and public relations, and William D. Parsons Jr., another assistant manager, who joined the company in 1952 after operating his own phonograph record distributing concern. A third, who recently left the home office to take over the California and Arizona territory from the veteran William E. Day, retired, is Jack B. Strange.

Jack Strange is the son of the widely known Gene Strange, an oldtime Kimball district sales manager, who for many years ably assisted in the training of younger men entering the wholesale division. The elder Strange is now being followed in these duties by Roy Johnson, another veteran district manager.

Among the other steps that President Kimball took to strengthen the company in 1955 was the hiring of Floyd Treat, retired general sales manager of the Athletic Shoe Company, as his special assistant. Although Treat gave valued counsel in the trying period of readjustment, his services were cut short by his untimely death in midsummer of 1956.

To gain a greater efficiency in the business office, the able Merton E. Rowan, a former controller of the DeVry Corporation, was brought in as controller.

With the piano business steadily on the upgrade in the spring of 1956, it became apparent to both President Kimball and his son Bill that immediate steps must be taken to assure the company's 500 dealers of adequate shipments during the impending period when factory operations would have to be transferred from the old factory to Melrose Park. Output at Twenty-sixth and California had been going along at full capacity on a five-day week basis since the preceding summer, but early in March the plant was put on a six-day work week. In addition to meeting the heavy current demands, substantial inventories had to be built up to assure uninterrupted service to dealers during the moving period. Proof of the success of this program is that the company was actually able to ship more pianos in 1956 than in 1955.

A few days after the six-day schedule was initiated, Alfred Leech, a writer for the United Press, got wind of it and sensed a story. His special feature article of March 16 carried around the world the story of W. W. Kimball's great confidence in the future of the music industry. It said, in part:

"The piano business is booming as it never has before.

"W. W. Kimball, Sr., president of the Kimball Piano Co., predicts that piano production this year will set a new record. . . .

"In short, the piano is making a comeback, and this would seem to refute the notion that Americans are becoming a passive herd of lookers and listeners.

"Not since the roaring twenties have piano makers had it so good. More than 350,000 pianos were built each year in that era of bootleg and boom, but more than half were player pianos.

"Kimball said the current revival is part of a general trend which finds Americans spending less on homes and automobiles and more on home furnishings, musical instruments and do-it-yourself projects.

" 'We expect sales this year to be 5 to 10 per cent over 1955, which was 28 per cent over the year before,' he said.

" 'This is significant in view of the fact some other industries are leveling off or have shown slight declines from 1955 records.'

"One deterrent to piano sales has been the trend toward smaller homes, some of which hardly have room for a piano. But magazines have shown how pianos can be used as room dividers, and the industry itself has offered a variety of sizes, from grands to waist-high spinets.

"Kimball said there are unmistakable signs of a widening interest in music. He cited attendance at symphony concerts, double

Mrs. Mamie Doud Eisenhower accepts scroll awarding her first piano from new factory. Making award are Earl Campbell (right) and John J. Noone Jr.
Bottom: W. W. Kimball presents watches at 1956 dinner to (l. to r.) Gustave Havemann, 64-year employe; Frank Boike and Peter Williams, 60-year veterans.

what it was a decade ago, and the boom in long-playing records and hi-fi sets."

A month later, the Chicago *Daily News* quoted President Kimball's statement that unit shipments from the Kimball factory in the first quarter of 1956 were up 13 per cent over the corresponding period in 1955. Unfilled orders at the time were 30 per cent higher. Part of the current stimulus to sales was coming from the introduction of three distinctive new piano models, including a 36-inch spinet and a new studio upright for schools.

As another vital evidence of the new road being taken, the company inaugurated in March a series of special award dinners at which it honored 275 veteran employes.

Ninety-five of these were men and women who had served for a quarter of a century or more. Twenty-nine had served forty years or more. The dinner for the ninety-five longterm employes inaugurated the Kimball Quarter Century Club. It brought together employes and former employes who represented a total of 3,320 years of service, or an average of thirty-five years for each of those listed on the dinner program.

Oldest of those attending was Gustave Havemann, a sixty-four year veteran who started to work for the company at age 13. Peter Williamson and Frank Boike were also included with Havemann in the ranks of those who had worked sixty years or more.

All ninety-five received service pins. The twenty-nine with forty years or more of service behind them were awarded personally engraved gold watches. Separate ceremonies honored the 180 other employes with from five through twenty-four years of service. In addition to alerting the Chicago daily papers to the honors, the company prepared and distributed to local and suburban newspapers personal stories about every employe concerned.

There was no mistaking the intense loyalties the Quarter Century Club ceremonies stirred among the employes and former employes. William Beeskow, a fifty-year veteran who flew in from his Fort Lauderdale (Florida) home for the ceremonies, commented: "I say the Kimball company is a good company. If I didn't feel it was absolutely tops in the piano industry all these years, I wouldn't be here right now. This pin has given me the opportunity to say it again."

As President Kimball rose at the long speakers' table, where the oldest of the Kimballites sat with him, his voice trembled and his blue eyes misted. There wasn't a man there who didn't always call him "Wallace." It was something he could be proud of.

"There's a lot more to life," he said simply and with sincere emotion, "than to just see how much money you can make and how many pianos you can sell.

"I've wanted to do this for a long time.

"You fellows—and you girls—are my business associates. Every day that has gone by one of you has been of help to me. This company couldn't be here without each of you."

In addition to Havemann, Boike, Williamson, and Beeskow, the roll call included these persons: John Harbison, Anton Przyborowski, and John Rezba, fifty years of service; Maurice Buckley, Ernest Carlstrom, Henry Osenberg, Herbert Sommers, Robert Vondriska, and Otto Weissbrodt, fifty years; Carl Behnke, Frank Benda, Stephen Kwiatt, Henry Lesney, Ivar Lindstrom, Andrew Nelson, Vaclaw Strohmayer, John Swanson, and George Timm, forty-five years: Carl Boncha, Charles Fiek, Walter Greinke, John Grimmenga, Elmer Henning, August Matz, and James V. Sill, forty years; Frank Bashin, Frank Cygan, Paul Davis, William E. Day, Walter Fickenworth, Martin Fjeld, Peter Gazda, Edward Hlinka, James Kacirek, Mike Knizkiancis, George Kranz, Arthur Kremske, Ernest Oehlke, James Steck, and Martin Strauss, thirty-five years; Frank Balla, Edward Ciz, Louis Calrizio, Stanley Dobek, Joseph Duslak, Benjamin F. Duvall, Joseph Gionnelli, Anna Gorak, Pete Gorrence, John Henning, Frank Kania, W. W. Kimball Sr., Leon Klimovich, Tore Kling, John Komarek, John Kremsreiter, Flore Krug, John Novitski, August Ratoike, Steve Redensek, Frank Rek, Stephen Renza, John Siegle, Otto Skoda, Helen Tarka, John Viduna, William Woeltje and Laddie Zalewski, thirty years; and Ivar Anderson, Harry Bernicchi, Harriet

309

Governor Stratton of Illinois (seated in Springfield office) presses Kimball piano key to send signal opening new plant on June 4, 1956. President Kimball watches. Right: Melrose Park's Mayor Frenzel receives signal and pushes switch as Vice President W. W. Kimball Jr. addresses workers and notables at ceremony.

Members of the Quarter Century Club—ninety strong—pose after receiving special awards for service to the company at dinner in 1956. All with more than 40 years' service got gold pocket watches.

Bojan, Julia Boutet, Theodore Gall, Frank Gritzmacher, Frederick Grosser, Anthony Janka, Roy Johnson, Virgil Kimball, William Kranskowski, John Lesziewicz, Earl Lorenzen, Stanley Matuszewski, Stephen Osoweic, John Pogorselski, John Ptaszynski, Walter Sandberg, Edward Schenekel, Fred Schraub, Oscar Steinhauser, Stanley Szczygiel, and Walter Zander, twenty-five years.

The long months of planning and the electric feeling of excitement that had been building up, both at the downtown headquarters and among the employes at the old plant, reached a climax on Friday, May 26, 1956.

It was M-Day—moving day—for the Kimball company. One of the office wags remarked that, having set almost every other kind of record, the Kimball company would now attempt the biggest piano-moving job in history. The jest was actually a fairly accurate description of what occurred.

For weeks the Kimball Building crew had been cleaning out desks, digging out material from decades-old files, and placing all properties in sturdy cardboard cartons. All were carefully labeled so that on Monday morning in the new plant each employe would find his own carton sitting beside his new desk.

"You certainly find odd things when you move," President Kimball told a reporter assigned by the Chicago *Daily News* to report the event. "I found the original building contract for Kimball Hall in our dead files, and also a contract to buy three boilers that have been heating the building all these years." The cost of the three boilers did not equal the cost of one of the boilers in the new plant.

While the transfer from downtown required only one weekend, the process of vacating the old factory required approximately a month and a half. A steady parade of trucks carried out the moving of pianos, machinery, and equipment. Vice President Bill Kimball directed the operation in easy stages, with the loss of a minimum amount of production time. Meanwhile, the careful building up of reserves permitted the maintenance of a normal shipping schedule until a regular production pace was established at the new plant late in July.

In an action that symbolized the importance of the new plant to Illinois and the nation, Governor William G. Stratton formally launched the $2,000,000 establishment into full production on Monday, June 4, from his offices in Springfield.

President Kimball stood by his side as Governor Stratton struck Middle C on a specially rigged Kimball piano key and sent an electrical impulse by telephone to the factory, 200 miles away, as a signal for production to begin. Mayor Andy Frenzel of Melrose Park stood by with Bill Kimball at a gathering of civic leaders and company employes to receive the signal and in turn press the button that started the great plant humming.

The face-brick and glass structure, equipped with the most modern piano making machinery, contains 175,000 square feet of floor space. One wing of the new building, which carries a partial second floor, houses the air-conditioned offices of the executive and administrative staff and the company cafeteria. On the main floor, to the left of the entrance, is a splendidly furnished retail wareroom. This facility supplements the retail business that continues in the downtown store and elsewhere in the Chicago area under the veteran retail sales manager, Rolla A. Burke.

One of the features of the factory is a completely soundproof acoustical laboratory which, as the *Piano Trade Magazine* has noted, is unlike any ever used before in the piano industry. Its walls are perforated and plastered with a pliable soundproofing compound that never completely hardens. Here, in this incredibly efficient silence, the great voice of a piano under test seems literally to speak to the listener, as Oscar Steinhauser, the German-born chief designer, recently demonstrated to the writer. An electrical instrument, the oscilloscope, however, substitutes for the human ear in the Kimball testing chamber and indicates sound values with unerring precision.

Describing the new headquarters as "the largest and costliest factory built in the piano industry since the decline of the player,"

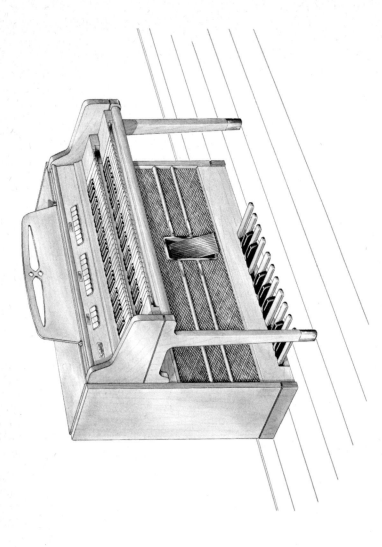

A new anniversary product—the revolutionary Kimball electric organ, which makes use of tone pictures to create its music. The case was designed by Arthur G. Haggstrom.

the *Piano Trade Magazine* of June, 1956, wrote of it as follows:

"Unquestionably the largest individual investment in the music industry in over three decades, the new Kimball plant is formidable proof of President William Wallace Kimball's faith in the expanding piano industry."

The first piano to be completed in the Melrose Park quarters was "put on casters" and rolled out for a first inspection by W. W. Kimball Jr., and Chief Inspector Robert Werderitch on June 11. A Colonial Modern Consolette, it was the 566,966th Kimball piano to be produced since the company began their manufacture. After seasoning, finishing, tuning, and regulating, it was given a final inspection by President Kimball on July 10 and then personally certified by him for shipment to the Campbell Music Company of Washington, D.C. Earl Campbell, president of the company and chairman of the board of the National Association of Music Merchants, accepted it in a special ceremony in Washington. Campbell has been a Kimball dealer since he established his business fifteen years ago.

This first piano from the new factory was presented by Campbell to Mrs. Mamie Doud Eisenhower on behalf of the Kimball company. She in turn gave it to the District Training School for Retarded Children in Washington and wrote to the company to express her gratitude for "the good which you have done with this act."

Thus the W. W. Kimball Company, in its one hundredth year of service to the music lovers of America and the world, expressed its abounding faith in the future with a fresh start in manufacturing. With its rich heritage of tradition, it had dared after World War II to undergo a critical self-examination and then to move with courage and freshness of spirit into an extensive program of improving its products and its methods.

Of such boldness and courage were created all the memorable achievements of the company's first century. It is those achievements that will provide the best measure for the company's efforts in the years that lie ahead.

The W. W. Kimball of today shares with the founder who bore that name a desire to move forward, a willingness to take calculated risks, and an ability to look beyond the next quarter's sales reports.

As 1957 began, the music industry was astir again with the sort of rumors and trade talk that enlivened the company's first half-century: "I hear that Kimball is going to do so and so." "Wonder what Kimball is going to do next?"

Without tipping the company's hand, it could be said as it began its Centennial Year that the rumors indeed had a basis in fact.

Among the things that are in the "Kimball Pattern of Progress" for the future is the manufacture and sale of a new type of Kimball organ, which is expected to be as revolutionary in its field as was the first Kimball portable pipe organ when it was presented at the World's Columbian Exposition of 1893.

It is unlike any other organ on the market and has been under development for more than two years. It will be offered in a full range of instruments for various uses—from the small residential organ to an instrument that will contain the potential of the largest of the great pipe organs for which the Kimball company has been famous.

As he proved in World War II, W. W. Kimball is a strong believer in improved management and in research and development, and the Kimball engineers and technicians have been at work in other fields as well. It seems certain that, as the second Kimball century unrolls, their continuing explorations will lead the company into the development of products outside the piano and organ business.

One thing is clear: There are new dynamics in the Kimball company's thinking. The pioneering spirit that moved its founder is still strongly alive.

INDEX

Kimball, William Wallace—
Continued
246, 253, 257, 265, 280, 283,
291, 298
Kimball, W. W. Sr., 186, 188,
190, 239, 246, 263, 266-67,
270-75, 278-81, 283-84, 286-
87, 290, 292, 294, 299-300,
303, 305-306, 308-309, 312-
313, 315-316
Kimball, W. W. Jr., 300, 303,
305, 312-13, 315
King, Ben, 230-31
Kingsley, H. M., 42
Kipley, Joseph, 253
Klimovich, Leon, 309
Kling, Tore, 309
Klug, F., 177
Knabe, William & Company,
160
Knight & Campbell Music
Company, 161
Knizkiancis, Mike, 309
Kohlsaat, Herman H., 196
Komarek, John, 309
Kranz, George, 309
Krause, S. A., 236
Kranskowski, William, 312
Krebs, H., 237
Kremske, Arthur, 309
Kremsreiter, John, 309
Krug, Flore, 309
Krumweide, Theodore H., 305
Kunkel, Charles, 122
Kurtzmann & Hinze, 45
Kwiatt, Stephen, 309

Lakes-to-the-Gulf Deep Water-
ways Association, 77
Lamp, S., 237
Landith, The Reverend Ira
D., 249
Lange, Paul, 175
Lawrence, Sir Thomas, 144
Leech, Alfred, 306
Le Gallienne, Eva, 260
Lehmann, Lilli, 120
Lenartson, C., 237
Lennisch, H. H., 237
Lennon, John B., 203
Lesney, Henry, 309
Lesziewicz, John, 312
Levinson , Becker & Peebles,
300
Lewis, Frank J. Foundation,
261
Liberace, 260
Liebling, Emil, 108, 110, 117,
119, 131, 133, 135, 163-64,
171-73, 176, 209, 237, 265
Liebling, George, 173
Life-Crowned Toneboard, 278-
79
Lighte, F. C. & Company, 20,
45, 49
Lincoln, Abraham, 39
Lincoln, Robert Todd, 216
Lindstrom, Ivar, 309
Liszt, 119, 173
Lockheed Aircraft Corpora-
tion, 275
Loesser, Arthur, 61, 119, 224
Logan, Emma, 23

WGN, 186
Wheaton Club, 217
Whelan, Eugene, 177, 241, 247, 253
Whelan, Josephine Kipley, 253
White, George, 252
White House, 209
White, Marian A., 265
White Piano Company, 252
Whitechapel Club, 230
Whitelaw, G., 237
Whitmore, Elizabeth, 252
Whitmore, Frank P., 209, 224, 241, 251-53, 263, 270, 272, 280, 295-96
Whitmore, Philip, 295
Whitney, Alvin, 195
Whitney, Arthur E., 195, 224-25
Whitney, Frank H., 195
Whitney, John H., 195, 225-26
Whitney Piano and Supply Manufacturing Company, 195-96
Wigwam, 39
Wild, Harrison M., 135
Wilde, Oscar, 185
Wilking, Forrest J., 296
Williams Piano Company, 287, 296
Williamson, Peter, 308-09
Willis, "Father," 190
Wilson, Richard, 144
Winter & Company, 246

Wise, H. A., 176, 179, 209, 216, 253, 259
Wizard Phonograph Company, 250
Woeltje, William, 309
Worcester (Massachusetts) Municipal Auditorium, 186, 191
World's Columbian Exposition, 56, 62, 118, 135, 157ff., 171, 203, 217
World War I, 212
World War II, 181, 269, 270, 272, 296, 303, 316
Woodruff, C. B., 177
Wright, John, 42
Wurlitzer, Rudolph Company, 25

Yale University, 246
Yates, Gov., 210
Yore, Luke, 177, 209
Young, Clarence, 221
Yount, Mrs. M. F., 187

Zalewski, Laddie, 309
Zander, Walter, 312
Ziegfeld, Dr. Florenz, 59, 119, 122, 127, 131, 133, 160, 164, 176
Ziegfeld, Florenz Jr., 163
Zoll, Clifford A., 300
Zion Industries, 267